THE SANTA FE HOUSE

Historic Residences, Enchanting Adobes, and Romantic Revivals

MARGARET MOORE BOOKER

PRINCIPAL PHOTOGRAPHY BY STEVE LARESE

RIZZOLI
NEW YORK

For my adorable husband, Marty

First published in the United States of America in 2009
by Rizzoli International Publications, Inc.
300 Park Avenue South | New York, NY 10010
www.rizzoliusa.com

© 2009 by Margaret Moore Booker

2009 2010 2011 2012 / 10 9 8 7 6 5 4 3 2 1

FRONTISPIECE *Adobe entranceway, Francisco De La Peña–
Frank Applegate House* Courtesy of the Gerald Peters Gallery

ABOVE *Rear portal, El Zaguán, Canyon Road*

LIBRARY OF CONGRESS CATALOGING-IN-PUBLICATION DATA
Booker, Margaret Moore.
The Santa Fe house : historic residences, enchanting adobes, and romantic revivals /
Margaret Moore Booker ; principal photography by Steve Larese.—1st ed.
p. cm.
ISBN 978-0-8478-3197-5 (alk. paper)
1. Architecture, Domestic—New Mexico—Santa Fe.
2. Santa Fe (N.M.)—Buildings, structures, etc. I. Larese, Steve. II. Title.
NA7235.N6B66 2009
728.09789'56—dc22
2009008506

ISBN 13: 978-0-8478-3197-5

PRINTED IN SINGAPORE
DESIGN BY SARA E. STEMEN

CONTENTS

INTRODUCTION

Upon arriving in Santa Fe, New Mexico, one immediately becomes captivated by the unique architecture in perfect harmony with its high desert surroundings. In the downtown area, graceful old adobe, stucco, and brick commercial buildings hug the central plaza, where ancient cottonwoods provide much-needed shade. In the surrounding neighborhoods, earth-toned residences crouch low on piñon-forested hills, amid endless stretches of yellow chamisa, purple sage, and prickly pear cactus. From everywhere, one has views of the stunning Sangre de Cristo and other impressive mountain ranges that encircle the city.

At first glance it appears all the houses conform to the same style and configuration: low, flat-roofed buildings with round-edged walls of adobe bricks (or material imitating adobe) painted in earth tones, with deep-set windows and protruding *vigas* (wood beams). But as you stroll further along the narrow, winding lanes, you discover that myriad architectural styles are present within the city. Amid the enchanting adobes are fine examples of romantic revivals and native styles of architecture. There are Queen Anne, Italianate, and French Second Empire houses of the Victorian era; early-twentieth-century California Mission revivals and Craftsman bungalows; and residences built in the Territorial and Spanish Pueblo Revival traditions—known collectively today as the "Santa Fe style."

Santa Fe—described by one nineteenth-century visitor as having "the charm of foreign flavor . . . [where] the soft syllables of the Spanish tongue are yet heard"[1]—has long been home to a multitude of people of varying ethnicities and cultures. Inhabited by Ancestral Puebloans for centuries, the *Villa Real de Santa Fe* (royal city of holy faith) was "founded" by Spaniards in 1609–10, and by the mid-seventeenth century it was home to Indian and mestizo residents, including Mexican Indians, Pueblo Indians and Plains Indians raised in Spanish households, and a few people of mixed African-European descent.[2] In 1846, after twenty-five years of Mexican rule, Anglo-Americans claimed the city and region as a territory of the U.S., and statehood arrived in 1912. Santa Fe's diverse cultural heritage and its many authentic historic residences and public buildings play a vital role in telling the city's story.

The "ancient city" of Santa Fe and its historic architecture, streetscapes, and cultural traditions have won national and worldwide acclaim. For example, in 2005 Santa Fe was the first American city to be designated a "Creative City" by UNESCO (United Nations Education, Scientific Cultural Organization), a global acknowledgment of its place at the forefront of folk art, crafts, and design. Two years later the American Planning Association (APA) named Santa Fe's Canyon Road "one of the 10 Great Streets" in the U.S. through its Great Places in America program. A renowned center for the arts, the almost four-hundred-year-old road has retained much of its original character with low-scale authentic adobe buildings, some dating back more than one hundred years.

For organizational purposes, the historic residences featured in this book have all been placed in chapters covering specific styles and time periods. But doing so has been a difficult task, for each house is an organic, living, breathing thing that reflects different generations of homeowners and their individual tastes. It is difficult to identify the precise configuration of the early buildings because of the vagueness of property descriptions, because later remodeling efforts have disguised original sections, and because of the fluid and flexible nature of adobe. It was relatively easy to add on rooms of mud and straw walls and timbered ceilings. Archaeological excavations in the city indicate there was a practice in Santa Fe of constructing new buildings on the ruins of older structures—the Palace of the Governors and the Cathedral of St. Francis are two examples. In addition, time and weather are the natural enemies of Santa Fe's primary early building material, adobe. Excessive exposure to water weakens adobe bricks and mud plaster finishes. Dating houses and individual architectural features within them is also problematic. Early Spanish deeds are confusing, and many historic structures have items that were salvaged from other buildings. To name just one example, the Borrego House on Canyon Road has a fireplace mantel salvaged from a circa-1870s Fort Marcy officers' home that was installed in the *sala* (main room) during a 1928–30 renovation.[3]

However, by drawing upon the information gleaned from early photographs, maps, legal documents, newspaper articles, personal diaries and letters, and measured drawings executed by preservationists, such as the Historic American Buildings Survey crews, the history of Santa Fe's oldest residences can be resurrected. Added to this is the all-important physical evidence extant in each house. For instance, in some houses the vigas in the ceilings have large holes at one end, where someone once attached a rope so the felled log could be dragged by burros from a mountaintop to Santa Fe. During the restoration of old structures in Santa Fe, various items (likely used as binding) have been found in the mud bricks, including shells, bones, hair, and corncobs.

Like most cities in America, Santa Fe has experienced periods of extensive growth and development, as well as changes in aesthetic tastes, all of which have endangered its historic structures. For example, much of Victorian Santa Fe was destroyed or stuccoed over in the early twentieth century, when many in the city advocated building residences and public edifices in the Spanish Pueblo and Territorial Revival styles. In later years, some complained about this attempt to unify the look of the city. In 1963, when asked about establishing a historic style ordinance, architectural historian Lewis Mumford declared, "Certainly I would have preserved here in Santa Fe some of the buildings of the middle nineteenth century that have been destroyed. That was part of the history of this community. You destroy the memory of the past if you ruthlessly wipe out all buildings of an earlier period in order to make the city look more uniform than any really living community should look."[4] Homeowners, city officials, and preservationists grapple with this same issue today.

In the late nineteenth century visitors noticed that Santa Fe's historic structures needed preserving. In 1880 writer Ernest Ingersoll noted that the city's old customs and ancient landmarks were being threatened by "the railroad [that] has penetrated her borders."[5] Thirty-six years later a writer for the *New Mexican* complained, "By the time the New Mexicans begin to cherish their romantic and historical landmarks, the landmarks will have disappeared!"[6]

In 1926 the city's preservation efforts began in earnest with the founding of the Old Santa Fe Association (OSFA). Established by architect John Gaw Meem and other civic-minded residents, OSFA intended to preserve and maintain the historical structures and traditions of "Old Santa Fe," and to guide its growth and development in order to sacrifice the city's unique charm as little as possible. Today OSFA, the Historic Santa Fe Foundation, and other organizations, aided by city and state ordinances, work exceptionally hard to protect landmarks and vernacular architecture.

In an effort to protect the city's architectural legacy, about 103 Santa Fe buildings have been individually listed on the New Mexico State Register of Cultural Properties since its inception in 1968, as well as hundreds more listed as contributing to one of the four historic districts. Since 1966 there have been about thirty buildings and four historic districts nominated to the National Register of Historic Places. In addition, the Palace of the Governors, Plaza, and Barrio de Analco are National Historic Landmarks—nationally significant historic places designated by the Secretary of the Interior because they possess exceptional value in illustrating the heritage of the U.S.

As a writer for the Santa Fe *New Mexican* stated back in 1889, this city offers "ancient buildings and modern in curious contrast for the sight seer."[7] Today this place, with its magical vistas of the Sangre de Cristo Mountains, brilliant sunshine, vivid blue skies, and varied landscape, continues to offer residents and visitors alike a feast for the eyes. Santa Fe—situated in a state appropriately nicknamed the "Land of Enchantment"—is indeed truly unique.

As Charles F. Lummis wrote in "The Land of Poco Tiempo," New Mexico is an "anomaly" in America, where the "opiate sun soothes to rest, the adobe is made to lean against, the hush of day... [will] not be broken." It is a place where the "enchanted light of its blue skies casts an eternal spell" upon the region's people and picturesque landmarks.[8]

CHAPTER I

LA VILLA REAL DE SANTA FE

A Spanish Colonial Capital, 1609–1821

THE ENCHANTING CITY of Santa Fe, New Mexico, lies at seven thousand feet in the foothills of the Sangre de Cristo (Blood of Christ) Mountains— so christened by the early Spaniards who observed that the heavily forested mountains turned a deep crimson when the sun set. South of the city are rolling hills dotted with piñon and juniper trees and a vista of the grand Sandia Mountains. On the northern horizon are the majestic Jemez Mountains.

In the winter of 1609–10, the first royal governor of New Mexico, Don Pedro de Peralta, established *La Villa Real de Santa Fe* as the seat of Spanish Colonial authority. This makes Santa Fe, after St. Augustine, Florida (established in 1565), one of the oldest European towns within the present-day United States.[1] The neighborhood south of the Rio de Santa Fe (Santa Fe River), Barrio de Analco, was established shortly after Santa Fe's founding, making it one of the oldest settlements of European origin in the U.S.

Situated on arable land on the banks of the river, La Villa Real de Santa Fe had an ideal location. Water from the river and nearby springs was carried into the new city through *acequias*, and the surrounding mountains provided an abundance of wild game and wood for buildings, furniture, farm implements, and carts. And the region was reachable by trails from all directions.

Upon their arrival in New Mexico, the Spanish found American Indians living in communal terraced houses—pueblos—two or more stories high, containing hundreds of rooms and housing thousands of people. The pueblo homes consisted of stone or "puddled" adobe for the walls;[2] vigas overlaid with *latillas* (wood saplings) for the ceiling; and a roof of poles, branches, and packed earth. The small, stacked rooms of the pueblo were accessed primarily through an opening in the ceiling by way of movable ladders (interior rooms were reached by doorways cut into adobe walls). A hole in the roof provided venting for the fire pits placed in the center or corner of each room.

The Spanish settling in New Mexico shared a similar tradition of earth, stone, and wood construction. However, by using the tools they brought with them they improved upon the Indians' building techniques. They used metal hoes to mix the mud and straw into adobe, and wooden forms to shape the adobe into bricks. Metal tools were used to shape timbers, and crowbars and pulleys to raise roof beams into place. The Spanish also introduced new architectural features: ground-level doors, corner fireplaces, *hornos* (beehive-shaped outdoor ovens), and wider rooms (a result of using metal tools to cut larger roof timbers).

Another early building technique used by both the American Indians and the Spanish in New Mexico was *jacal*—vertical wood poles set side by side in a trench, capped by horizontal bond beams, and finished with a thick coat of mud inside and out. The roofs of the *jacales* consisted of vigas resting on bond beams and spanning the structure, then a layer of latillas, grasses, and finally packed dirt. One early visitor to San Juan Pueblo described seeing structures of this type: "The houses here are built of mud and palisades. They appear to have a dry trench, in which a row of palisades, from six to eight inches in thickness, is planted; the interstices of which are daubed with the clayey earth from which they make the 'adobes' that are used in building their walls."[3]

With the exception of the much-remodeled *El Palacio Real de Santa Fe* (Palace of the Governors), little survives of the original fabric of Spanish Colonial Santa Fe. In some cases all that remains are massive cobble foundations, such as those discovered during a 2003–04 excavation of the area behind the palace.[4] Thick adobe walls that likely supported a second story once rested on the two-to-three-foot-wide foundations of river cobbles weighing between ten and one hundred pounds each—tantalizing evidence of pre-1680 Spanish Colonial Santa Fe.

Most of seventeenth-century Santa Fe was in fact destroyed during the Pueblo Revolt of 1680. Buildings that survived the event were later remodeled or superimposed with new structures that all but obliterated the original materials and forms. The fugitive nature of the primary building material—mud bricks—also contributed to the loss of the city's earliest buildings. Almost as soon as they are constructed, adobe houses begin to disintegrate from exposure to sun, wind, and rain. When the royal *presidio* (fortress) was being rebuilt in Santa Fe in 1790, construction work was delayed when about 100,000 adobes that had been stacked for curing were dissolved by unrelenting rains.[5]

The history of New Mexico's earliest residences, therefore, must be reconstructed from the data gathered during archaeological excavations, from documents in the Spanish Archives of New Mexico, from maps and firsthand accounts, and from the original fabric remaining in a handful of existing structures. Dendrochronology—the study of tree rings—using specimens from log ceiling beams has been crucial for dating some of Santa Fe's earliest houses. From these various sources we know that domestic architecture of the period arose from vernacular building traditions that were practiced by the people who settled the region.

In designing the new capital—the first planned Spanish settlement on the northern frontier of New Spain—Don Pedro de Peralta followed the 1573 *Ordenanzas de Descubriemiento* (Ordinances of Discovery), or royal decrees of King Philip II, which detailed the laying out of Spanish towns in the new world. In accordance with the decrees, the villa was arranged around a central plaza, and public, commercial, and institutional buildings were built facing it. Santa Fe's rectangular plaza served as the military parade ground—or *plaza de armas*—of the Spanish garrison. As the central meeting place, it was the starting point for military expeditions and the destination point for supply trains.

One of the first *casas reales* (royal houses) erected by Don Pedro was *El Palacio Real* (Palace of the Governors) on the north side of the plaza, with the presidio on the west side. The presidio included barracks, a guardhouse, and eventually a

TOP

Acoma Pueblo, ca. 1883

Photograph by Ben Wittick, courtesy Palace of the Governors Photo Archives (NMHM/DCA), 016042

BOTTOM

Jacal barn, 519 Canyon Road

high protective wall with towers. Later additions housed the chapel, jail, storage rooms, stables, kitchens, forge, tannery, and slave and servant quarters. Don Pedro also ordered the construction of guarded gates at the plaza's corners and sides that led to various trails and a well-fortified main entrance on the south side that opened onto *El Camino Real* (Royal Highway). Goods from Mexico City were brought to Santa Fe by ox-driven freight wagons along the El Camino Real, and some Spanish colonists of the villa produced furs, hides, and weavings for export to Mexico. The 1,800-mile trip over rough terrain took a grueling six months and was made infrequently; some deliveries were five or six years apart.

The fifty or so Spaniards who relocated with their families to the new capital in 1609 were allotted two lots for a house and garden, two contiguous fields for vegetable gardens, two others for vineyards and olive groves, and four *caballerias* (about 133 acres) of land, as well as water for irrigation.[6] Generally, only prominent citizens were given the land facing the plaza.

Spanish colonists with homes on the plaza and principal streets were required to build *portals* (covered porches) for the "considerable convenience to the merchants who generally gather there."[7] Constructed of hand-hewn log posts topped by *zapatas* (carved ornamental brackets or corbels) and spanned by horizontal beams, the portals were roofed like normal rooms and provided shelter from the blazing sun or monsoon rains.

Within a few blocks of the plaza, Santa Fe's streets gave way to dirt paths that wound around the hills to the east and west along the banks of the Rio de Santa Fe, where the Mexican, Indian, and mestizo settlers built their homes. Clearly, Santa Fe's *vecinos* (citizens) did not abide by the royal ordinance that specified creating a grid of streets radiating from the central plaza. To protect their crops and stock, and to carry on friendly trade with nomadic Indians, they instead built structures near their fields and corrals.[8] As Fray Dominguez noted in 1776, "[T]he Villa of Santa Fe (for the most part) consists of many small ranchos at

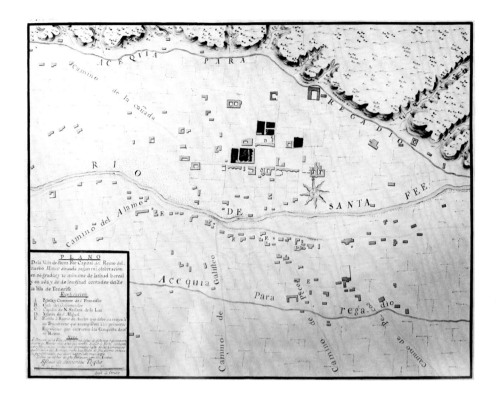

Josef de Urrutia, Plano de la
Villa de Santa Fee Capital del
Reino del nuevo Mexico, *ca. 1766*

Courtesy Palace of the Governors Photo
Archives (NMHM/DCA), 015048

various distances from one another, with no plan as to their location, for each
owner built as he was able, wished to, or found convenient . . . for the little farms
they have . . . for the small herds of cattle they keep . . . or else for other reasons."[9]

The earliest known map of the city, *Plano de la Villa de Santa Fee*, drawn by
Josef de Urrutia in circa 1766, gives an indication of the number, location, and
overall shape of homes in the Spanish Colonial village. It shows that the plaza was
much larger than it is today, extending farther east to about Cathedral Place. It
illustrates the major streets, acequias, and Rio de Santa Fe, and includes a legend
of the most important structures in the village: A) church and convent of St. Francis, B) *Casa del Gobernador* (Palace of the Governors), C) *Capilla de N. Señora de la
Luz* (Church of Our Lady of Light), D) Church of San Miguel, and E) *Pueblo ò
Barrio de Analco*. The cartographer also noted: "to the east of the Villa, about a
league distant, there is a chain of very high forested mountains" and "all the buildings of this place are of adobes."[10]

Comments from eighteenth-century visitors to New Mexico also give an
idea of Santa Fe's early appearance. Virginia native John Rowzee Peyton noted in
1773 that "though a place of inconsiderable size, Santa Fe has been laid out on a
grand scale."[11] Three years later, Fray Francisco Atanasio Dominguez, who
stopped in Santa Fe during his tour of New Mexico missions, described seeing
only one "quasi-street" in the villa that "lacks orderly rows, or blocks, of houses"
and a main plaza surrounded on three sides by "the houses of settlers with alleys
between them. . . . The other side is the government palace, which, with its barracks, or quarters for the guard, and prison, is opposite the chapel [of Our Lady of

Light]." He further explained: "its appearance, design, arrangement, and plan do not correspond to its status as a villa nor to the very beautiful plain on which it lies, for it is like a rough stone set in fine metal. . . . Its appearance is mournful because not only are the houses of earth, but they are not adorned by any artifice of brush or construction."[12] He concluded there was generally "nothing worth noting" about the architecture of New Mexico.

Despite these complaints, it was apparent to Spanish colonists that adobe homes, with walls about two to three feet thick, proved to be uniquely suited to the arid high-desert climate of Santa Fe. The mud walls held the warmth of the day into chilly nights and provided protection and coolness from the midday heat.

The process of making adobe walls is the same today as it was centuries ago. First, earth is dug up and mixed with a little straw and water. Next, the mud mixture is shoveled into rectangular wood frames. Immediately the frames are lifted up and the bricks are laid flat to dry in the sun. After a couple of days the bricks are turned on their edges, and the drying process continues. After a few more days, the bricks are stacked. Builders then lay the bricks in courses using the same mud mixture for mortar. They start the walls directly on the ground or on a stone foundation.

A layer of earthen plaster was typically hand applied to the adobe bricks to protect them from wind and rain erosion. This mud plastering was usually reapplied annually. The mud plastering of walls was usually done by women—a tradition that continues in New Mexico's Puebloan and Hispano communities today. Known as *enjarradoras*, these women work with adobe, mud plaster, clays, and *alízes* (slips) to create functional and beautiful wall finishes. The indelible imprint of their hands is visible on adobe facades across the region.

Santa Feans were rather particular about where they obtained the earth for their bricks and plaster. For example, in 1716 Don Felix Martínez, then governor of Santa Fe, discovered that the best dirt for his building needs was located in the middle of a street adjacent to the plaza. He hired workmen to dig a deep hole in the street and extract the earth for his adobe bricks.[13]

Various sources indicate that the typical home in Spanish Santa Fe was a flat-roofed adobe, consisting of a single file of rooms built around and opening into a *placita* (small plaza or courtyard). By designing the house to open outward, builders were taking advantage of the moderate climate. The rooms were built one or two at a time, initially creating an L-shaped and then a U-shaped house, and sometimes, if resources allowed, a fully realized placita.[14] These house configurations are visible in Urrutia's map.

The flat roofs were constructed of a thick layer of dirt, brush, and branches supported by a ceiling of vigas and *tablas* (split, hand-adzed boards) or latillas. The width of a room often depended upon the length of the vigas. Settlers dragged the felled logs down from the mountains; in rare instances the holes used to tie the rope through the beams are still visible in the vigas of historic Santa Fe homes.

To conserve heat and for defensive purposes, doorways and windows were relatively small and faced into the placita. Sheets of selenite or animal skins were used to cover the windows. Hand-adzed lintels and raised sills were common. In larger homes, a *zaguán* (covered gateway) allowed for horses, wagons, and residents on foot to pass into the placita. Among the few embellishments on the sparse adobe exterior was the portal—a simple type of portico or porch with wooden corbels, columns, and beams that were left plain or decorated with hand-chiseled designs (see above left).

The Spanish Archives of New Mexico provide enlightening details relating to Santa Fe's earliest residences. Most homes were modest, like the one sold in

LEFT

*Adobe residence with portal,
Arroyo Tenorio Street, Santa Fe*

Photograph by Jesse Nusbaum, courtesy Palace of the Governors Photo Archives (NMHM/DCA), 015030

RIGHT

Placita in Santa Fe house, ca. 1882

Photograph by William Henry Jackson, Colorado Historical Society, Denver, Colorado, CHS.J1351

Woman plastering fireplace in New Mexico

Photograph by Jesse Nusbaum, courtesy Palace of the Governors Photo Archives (NMHM/DCA), 061635

1706 by Roman Garcia Juarado that "on one part borders with the royal road that goes to Tesuque" and consists of "three rooms, two middling ones and a capacious sala."[15] The *sala*, or parlor, was usually a large multipurpose room where guests were entertained, food was cooked and served, and the residents sometimes slept. It was the most elaborate, formal room in a dwelling and often contained more woodwork and a finished ceiling of tablas.

At the other end of the spectrum was the spacious, more luxurious residence of Governor Don Felix Martínez. When he died in 1738, his Santa Fe property reverted to the Spanish crown and was inspected by Captain Antonio Montoya of the survey office. The house had not been occupied for several years and was in a state of ruin. Captain Montoya reported that the adobe walls had crumbled because they had "no cornice, no doors nor window sashes."[16] He also stated, "Said house consists of 11 rooms, 5 partly roofed, and contains 105 carved vigas, 574 boards, 212 corbels. The other six rooms have 59 round vigas, and the roofing is of raja [hewn logs], also 2 hallways, one of which has a roof and the other has none, with 1 viga less."

In studying the twenty-eight New Mexican homes described in the Spanish documents, architectural historian Chris Wilson discovered that twenty-four had a sala, nineteen had a *cocina* (kitchen), sixteen had one or more *dispensas* (store-rooms), and fifteen had an *aponsento* (a lodging room, or bedroom).[17]

Spanish Colonial home interiors were generally stark, with compacted-dirt floors and small window openings. The color of the mud-plastered adobe walls was determined by what clay was available. Some clay deposits in the villa were valued for their particular hues—pinks, browns, dark purples, and yellows (*tierra amarilla*), or *jaspe* with flecks of mica.[18] The only decorations were the *retablos* (two-dimensional religious paintings) and *bultos* (three-dimensional religious sculptures) typically found in the *nichos* (spaces carved out of the adobe wall). The Spanish also tended to whitewash the interior surfaces and the walls under open portals with a form of gypsum known as *tierra blanca*.[19]

The simply constructed adobe *fogónes* (fireplaces) were generally placed in the corner and, like the exterior walls, required yearly replastering and repair. Again, the mud plastering of the fogónes was traditionally done by women. In some instances, an elevated shelf or "shepherd's bed," constructed of wood posts and adobe, was built near the fire. The shelf may have been used for sleeping or as a place to prepare meals. One still exists in the De La Peña–Applegate House (see Chapter 2, page 49), and evidence of a similar shelf was found during the 2003–04 excavation of the site behind the Palace of the Governors.[20]

The earliest homes were simply furnished with a few pieces of native pine, but eventually high-quality goods were brought to the region through trade with Mexico along El Camino Real. New Mexicans made pilgrimages south each January to a trade fair in Chihuahua to barter sheep, hides, and blankets for such sought-after luxuries as fine clothing, shoes, iron tools, chocolate, sugar, tobacco, books, porcelain dishes, and leather chests.

More than one hundred wills and fifty estate inventories from New Mexico, dating from the 1693 Spanish reoccupation of the region to Mexican independence in 1821, provide a glimpse of how the earliest Hispano homes were furnished and

decorated.[21] The Museum of Spanish Colonial Art in Santa Fe has re-created an interior of a wealthy colonist's home based on the will and estate inventory of Santa Fe Captain Manuel Delgado (1739–1815).

Towering above the single-story adobe residences of Spanish Colonial Santa Fe were houses of worship. As Zebulon Pike observed in 1806, "There are two churches the magnificence of whose steeples form a striking contrast to the miserable appearance of the houses."[22] One was the *parroquia* at the head of San Francisco Street, which was built by 1627. The earliest photograph of the church shows a fortresslike edifice with crenellated towers and cornices. A small rose window is above the main entrance, the openings in the bell towers have Gothic-style pointed arches, and the grand main doorway is framed by a rounded arch.

The other main church was San Miguel; first built around 1645 by Franciscan Brothers, it faced a modest plaza south of the river in Barrio de Analco. After much of it was destroyed in the Pueblo Revolt of 1680, it was rebuilt in 1710–11 under the supervision of Andres Gonzales, *maestro de la obra* (a "master-mason"), who was in charge of the overall design.[23] Eventually it featured a three-tiered tower (with the upper tower added in the early 1800s). Although it has been extensively renovated over the centuries, San Miguel chapel is an excellent example of Spanish Colonial

Re-creation of late-eighteenth/early-nineteenth-century interior of Captain Manuel Delgado's Santa Fe home, Museum of Spanish Colonial Art

Mission churches and is one of the few remaining eighteenth-century structures in
Santa Fe. By 1880 the church was advertised as one of Santa Fe's most important
landmarks; professional photographers featured different views of the building in
stereographs. One of the first Santa Fe structures to appear on a postcard, San
Miguel is today considered one of the oldest churches in the U.S.

Among the major events that changed the fabric of Santa Fe was the Pueblo
Revolt of 1680. After decades of repression of their families, their culture, and their
native religion, American Indians living along the upper Rio Grande joined forces
to drive out the colonists and Franciscan missionaries. The Tano, Tewa, and other
Puebloan Indians seized Santa Fe and destroyed several of the casas reales. Later
they rebuilt the Spanish seat of government (Palace of the Governors) into a
pueblo featuring two plazas. They piled third and fourth stories onto the Spanish
structure and divided the large interior rooms into more compact, Pueblo-style
living and storage spaces.

In 1692 the king of Spain, out of pride and the need to protect his settlements
in New Spain, issued orders to reconquest the province of New Mexico. Don
Diego de Vargas, a member of one of Spain's leading families, was appointed governor and captain general of the province. He marched into New Mexico with
two hundred soldiers and two cannons to reclaim the capital of Santa Fe. In late
December of 1693 Don Diego and his troops fought a bloody battle with the
Pueblo Indians and accomplished their goal. The fight was personal for Don
Diego, who wrote, after all "it was my palace and casas reales that they had made
into a pueblo."[24] In 1697 Diego's successor, Don Pedro Rodríquez Cubero, demolished the pueblo, built new two-story casas reales, and opened the perimeter of the
plaza for grants to Spanish colonists.

In 1705 Governor Cubero y Valdez issued a *bando* ordering Santa Fe residents
to build their houses and corrals on the royal plaza and four public streets of the
villa so they could be more easily defended from attacks by neighboring Indians.
The royal presidio, including housing units for the troops and their families, was
rebuilt from 1789 to 1791. The following is a list of construction equipment and
material purchased for the builders of the large, rectangular structure: oxen, hand-
barrows, scoops, adobe molds, mixing paddles, axes, straw, mud, iron, and
lumber.[25] Tens of thousands of adobe bricks were manufactured and stacked to dry
for the large military complex.

In 1807, when Zebulon Pike was led into Santa Fe under military escort, he
observed that the villa had a population of about "4,500 souls," all the streets were
very narrow except for three main boulevards, and the houses were decorated with
"a shed before the front" and some had adobe brick flooring.[26] Despite his lacklus-
ter description, by this date Santa Fe was the territory's civil, religious, and social
center and the largest urban center in the west.[27] The Governor's Palace, with its
newly attached presidio that housed one hundred soldiers and their families and
servants, was the royal military and government seat. In addition to numerous
barrel makers, weavers, carpenters, cobblers, blacksmiths, tailors, and mule driv-
ers, the villa was home to wealthy landowners, some of whom maintained both a
town home and country house.[28]

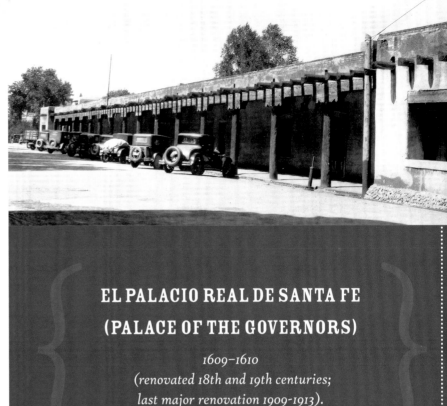

EL PALACIO REAL DE SANTA FE
(PALACE OF THE GOVERNORS)

1609–1610
(renovated 18th and 19th centuries;
last major renovation 1909-1913).

El *Palacio Real de Santa Fe* (Palace of the Governors)—the long, low, flat-roofed adobe with a portal stretching its entire length gracing the plaza's north side—is Santa Fe's most famous landmark. Originally built in 1609–10 by Don Pedro de Peralta, New Mexico's second official governor, the palace is the oldest continuously used public building in the United States. From the beginning it was the central focus of the plaza and the center of communal, economic, and social activity in Santa Fe. It is all that remains of Spain's casas reales.[29]

Today home to the New Mexico History Museum, for over three centuries the palace was the official residence of governors; governors from Spain, Mexico, and territorial New Mexico resided there. The building has also housed various executive, judicial, legislative, military, and other civic offices that reflected the changing roles and civic needs of each successive New Mexico government.[30]

The palace building has been radically altered throughout the centuries, but archival material and archaeological excavations have

LEFT
Palace of the Governors

ABOVE
Palace of the Governors, ca. 1920s
Collection of the author

Postcard, "Greetings from the Old City of Santa Fe," 1905
Collection of the author

enabled historians to re-create some aspects of the original structure. It is believed that the rock foundations for the palace were laid in the winter of 1609, and with the assistance of Tesuque laborers construction was underway by the spring of 1610. The earliest sections were likely built of jacal—with upright, mud-plastered timbers set in trenches—and over the next decades more substantial adobe bricks were added.[31] Most of the floors were likely packed earth, though recent excavations have shown that some palace rooms had patterned adobe brick floors. All the windows and doors opened onto a plaza and enclosed courtyard.

Archaeological excavations at the palace in 1974–75 uncovered Spanish Colonial–era cobblestone and adobe mortar foundations that extend beyond the present-day building. The foundations are one meter or more in width, indicating that the palace—or a portion of it—was originally two stories in height and larger overall.[32] Excavations in 2003–04 of the area behind the palace, in preparation for the building of the new history museum, uncovered massive cobble foundations—again evidence of pre- and post–Pueblo Revolt Spanish Colonial and Territorial period structures (see page 3).[33]

Following the Pueblo Revolt of 1680, when more than one thousand Spanish colonists fled to its walled plaza for protection from Indian warriors, the palace was largely destroyed. The victorious Pueblo Indians adapted the Spanish royal compound for their own use: it was remodeled into a three-to-five-story, E-shaped pueblo fortress with numerous small living rooms and large storage and fire pits.[34] More than one thousand Tano and Tewa Indians occupied the new pueblo. In 1693 Don Diego de Vargas recaptured Santa Fe and the former palace. Diego's successor, Governor Pedro

Detail, Palace of the Governors

Rodríguez Cubero, replaced the multistory pueblo with six smaller buildings.

The next significant document relating to the palace is Governor Don Felix Martínez's inspection report of 1716. He describes how the main palace entrance opened onto a courtyard with a guardhouse, "coachroom," and "two rooms, one above and one below, of adobes in which General Juan Flores had ... a flourmill."[35] He further reported that there was only one usable room with an intact ceiling.

Another document dated 1720—a report of the criminal case against Ysidro Sánchez, who robbed the palace storeroom—indicates that the south facade of the palace had a second-story balcony with a window that overlooked the plaza.[36] The court reported that Sánchez, "deceived by the devil," climbed up to the balcony and inside the window and then walked down the stairs to the first-floor store, where he stole "*campeches*" (blankets) and other items. He later escaped through a door on the ground floor. In addition to the clear reference to a second story, it is fascinating to note that the court record also mentions that when Sánchez hid some of his stolen goods it was behind "vigas that were on the plaza"—a rather surprising place to store vigas.[37]

Fifty-six years later, Fray Dominguez was disappointed with the mud structure: "The government palace is like everything else here, and enough said."[38] The Urrutia map drawn around the same time shows the palace as a single rectangular building facing the plaza, with outbuildings, gardens, and orchards behind.

As the royal palace was enlarged and improved over the following decades, it came to symbolize Spain's power and formidable presence on the remote frontier.[39] It was lavishly furnished and had formal dining rooms for entertaining important visitors. The governor's residence consisted of living rooms, slave and servant quarters, kitchens, banquet halls, gardens, stables, and patios. And the capital government quarters consisted of meeting rooms, a dining hall, a ballroom, and storage rooms.

When an inspection was made of the palace in 1810, the building was described as "suffering from being in ruins, and the exterior crumbling from the continual snows of winter and rains of summer."[40] The inspector also noted that donkeys, pigs, and other animals were often seen running amok in the building. In 1832 it was still "partly in ruins and in a general state of neglect."[41] Despite its condition, some found the old decrepit building romantic. In the early 1850s Marian Russell thought the palace "looked as if it might have been transplanted from medieval ages."[42] Until 1885 the palace served as the seat of the Territorial legislatures, and even after the completion of the capitol building in 1885, the palace continued as the governor's residence for another twenty-four years.

Within years of Santa Fe becoming a territory of the United States, modernization of the palace building began, and each remodeling effort removed layers of authentic details.[43] In 1879 a writer for *Harper's Weekly* declared, "This interesting old building, on account of the repairs repeatedly made upon it nowadays, is fast losing its antique appearance and internal arrangements."[44] An early postcard of "The Old City of Santa Fé" includes a drawing of the Palace of Governors and its fancy Victorian-era facade.

The most radical changes to the palace occurred from 1909 to 1913, when overzealous "restorers" led by Jesse Nusbaum attempted to return the building to what they considered to be its original appearance. The twenty-nine, one-story, adobe-walled rooms were clustered around an interior courtyard that was fronted by a new Spanish Colonial portal.

In 1934 the Historic American Buildings Survey (HABS) recognized the importance of the Palace of the Governors and sent a survey team of Colorado architects and drafters to measure the building. Five years later their measurements were transformed into detailed, scaled drawings. Founded in 1933 as a federal assistance program and still in existence today, HABS identifies and documents surviving architectural masterpieces of the past, particularly those that might be threatened with demolition or development. The twelve HABS photographs and twenty-six sheets of drawings capture the palace as it existed in the early Depression era, when it was a monument to the popular Spanish Pueblo Revival style.

Despite the many remodels, the Palace of the Governors is still an excellent place to learn about Santa Fe's earliest building practices. Small exhibits literally provide a window into the past. For example, by the entrance is a glass-covered doorway that shows a mud-plastered adobe wall and the various finishes added in later years. Elsewhere is an example of a nicho and a Spanish Colonial–era ceiling of hand-adzed vigas and hand-hewn tablas. In 1960 the Palace of the Governors was named a National Historic Landmark—an important designation given by the U.S. Secretary of the Interior for buildings that possess exceptional value in illustrating America's heritage.

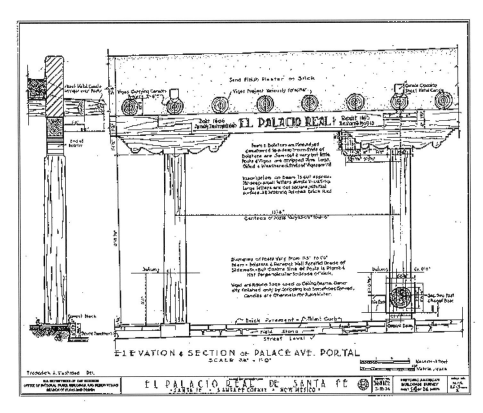

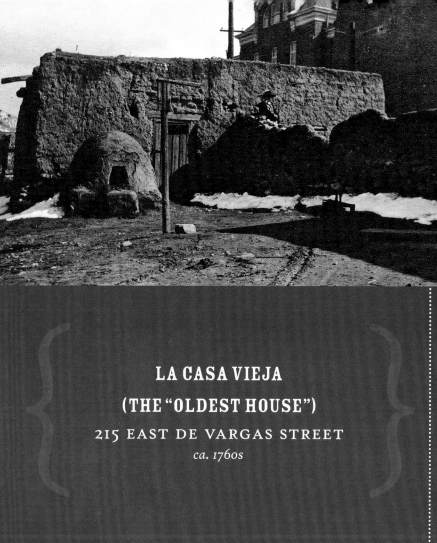

LA CASA VIEJA
(THE "OLDEST HOUSE")
215 EAST DE VARGAS STREET
ca. 1760s

For more than 130 years, this structure, located in one of Santa Fe's oldest neighborhoods—the Barrio de Analco—has been known as *La Casa Vieja*—or the "Oldest House." Although some have claimed that it is the oldest house in the entire United States, most historians today believe that the Gonzales Alvarez House built in St. Augustine, Florida, in the early 1700s, is the oldest surviving Spanish Colonial dwelling. In fact, there are more legends and stories relating to Santa Fe's "Oldest House" than actual records that outline the structure's true history. Still, as a remnant of the type of building once prevalent in the city and as a landmark of the city's cultural history, La Casa Vieja is an important building.

Stylistically part Native American and part Spanish, the house has crudely built adobe-brick walls, low ceilings, hand-hewn vigas, and dirt floors. There once was a traditional horno oven outside. Early photographs indicate that the lower walls of the house may have been

LEFT

The Oldest House

ABOVE

The Oldest House, early 1900s

Photograph by Katherine Stinson Otero, Otero-Stinson Family Papers, MSS 506 BC, The University of New Mexico, University Libraries, Center for Southwest Research

constructed of "puddled" adobe. The structure was originally two stories, but by the early 1900s the second story had been removed. It was built in an area once occupied by the Pueblo Analco in about 1200 AD. Historians based this theory on pottery fragments unearthed in the neighborhood that date from 1100 to 1200 AD.

Dating the house is indeed problematic. Archaeologists Adolph Bandelier and Edgar Lee Hewett agreed that it belonged "mainly to the historical period (or later than 1610)."[45] When Hewett thoroughly examined the walls in 1902, he recorded evidence of early construction: "(1) numerous fragments of recent Mexican adobe work, the result of occasional repairs; (2) large portions, perhaps three-fourths of the entire structure, of old Mexican adobe masonry and (3) in three places, forming the foundation and at no point exceeding eighteen inches in height, considerable fragments of the original pueblo wall, the adobe masses exactly corresponding, in texture, dimensions, and mode of construction, with those in the remaining walls of the pueblo of Kwapoge on the hill formerly occupied by Old Fort Marcy."[46]

Tree-ring specimens taken from vigas in the ceiling of lower rooms in the house indicate an approximate cutting date of 1740 to 1767.[47] The Josef de Urrutia map of circa 1766 (see page 4) shows a structure near San Miguel Chapel that could be the Oldest House. J. J. Stoner's 1882 bird's-eye-view of Santa Fe (see page 94) is one of the first documents to label the building at 215 East De Vargas the "Oldest House." The building also appears in many early photographs of the San Miguel Chapel.

A property deed indicates that Bishop Lamy of Santa Fe purchased the Oldest House from Don Simon Delgado and Dona Peregrina Campbell Delgado in 1859.[48] In 1881

the house, along with San Miguel Chapel and the surrounding property, was sold for around $3,000 to the Christian Brothers, who still own the building today.[49]

By the late 1870s this building was being touted as "the oldest inhabited house in America" in newspaper and journal articles and on postcards and city maps. A romanticized portrayal of the building appeared in *Harper's Weekly* in September 1879. The "oldest house" designation was encouraged by city officials, who hoped to lure tourists to Santa Fe to see its unique historic buildings. In the Santa Fe *New Mexican*'s column featuring information for tourists visiting the city, the "oldest dwelling house in the United States" was listed as a primary point of interest in the "ancient city."

The same engraving of 1879 appeared in *Harper's Weekly* in a July 14, 1883, article about Santa Fe's "tertio-millennial" or 333-year celebration of its founding. The Oldest House was illustrated as an example of what the author called Santa Fe's "ancient and somewhat shabby picturesqueness." The whole celebration, however, was concocted by city leaders to bring more visitors to Santa Fe—the city's founding was not in 1550 as the event claimed, but in 1609–10.

Many photographers of the era captured the house in views intended for tourists, including George C. Bennett, Ben Wittick, Dana B. Chase, William Henry Brown, and William Henry Jackson.[50] In William Ritch's 1885 *Illustrated New Mexico, Historical and Industrial*, the house is again featured as a tourist attraction. "Adjacent to the old church you can see 'The oldest house in America,'" wrote Ritch. "It is a low, two-story structure, the last remains of the ancient Tegua pueblo of Analco. Formerly it was entered as all pueblo houses originally were, from a scuttle in the roof. The sides have since been pierced with doors and windows,

which give it a more modern appearance. Two of the old women still living in the house are claimed to be lineal descendants of the aboriginal occupants."[51]

The advertisements were a success, for indeed the house was on every visitor's itinerary. In 1881 Captain John G. Bourke examined the old structure carefully and "found it to be an extremely antiquated two-story edifice, with *round* rafters thickly encrusted with grime and soot; the second story was reached by a ladder."[52] When Caroline Douglass visited her uncle, Colonel Henry Douglass of the Tenth U.S. Infantry at Fort Marcy in 1889, she wandered through the Barrio de Analco and saw the Oldest House, which she described as "an old Indian adobe dwelling of two stories—from the upper window of which protruded the head of an Indian with his hat on."[53]

Numerous physical alterations to the building have occurred during its lengthy history. In 1892 the *New Mexican* noted that "The oldest dwelling house on American soil is being adorned with a new roof. The vigas which have been used for the past 100 years are as sound as when they were originally cut."[54] Six years later the newspaper described the house as "deserted" and ominously warned that "unless it is looked after at once [it] will go to ruin. This is one of the Santa Fe historic attractions and should be taken care of."[55]

In 1925–26, five members of the Christian Brothers order rebuilt a second story; one of them left a note "expressing some guilt that they might have changed history."[56] In 1928, when Francisco Delgado and his son Eddie were in charge of the house, they opened a curio shop in part of the structure and advertised that they would "give all information desired concerning the history of the most ancient European house in America."[57]

In 2003 the Hampton Inn's Save-A-Landmark Program donated funds to restore the building, especially the interior, which was in a dilapidated condition. The work was completed by volunteers and the Olin Construction Company of Santa Fe, under the supervision of Cornerstones Community Partnerships. Interior walls were replastered, rotting vigas were cleaned, and doors and other fixtures were replaced. On the exterior, the concrete covering the foundation on the facade was replaced with round river rock and sand. In August 2006, when an adobe craftsman was fired for inappropriate changes (including cutting off exposed viga ends), Cornerstones once again stepped in to help preserve the building. Today the house is still owned by the Christian Brothers and the eastern portion is rented as a curio shop, while the western portion remains open to tourists as an example of early Santa Fe architecture.

GREGORIO CRESPIN HOUSE
132 EAST DE VARGAS STREET
ca. 1720–50

One of the unique ways to date Santa Fe's earliest houses is by tree-ring dating, or dendrochronology. Samples taken from timbers used to construct buildings reveal the year in which the timbers were felled. In 1961 core specimens were taken from the vigas in the oldest part of the Crespin House and examined by specialists at the University of Arizona.[58] It was discovered that the cutting period of the vigas was between 1720 and 1750, making the adobe Crespin home, with its distinctive long portal, older than the "Oldest House."

Seventeenth- and eighteenth-century land grant documents in the Spanish Archives of New Mexico list the first owners of this property, which is on the western end of the Barrio de Analco. Among the earliest was Juan de León Brito, who was granted the land by General Don de Vargas. A Tlascala Indian who participated in the reconquest of Santa Fe in 1693, Juan and his brother Diego are mentioned in the "Affidavit of Expenses" for the 1710 rebuilding of San Miguel Church as having contributed 1,500 adobe bricks toward its construction.[59]

LEFT
Gregorio Crespin House

ABOVE
Detail of Territorial-era window,
Gregorio Crespin House

By 1742 the property was owned by Gregorio Crespin, who may have inherited the land from his mother, Sebastiana Flores.[60] Little is known about Crespin, except that he was born in Santa Fe in about 1707, and when the city census was taken in 1790 he was eighty-three years old, a widower, and living with three daughters. In September 1747 he sold the house with "lands and an apricot tree" to Bartolomé Márquez for fifty pesos.[61] Between 1850 and 1862 the property was owned by Don Blas Roibal, whose son Benito sold it to Don Anastacio Sandoval in 1867. At that time the house consisted of five rooms with a portal on the north side and a small placita.[62] When Roberta and George Van Stone purchased the house in 1916, it had been enlarged to twelve rooms.

At some point in the late 1800s the adobe bricks were smooth plastered on the exterior and painted a brick color over which white lines were painted, simulating brick mortar. By disguising the locally made mud bricks with "tattooing" or "stenciling," as it was called, the owners expressed their preference for a more eastern style of building. Likewise, the addition in the mid- to late-1800s of the fired brick coping crowning the north, south, and west walls, the slender rectangular posts supporting the portal, and the Territorial-style trim around the windows and doors reflected Santa Fe's version of the eastern classical Greek Revival manner.

Throughout the house are adobe fireplaces, some with traditional curved openings. One distinctive feature of the interior is an elaborately hand-carved viga, with a stylized four-petal flower and diamond pattern, installed alongside plain vigas in the ceiling of the sala. One source speculates that it may have come from the original San Miguel Church, which was rebuilt in 1710 and is a short walk from the Crespin house.[63] Indeed, the viga is similar to those found under the floor of the church in 1927 that are believed to have been used for the church's ceiling.[64] Perhaps the same artisan carved them in the late seventeenth or early eighteenth century. A similar four-petal flower and diamond pattern can be seen on the beams in the Church at San Ildefonso Pueblo.[65] It seems likely that originally all the vigas in the Crespin ceiling had a similar stylized diamond and floral pattern, and at some point they were replaced with the simpler hand-adzed beams that can be seen there today.

LEFT

Detail of hand-carved viga, living room, Gregorio Crespin House, 1974

Photograph by Susan Olup, courtesy of the Historic Preservation Division, Santa Fe, SF.147

BELOW

Living room fireplace, Gregorio Crespin House, 1974

Photograph by Susan Olup, courtesy of the HistoricPreservation Division, Santa Fe, SF.144

OPPOSITE

Detail, Gregorio Crespin House

PIT HOUSES AND PUEBLOS
SANTA FE'S EARLIEST RESIDENCES

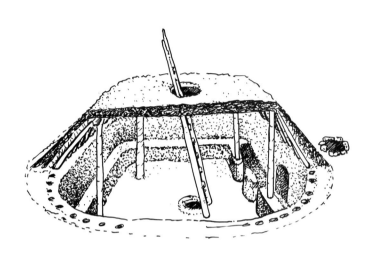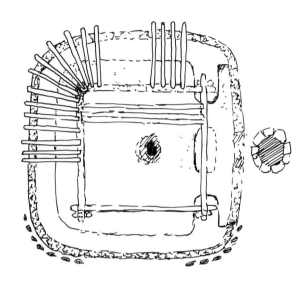

Elevation and aerial views of pit house construction typical of the ancestral Puebloan era

Drawings by Rose Gonnella, 2008

The story of Santa Fe's architectural heritage begins with its earliest inhabitants. As New Mexico State Historian Estevan Rael-Galvez has stated, "The stories of the indigenous people are so essential for understanding this place we now call Santa Fe. The memory, like the built environment, is deeply layered, and remembering the detail of each of those layers will reveal the fullness of a living history."[66]

We must bear in mind, therefore, that throughout the city, hidden beneath multistoried buildings and layers of dirt and rubble, are the ruins of villages that were occupied by Ancestral Puebloans between A.D. 850 and 1425. Among the earliest archaeologists to study these communities was the Swiss-born Adolph Bandelier. In the 1880s, after speaking with local Tewa Indians and analyzing artifacts and other material he observed at several ruins, he concluded that the remains of an ancestral Puebloan village called by the Tewa name O'gha po'oghe ("down at the Olivella shell-bead water") were located under downtown Santa Fe.[67]

In more recent times, tantalizing evidence of the city's prehistoric structures has been unearthed during excavations for various public and private construction projects. Due in part to city and state ordinances passed in the late 1980s requiring that professional archaeological and historical studies precede all private developments, these archaeological digs have deepened our knowledge of Santa Fe's first architecture.

Scholars have learned that ancestral families established permanent settlements on the hills just north of Santa Fe center between 850 and 1000.[68] Subsisting primarily on farming and hunting, they lived clustered together near their fields in pit houses—circular spaces dug from the earth (about fourteen to twenty-two feet in diameter and at least three feet deep) with upright posts that supported a roof of wood limbs, reed mats, and mud. The houses were entered through an opening in the roof that also acted as a smoke hole. A central fire pit provided warmth; smaller, rock-lined pits were used for cooking; and small floor pits and wall niches served as storage areas. Remnants of pit houses of this type have been uncovered at various sites in Santa Fe, including on land near the Federal Courthouse.

Further discoveries suggest that by the early 1100s families had moved to the piedmont hills north of the Santa Fe River, where they built small, above-ground houses with puddled-adobe (hand-shaped mud) walls and roofs of log beams covered by branches, grass, and mud. Like the earlier pit houses, these were purely functional structures. Most rooms were small and dark, with few if any windows, and were accessed either through an opening in the roof or through interior doors. Single families had the use of two to four rooms, with spaces used for living and cooking containing hearths and underground storage pits.

Over time, as the population grew, Ancestral Puebloans built larger, multistoried, terraced villages (called pueblos by the Spanish) grouped around communal open spaces (plazas), with kivas (below-ground chambers, usually circular) for religious and social activities. Consisting of stone set in mud mortar or mud mixed with ashes or dried plant material, the pueblos were built by everyone in the community—men, women, children, and the elderly participated.[69] The society was based on communal farm-

ing and worship. Artifacts and the remnants of buildings and storage pits belonging to a village of this type were unearthed during the 2006 and 2007 excavations of the property where the Santa Fe Community Convention Center now stands. Conducted by the Office of Archaeological Studies, the study revealed that "El Pueblo de Santa Fe" was occupied between 1250 and 1425.

For the early Puebloans the built environment was a reflection and an extension of the natural environment. As writer Rina Swentzell of Santa Clara Pueblo explains, "The adobe structures flowed out of the earth, and it was often difficult to see where the ground stopped and where the structures began. . . . We are synonymous with and born of the earth, so are we made of the same stuff as our houses."[70] Swentzell also observed that "The entire community was the house," and indeed the pueblos were and continue to be communal, interconnected structures where daily life is shared by all.

After a twelve-year drought forced the occupants of El Pueblo de Santa Fe to leave, Santa Fe served as a temporary home to indigenous travelers passing through the region.[71] By the time Don Pedro de Peralta and his caravan of Spanish colonists arrived in 1609 to establish La Villa Real de Santa Fe, all that remained of the ancestral villages were subtle mounds of earth scattered across the hilly landscape. The mud structures had disintegrated into the earth from whence they came and became the foundation on which future dwellings were built. We must respect and remember these hallowed grounds.

CHAPTER 2

A MEXICAN TOWN

1821–46

T HE NEWS OF Mexico's independence from the Kingdom of Spain reached La Villa Real de Santa Fe in September 1821. The Mexican flag was raised in the Plaza de Santa Fe, and all local government officials swore allegiance to *la Independencia del Imperial*. Then in January of 1822, as demanded by decree from the Mexican government, the city celebrated in grand style. Citizens braved the frigid winter temperatures to enjoy the bell ringing, music, orations, dramatic presentations, military parades, Pueblo Indian dances, and a lavish ball at the old adobe Palace of the Governors.

At the beginning of Mexican rule the population of Santa Fe was about five thousand souls. The governor for much of the period was Manuel Armijo, who was born into a wealthy Albuquerque family and became a fine administrator and clever politician. He was also known to be arrogant, quick tempered, and tough. Armijo was not popular with Anglo-Americans, who described him as a greedy tyrant. When the governor attempted to stop illegal fur trapping by Americans in Mexican territory, Armijo further angered the visitors from the States.[1]

Following independence from Spain, Mexico legalized foreign trade. Within months, Anglo-Americans from the East, riding in wagons laden with goods, traveled down the Santa Fe Trail to sell their calicoes, tools, medicines, and other items in the plaza. The traders left the city with ox-driven wagon loads of gold, silver, buffalo hides, woven blankets, and wool. Goods also continued to move north and south along El Camino Real, Santa Fe's link with Mexico. As a result of the increased trade, Mexican-era Santa Fe prospered and grew.

To accommodate the new business, merchants erected large buildings along the south side of the plaza to serve as retail stores and warehouses. Second stories were built for extra space. In addition, hotels, stables, wagon repair shops, and other businesses were built on or near the plaza. Officials in the Palace of the Governors regulated prices, collected freight taxes, and distributed mail.[2]

Santa Fe during this period still consisted primarily of mud residences with pine beams supporting flat roofs and mica windows. Mica, readily available in New Mexico and easily separated into thin, transparent sheets, proved to be an ideal window covering. Although they lacked decoration, the houses possessed a striking sculptural quality in the rounded edges of the adobe walls and fireplaces. There were also several stone and adobe churches in the Mexican town, including La Castrense, a military chapel facing the plaza. With its Spanish paintings brought from Cadiz in 1812, this chapel was considered the handsomest building in town.[3]

OPPOSITE

Sala, with Boris Gilbertson fireplace, Vigil-White House

Home interiors of the period were whitewashed, sparsely decorated with retablos and other religious objects, and meagerly furnished with simple pieces of native pine, animal skins, and *jergas*—carpets made from coarse, locally woven textiles. Openings between rooms were closed with pieces of fabric or hide, and floors were still packed earth. Most residents slept on the floor on mattresses that were rolled up and used as settees during the day.[4] Trade with the States brought some improvements for Santa Fe homes: calico and gingham to tack on the walls, looking glasses, colored prints of Catholic saints, and an occasional piece of fancy furniture.

On the bare and dusty plaza where the flag of Mexico was raised, animals wandered unattended and a few fledgling cottonwoods struggled to grow. Antonio Barreiro observed in 1832 that Santa Fe's main plaza was "quite extensive," the streets off the plaza were "irregular," the main street and plaza were "bordered by frame porticoes," and "around the plaza are scattered many houses without any order and at distances which make frequent and daily communication inconvenient."[5] Twelve years later, Anglo-American trader James Josiah Webb found that Santa Fe "houses were nearly all old and dilapidated, the streets narrow and filthy."[6] However, he did come across several "grand houses for the time" with small farms and orchards that were built not far from where the Presbyterian Church now stands. He found only a handful of Americans who lived in the city as permanent residents.

The governor's residence was still called the casa real, but it was in very poor condition.[7] The governor's family and servants were forced to move from room to room as repairs were made to the dilapidated edifice. The ballroom still had a packed-dirt floor and door panels made of tanned hide that were faux painted to look like wood. By the 1840s pine portals had been built along the east, south, and west facades; public meetings and food markets were held out front and at the west end. Much of the nearby presidio was also in ruins. To raise some revenue the city council discussed selling the remaining adobe bricks of the wall that surrounded the barracks—most of the bricks had already been hauled away by residents for new structures.[8]

As the century progressed, Anglo-American visitors continued to be disdainful of the city's buildings. In the early 1840s, Josiah Gregg observed, "In architecture, the people [of Santa Fe] do not seem to have arrived at any great perfection, but rather to have conformed themselves to the clumsy style which prevailed among the aborigines, that to waste their time in studying modern masonry and

Adobe buildings on San Miguel Street (now East De Vargas), ca. 1890
Photograph by Dana B. Chase, courtesy Palace of the Governors Photo Archives (NMHM/DCA), 0110509

Wagon trains, south side of the plaza, San Francisco Street, 1873
Courtesy Palace of the Governors Photo Archives (NMHM/DCA), 0144637

the use of lime. The materials generally used for building are of the crudest possible description; consisting of unburnt bricks, about eighteen inches long by nine wide and four thick, laid in mortar of mere clay and sand. These bricks are called *adobes*, and every edifice, from the church to the palacio, is constructed of the same stuff."[9] Gregg also found that in general New Mexican carpentry and cabinetwork consisted of timber that was "hewed out with the axe."

Perhaps the most interesting document pertaining to Mexican-era Santa Fe is the code of municipal ordinances drafted in 1845 by the town council (*Muy Illustre Ayuntumiento*) to encourage cleanliness and morality among the population and make Santa Fe a more livable and attractive place.[10] To administer the ordinances the council divided the town into four barrios: San Francisco, San Miguel, Nuestra Señora de Guadalupe, and Torreón. An *alcade* was assigned to each barrio and was responsible for reporting violations of the code. The council ordered the alcades to keep their neighborhoods under surveillance, watching out for vagabonds, thieves, rustlers, and other *malhechores* (malefactors). The council ordered the alcades and the citizens of each barrio to keep the streets clean and in a state of good repair; plant trees whenever possible; repair or tear down dilapidated structures; and discontinue the practice of tying up pack mules and saddle horses to the columns supporting the portals around the plaza (as it was causing the roof to sag).

The council devoted several articles in the code to the improvement of personal behavior. The following are just a few of these demands: during religious processions officials were ordered to maintain an atmosphere of reverence and decorum in Santa Fe; after nightfall all loud shouting and the indiscriminate discharge of firearms was forbidden; tightrope walkers, acrobats, and other public entertainers were required to obtain permits; and during the day, horse racing and cockfighting were not allowed on the city streets, which were also to be kept clear of drunkards and prostitutes.

One of the neighborhoods the town council sought to control was the Barrio de Nuestra Señora de Guadalupe, a Hispano farming community that developed around the Santuario de Guadalupe (built in the late 1700s by Franciscans and remodeled in 1881 and 1922). Using water from the acequias along Alto Street and El Camino Real (today called Agua Fria Street), the families of this barrio grew alfalfa, corn, chili, and fruit trees.[11] When feast days such as *el dia de Guadalupe* (December 12) were celebrated, parishioners walked from the Santuario to the altars they had erected in their homes. The houses built in this neighborhood shared the same aesthetic as the rest of Santa Fe: they were simple, sparsely decorated, earthen-hued, and flat-roofed adobes that generally fronted directly onto the road. Some were embellished with portals.

Again, like in the Spanish Colonial period, no unremodeled houses of the Mexican era exist. However, some streets in the Barrio de Guadalupe retain the flavor of this early period. And the Donanciano Vigil house on Alto Street, being preserved by the Historic Santa Fe Foundation, is an excellent example of life in the Mexican barrio.

DONACIANO VIGIL–
CHARLOTTE WHITE HOUSE
518 ALTO STREET
ca. 1820s (renovations 1960s–1980s)

Described as a "retired, quiet retreat, once abounding in magnificent trees, planted by the hands of Judge [Juan] Vigil,"[12] the Vigil-White homestead is situated in the ancient Barrio de Guadalupe, near the Santuario de Guadalupe. The house is named for both one of the earliest owners, Donaciano Vigil, who served as military secretary to Governor Manuel Armijo during Mexican rule, and one of its last owners, Charlotte White, who with her partner, Boris Gilbertson, lovingly restored the old adobe in the mid-twentieth century.

Today the house is owned by the Historic Santa Fe Foundation (HSFF) and is considered to be one of the most significant structures in the city. It is one of a handful that still has authentic mud-plastered walls on the exterior. Shards and flints were discovered on the land dating to the 1300s, indicating that Indians were actually the very first inhabitants of the site.[13]

In the early 1800s Don Juan Cristóbal Vigil built the first house on the property in the typical Spanish Colonial manner: a single-

LEFT
Zaguán with penitentiary brick flooring, Vigil-White House

ABOVE
Charlotte White in doorway of Vigil-White House, ca. 1959

Courtesy of the Historic Santa Fe Foundation

story, four-room, adobe-walled structure built around a placita. The house faced the Santa Fe River, which then flowed heavily with water draining from the mountains. Vigil described the property in his will of 1832: "I declare for my goods the house of my adobe which is composed of four parts and an orchard with five fruit trees, and in addition to this a plot of land close by, and contiguous to the said land a large room and another structure which because they are old have been assigned as a stable for the animals and a barn."[14] An important soldier and local government official, Juan Vigil lived in the home with his wife, María Antonia Andrea Martínez, and their brood of ten children.

In 1842 Juan and Maria's son Donaciano Vigil (1802–1877), who was likely born in the house, inherited a portion of the building. Over the next year he gradually purchased additional rooms and adjacent lands from relatives, until he was the sole owner of the extensive riverfront property. Including the sizeable orchard planted by his father, the property was likely the largest in the Barrio de Guadalupe.[15]

Donaciano was one of the most important military and political figures of his day. From 1842 to 1846 he served as captain of the Presidial Company of San Miguel del Vado, and as military secretary to Governor Armijo. After American occupation in 1846, he was appointed secretary of the new territory of New Mexico by General Stephen Watts Kearny. After the assassination of Governor Charles Bent in 1847, Vigil took over as acting civil governor, a post he held until the Treaty of Guadalupe Hidalgo in 1848. From 1848 to 1850 he served as secretary of the territory and as registrar of land titles. In a way, Vigil was also one of Santa Fe's first historic preservationists. In 1851 he organized local opposition to the U.S. Army's plans to use the old military chapel of La Castrense for secular purposes.

Naturally, Donaciano and his wife, Refugia Sánchez Vigil, made their own alterations to the property. They added space for entertaining guests, as their home was then one of the centers of civic and political activity in Santa Fe. The couple lived there until 1855, when Donaciano retired from public life and they moved to a ranch on the Pecos River. The following year they sold the Alto Street property for $250 to Vicente Garcia.

The Vigil homestead was altered significantly—but sensitively—by subsequent owners.[16] In 1946, when architect and artist William T. Lumpkins purchased the property for $700, the old adobe was in a dilapidated condition. He began a major renovation, but due to financial difficulties was

ABOVE
Window detail, south wall of placita, Vigil-White House

OPPOSITE
Vigil-White House

unable to complete the project. When Charlotte White and her longtime companion, the celebrated artist-sculptor Boris Gilbertson, purchased the house in 1959 for about $4,000, it had been abandoned for many years and was in very poor condition. "The roofs were leaking, the walls were falling down and there were tin cans everywhere. Nobody wanted it. They thought it was hopeless," recalled White.[17]

Over the next two decades, she and Gilbertson lovingly restored every inch of the property, using traditional materials of northern New Mexico and employing local craftsmen to replace adobe and vigas. The property then included the main building (where the sala is located) and an unconnected building behind it. The couple focused their attention on the main building first, where they lived among the debris and chaos during the twenty-year-long renovation. Throughout this time, White held down various jobs in Santa Fe and Gilbertson struggled to make a living as an artist. Some of his whimsical animal sculptures are still on display in the Alto Street home. His skills can also be seen in the carvings on the massive front door, in the portal of the zaguán, and in numerous other handcrafted features.

In restoring the spectacular rectangular sala, with its twelve-foot-high ceilings and massive adobe walls, Gilbertson removed a northwest door to build a traditional corner fireplace, replaced rotting window frames, and relocated some windows and doors. Just outside the sala, he tore down a wall to reveal the original zaguán—the long, covered passageway that connects the front and back buildings—and built a wood portal that opens onto the placita. When nearly two feet of dirt was removed from the placita, Gilbertson and White uncovered Vigil's river-rock well.

Among the features that White and Gilbertson inherited from the Lumpkins renovation were the more than one-hundred-year-old wood doors and window frames that he salvaged from either the Victorian-era St. Michael's

College (1878) or Loretto Academy (1881).[18] The Territorial-style window frames are notable for their round-arched shape and unusual undulating outer frame. Gilbertson and White used many recycled materials as well.[19] For example, they used red bricks from the old state penitentiary (built in 1884–85 on Cordova Street and torn down in the mid-1950s) for the patio and flooring. They also used penitentiary bricks, costing one cent a piece, for several courses of brick coping on the adobe parapets. This decorative detail, which also helped prevent the adobe walls from eroding, was typically found in Territorial-style buildings in Santa Fe after 1846—a result of American influence and the availability of brick in the city. Last but not least, Gilbertson created a pathway of cut stones, also from the penitentiary, to replace the cement steps that led from Alto Street into the house.

Determined to maintain the historic integrity of the house, White arranged to have the exterior adobe walls repaired and finished in authentic mud plaster. In her memoirs, she described hiring two women from the village of Cañones to apply the final coat in June 1961. White explained, "We built a fire in the patio for the finishing coat. They got a big kettle and made a paste out of tortilla flour and water, which they mixed with mud....It dried like cement and lasted for years."[20] The HSFF continues to preserve and repair the mud-plastered facade.

The last section to be restored by Gilbertson and White was the south or back building that was roofed but had no ceiling. It was likely used by the Vigils as stables. By the late 1970s, this building had been transformed into a kitchen, bedrooms, and a dining area.

In 1969 the house was one of the first sites to be placed on the State Register of Cultural Properties, after the passage that year of New Mexico's historic-preservation bill, and in 1972 it was added to the National Register of Historic Places. After Gilbertson died in 1982, White lived in the house until her death in 2002. Fearing what might happen to the beloved historic house, she bequeathed the property to the HSFF. The latter takes very seriously its role as steward of White and Gilbertson's interpretation of a Spanish-era dwelling.

JOSÉ AND ISABEL SENA
HOUSE AND PLAZA
PALACE AVENUE
ca. 1840 (restoration 1927)

In the spring of 1882, Major José D. Sena put his Palace Avenue mansion up for rent. In the advertisement he described it as "A large and commodious house consisting of twenty-three rooms, a corral, and an orchard bearing fruit with seventy-three fruit trees, known as the Sena building . . . north and opposite the Catholic Church."[21] This luxurious-sounding property in fact evolved from just a few simple square adobe houses that date to the early 1800s, when Santa Fe was under Mexican rule.

The land on which the Sena House and Plaza stand can be traced even earlier, to the late 1600s, when a Spanish conquistador named Don Arias de Quiros was awarded the property by General Don Diego de Vargas as a reward for helping retake the Villa de Santa Fe from the American Indians in 1693.[22] The next document relating to the land dates to 1796, when it was owned by Don Juan Estevan Sena, a descendant of Bernardino de Sena who had come to New Mexico in 1693.

LEFT
José and Isabel Sena House and placita, Palace Avenue
Courtesy of the Gerald Peters Gallery

ABOVE
Sena House placita, ca. 1935
Photograph by T. Harmon Parkhurst, courtesy Palace of the Governors Photo Archives (NMHM/DCA), 051558

Trader James Josiah Webb observed in 1844 that Don Juan's house was one of only three on east Palace Avenue (between Washington Street and the *ciénega*, or marshland). He also recalled that on the southeast corner of the plaza there was "a store occupied by Don Juan Sena as agent of Don José Chávez. This was the second-best store in town, and floored with plank—the only plank floor in New Mexico."[23]

Don Juan and his wife gave the Palace Avenue land and a modest adobe house, in 1867, to their son, Major José D. Sena. A Civil War hero who had served with distinction in the Union Army under Kit Carson, José served as sheriff of Santa Fe County in the 1860s. The *New Mexican* reported on his peace-keeping duties: "The plaza was enlivened by a fierce encounter between two pugilists of the female persuasion, and hair pulling was the order of the day until Maj. Sena arrived . . . and led the combatants to quarters in the county jail."[24] During his active political career, he became known as a renowned orator in both Spanish and English. Notably, he gave an address in Spanish at the 1875 celebration of Jean-Baptiste Lamy's elevation to archbishop. In the summer of 1883, attired as a "Spanish Chieftain" in crimson, black, and gold, with boots, helmet, and sword, and riding a "spirited charger," Sena acted as chief marshal of Santa Fe's Tertio-Millennial celebration.[25]

After Major Sena and his wife, Doña Isabel Cabeza de Vaca Sena, moved into the Sena family home in the late 1860s, they added on more adobe-walled rooms to accommodate their growing family. Eventually they had twenty-three children, all of whom were born in the house. Over time the house expanded into a U-shaped mansion with twenty-three rooms grouped around a large placita. The family lived in rooms on the south (along Palace Avenue) and in the two-story west wing and single-story east wing. On the north side of the courtyard were the outbuildings: stables, storerooms, servant quarters, and two wells.

By 1868 the family had a ballroom built on the second story of the west wing that was occasionally used for public events. It was not unusual in the frontier Territorial period

OPPOSITE

Second-floor ballroom, Sena House
Courtesy of the Gerald Peters Gallery

RIGHT

Detail of brick coping and canale, Sena House
Courtesy of the Gerald Peters Gallery

Sena House (right side of photo), ca. 1915
Courtesy Palace of the Governors Photo Archives (NMHM/DCA), 093165

for residences to serve as sites for multiple civic and social activities.[26] The events held at the Sena house were recorded in the *New Mexican*; for example, in July 1868 it was noted: "A grand entertainment will be given at Sena's Hall this evening, by Professor Pollock of Vocal and Instrumental Music."[27] The newspaper also made note whenever improvements were made to the property. In 1869 it reported: "Major J. D. Sena is one of our most enterprising citizens. He has done as much as any other man towards improving Santa Fé. This spring he has beautified his grounds by planting a great many fruit trees, rose bushes, etc."[28] And many years later, when Sena laid the first brick pavement in Santa Fe, in front of his house, the paper wrote: "It is a great improvement and other property owners should follow suit."[29]

Devout Catholics, the Sena family contributed to the annual Corpus Christi celebration by building an altar under the portals of the Palace of the Governors.[30] Eventually, after the children matured and left home, the Senas rented out various rooms. For instance, in 1872 John P. Clum started Santa Fe's first school conducted entirely in English in one of the rooms, and in 1892, after the Territorial capitol burned, the second-story ballroom served as a meeting place for the Territorial Assembly.

Until about 1870, because of the ciénega to the east, Palace Avenue ended approximately where the Sena house was built. Gradually the area was filled in, the street extended eastward, and a fashionable residential area developed, where wealthy merchants such the Spiegelbergs and Staabs built their mansions.

Like most Santa Fe buildings the Sena house has gone through various architectural transformations. During the American Territorial period, a provincial Greek

José and Isabel Sena House
Courtesy of the Gerald Peters Gallery

Revival–style portal supported by square posts of white-washed lumber capped with simple molding was added to the facade, and pedimented lintels were placed over windows and doors. In addition, brick coping resembling Greek Revival–style dentils was installed on the adobe walls. In the 1880s and 1890s, when Santa Fe was undergoing "Americanization," various improvements were made to the Sena house, including the removal of the 1840s–50s Territorial-style portal.[31]

By the 1910s the house was in poor condition, with its mud-plaster facade disintegrating into the dirt of Palace Avenue. In 1927 the Sena family heirs deeded the property to Senator Bronson M. Cutting and the sisters Amelia and Martha White. Two years later they hired William Penhallow Henderson to remodel the hacienda. An artist, furniture maker, and architect, Henderson established the Pueblo-Spanish Building Company in 1925, through which he designed, built, and restored many residences and public structures in Santa Fe.

Henderson restored the older sections of the Sena house, including reinstating the whitewashed Territorial-era porch. He also designed and constructed a two-story wing at the rear of the building that enclosed the placita completely. The final result is a harmonious building design, with the old and new sections unified by Henderson's use of light stucco, heavy posts and lintels, and Territorial-style brick dentil coping.[32] Around the same time Henderson was remodeling the Sena house, it became a commercial complex with shops and offices. Since 1981 the property has been owned by a private business.[33] Known as Sena Plaza, it continues to house shops, and a restaurant graces a corner of the serene placita.

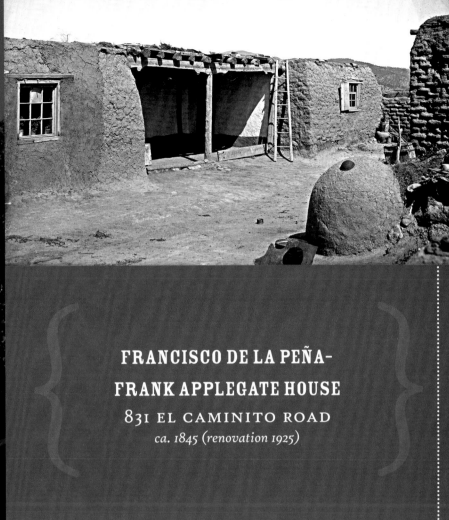

{ FRANCISCO DE LA PEÑA– FRANK APPLEGATE HOUSE

831 EL CAMINITO ROAD

ca. 1845 (renovation 1925)

I n the early 1800s the De La Peña property, with its numerous acequias, was one of the largest sheep ranches in Santa Fe. The earliest
record of the property indicates that it was sold by Tomas de Jesus
Lopez to Francisco De La Peña in May of 1845 for $114. Typical of
Mexican-era Santa Fe, the original building was rustic, single-story,
and flat-roofed, with the softly undulating walls of handmade adobe.
It contained three and a half rooms and featured an open portal off the
east end for corralling the sheep at night and a portal at the front, with
whitewashed walls and beautifully hand-carved zapatas. A horno oven
was in the front yard.

A distinguished officer in the Mexican Army, Sergeant Francisco De La Peña lived in the adobe with his wife, Isabelita, and
their many children. Francisco was involved in several campaigns
against American Indians in the region and received the Shield of
Honor award for his bravery in fighting against the Texas Expedi-
tion of 1841. He served in the presidial companies of Santa Fe and

LEFT

*Applegate additions with Spanish
balconies, De La Peña–Applegate House*

Courtesy of the Gerald Peters Gallery

ABOVE

De La Peña–Applegate House, 1912

Photograph by Jesse Nusbaum, courtesy Palace of the
Governors Photo Archives (NMHM/DCA), 061508

Frank Applegate, ca. 1920

Frank Applegate Photographic Collection,
Item #000-097-0008, Center for Southwest Research,
University Libraries, University of New Mexico

De La Peña–Applegate House, July 1937 (taken for the Historic American Buildings Survey)

Photograph by Frederick D. Nichols, courtesy Palace of the Governors Photo Archives (NMHM/DCA), 132158

San Miguel before the Americans took control of New Mexico in 1846. By the time Francisco died in 1887, his home had grown to accommodate his family of ten. When Isabelita died in 1909, the property was divided among the six surviving children.

Frank Applegate (1881–1931), a ceramist, teacher, painter, and important early member of the Santa Fe artists' colony, purchased the house and land in 1926. At that time the Santa Fe *New Mexican* called the property "perhaps the last large old Spanish hacienda available in the city."[34] Head of the sculpture and ceramics department at Trenton (New Jersey) School of Industrial Arts, Applegate first came to Santa Fe in 1921 with his wife, Alta, and daughter during a tour of the country to study native clays.[35] After one short week of camping in the orchard of Gerald and Ina Sizer Cassidy on Canyon Road, the Applegates decided to uproot their lives and move to Santa Fe.

Once settled in the city, Frank became acquainted with Los Cinco Pintores, five young, male artists living and working in the Camino del Monte Sol area. A student of architecture in college, Applegate gave advice to the painters when they restored old adobe homes. The latter were called "five little nuts in five adobe huts."[36] An ardent preservationist, Applegate amassed a large collection of Spanish handicrafts

and participated in a movement to restore Northern New Mexico churches. He also helped establish, along with his good friend the writer Mary Austin, the Spanish Colonial Arts Society in 1929 to encourage and promote traditional Hispano arts.

In designing his new-old home, Applegate made many alterations to the De La Peña property: he built a second story, added additional rooms at ground level, and thickened the parapet over the portal. He also shifted the original ground-floor, hand-hewn portal lintel up to a new second-story porch and placed a replica on the first floor. As with most authentic historic adobe homes in Santa Fe, rooms were added (by Applegate and later owners) organically, so that the house wraps in a U-shape around the original front placita.

Determined to preserve the original character of his home as much as he could, Applegate incorporated authentic details, such as wood Spanish Colonial balconies that he rescued from an old building about to be demolished. He also had several old New Mexican *alacenas* (cupboards) built into the walls, and he replaced rotting log vigas with squared-adzed beams and antique carved corbels in the ceilings. He retained the three-foot-thick adobe walls in the oldest sections of the house, which create wonderfully deep win-

Alacena in the dining room, De La Peña–Applegate House

Courtesy of the Gerald Peters Gallery

Detail of living room beams and corbels, De La Peña–Applegate House

Courtesy of the Gerald Peters Gallery

dowsills. The present living room was one of the original rooms and today exhibits the success of Applegate's restoration and later owners' preservation of the space.

One of the most remarkable features of the house is the "shepherd's bed," built in the east portal that was enclosed sometime in the early 1900s. According to local tradition, such beds or platforms were placed adjacent to the corner fireplace to keep the shepherd warm while tending to his flock at night. In 1912 Jesse Nusbaum captured a wonderful image of this room, which has been so well preserved by Applegate and subsequent owners. In a 1926 editorial about how "picturesque features of the old houses are being used intelligently and effectively" by Santa Feans, Applegate's efforts were praised. "In the ancient Peña house being remodeled by Frank Applegate, there is even an adobe bed of some centuries standing which is being preserved."[37]

The Applegate home drew national attention as an excellent example of Spanish Pueblo architecture. In 1929 *House and Garden* magazine published photographs of the exterior and interior, including shots of the Applegate's American Indian and Spanish Colonial art collections. The following year *Ladies Home Journal* printed pictures of the house taken by famed photographer Ansel Adams.[38]

By the time of Applegate's untimely death in 1931, the De La Peña house had quadrupled in size.[39] Seven years later, the remodeled building caught the attention of the Historic American Buildings Survey (HABS) as a significant building worthy of recording for preservation. When architect and Yale graduate Frederick D. Nichols, of the Washington HABS office, was sent to New Mexico to document various structures, he took four photographs of the De La Peña–Applegate House, three exterior (see page 46, top right) and one interior of the sala corner fireplace.

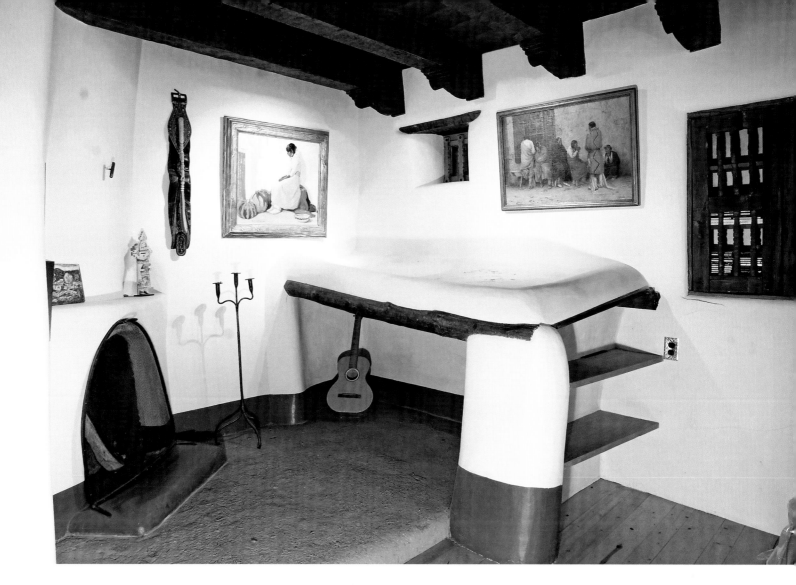

CORBELS
A KEY FEATURE IN NEW MEXICAN ARCHITECTURE

By James Hare,
Executive Director, Cornerstones Community Partnership, Santa Fe

An intricately carved corbel supporting the choir loft in the Santuario de Guadalupe, Santa Fe

Handcrafted corbels are frequently the most decorative wooden elements found in adobe architecture of northern New Mexico. They also perform the essential function as brackets that distribute the heavy load of the flat earthen roof system. In exterior portals, double-ended corbels—locally termed *zapatas*—are employed as capitals between the post-and-beam system utilized to support the portal roof. They also provide a surface area for carved and painted decoration—executed with knives, chisels, and scribes and colored with earth pigments. In the interior, corbels support vigas (roof timbers) and side walls, and once again provide a surface for embellishment.

Because the function of support increased in importance as the width of the space being enclosed grew in size, the most impressive examples of corbels created with adze and chisel are found in the missions, churches, and chapels of the region, the largest of which have roof timbers approaching thirty feet in length.[40] The corbels in domestic buildings—including some structures in Santa Fe—are usually carved from a single piece of local pine, while those of the larger religious buildings are often composed of several separate pieces of wood joined together in an upside-down step fashion. The resulting composite element is structurally more capable of supporting and anchoring massive roof beams as well as visually satisfying the proportions of grand interior volumes.

Regardless of the purpose of the building for which they were created, the form of New Mexican corbels invariably approximates the scrolled volute form that originated in corbels associated with the Mujédar architecture of Moorish Spain and which was imported by the Spanish to the New World along with the requisite vernacular interpretation. A fine example of Mujédar influence can be found in the late-eighteenth-century mission church of San José de Gracia in the village of Las Trampas between Santa Fe and Taos.

Elaborate carved and painted decoration enhances the surface of many corbels, particularly those remaining from the eighteenth century. However, in New Mexico the effect is less elaborate than the contemporary examples from the remaining flat-roofed churches of Mexico. Stunning examples can be found in the sixteenth-century church of San Esteban; Tizatlán in Tlaxcala, Mexico; and Nuestra Señora de Guadalupe at El Paso del Norte (present day Juarez, Mexico), where the Camino Real crossed into New Mexico to begin its arduous journey to Santa Fe.

Domestically, corbels would have served the same structural purpose found in the ecclesiastic architecture, however, the smaller volume of the typical Spanish Colonial house made their structural function much less important. There are few if any extant examples of the domestic interior use of corbels from the seventeenth and eighteenth centuries in New Mexico. As architectural historian Bainbridge Bunting emphasizes, "less is known about the homes in which the Spanish colonists lived than about Indian dwellings of the previous thousand years."[41] We can only suppose that when they were used in domestic interiors it would have been more for luxury than necessity. The extra expense and effort required to produce and decorate corbels for domestic consumption would most certainly have emphasized the wealth of a homeowner and served to formalize the most important room in the house—the sala (living room).

That corbels were highly valued is evidenced by their salvage and reuse. In Santa Fe the corbels supporting the choir loft in the early-nineteenth-century Santuario de Guadalupe were originally created in 1760 for Nuestra Señora de La Luz, the military chapel also known as La Castrense, which stood on the south side of the plaza until it was demolished in 1859. We also know that the roof timbers and corbels at the mission in Santo Domingo Pueblo were salvaged from an ancient Spanish Colonial church that was washed away by the Rio Grande flood of 1886.

Because so few domestic examples of interior corbels from the Spanish Colonial period remain, the prevalence of their use in the interiors of twentieth-century Santa Fe houses is the result of a romantic adoption of the Spanish Colonial architectural elements observed in missions and churches by the Anglos, who streamed into the area in the 1920s and '30s and popularized the Spanish Pueblo revival style. Excellent examples of decorative interior and exterior corbels abound in Santa Fe from this period forward. What was once handcrafted, however, is now mass produced. As a result, corbels remain a key feature of traditionally styled homes and buildings in New Mexico today.

CHAPTER 3

FRONTIER CLASSICISM

The Territorial Style, 1846–75

U.S. LIEUTENANT JOHN JAMES ABERT wrote in the autumn of 1846, "About 5 o'clock I came in sight of a square block of mud buildings one story high. In a little while after, I caught sight of the flag of my country waving proudly over some low flat roofed buildings that lay in the valley. I knew this must be Santa Fé."[1]

In the summer of 1846, several months after the United States declared war on Mexico, the U.S. Army marched westward over the Santa Fe Trail to occupy Santa Fe. On August 18, General Stephen Watts Kearny led a troop of cavalry into the city to claim the region for the United States. By sunset the soldiers had raised the American flag on the plaza and fired a celebratory salute. Two years later the Treaty of Guadalupe Hidalgo made New Mexico officially a territory of the United States, but statehood would remain elusive for another sixty-four years.

The U.S. Army used the Palace of the Governors for its headquarters, as the Spanish and Mexicans had done before, and began building Fort Marcy on a high bluff with a commanding view of the city, just a few hundred yards from the plaza. The structures were designed by First Lieutenants John F. Gilmer and William H. Emory. To expedite building the new military reservation, the Army built sawmills to provide milled lumber for pitched roofs, ornamentation, and trim.

American military occupation altered the dynamics of the economic, political, and social activity of Santa Fe. The Anglo-Americans brought new ideas, technology, and goods to the region. As the population grew, the town's economy diversified, and it became an important retail and wholesale center of commerce. Traders made their fortunes bringing wagonloads of goods over the Santa Fe Trail from Missouri to New Mexico, supplying military forts and retailers. The change was noticeable in the architecture, too. In the spring of 1848 the *Santa Fe Republican*, a new American newspaper, reported that "marks of improvement that strike the eye everywhere indicates a most rapid improvement. The ruins of old houses which were scattered all over town, have given place to new and better built ones. . . . If things continue, in one year more, the whole appearance of the city will be changed."[2]

Several interesting documents of 1846 give us a sense of what the villa looked like shortly after the Americans took control. Lieutenant John F. Gilmer, of the U.S. Corps of Engineers, drew a "Plan of Santa Fé" that shows a concentration of structures around the plaza; houses built along radiating roads, especially south of the river; the plaza reduced in size (in the same configuration it has today); San

OPPOSITE

Zaguán at El Zaguán, Canyon Road

"La Ciudad de Santa Fé," 1846–47.
Lithograph by C. B. Graham, sketch by
Lieutenant John James Abert, for "Report
of Lt. J. W. Abert of his Examination of
New Mexico in the Years 1846–1847"
(Washington: 1948)

Courtesy Palace of the Governors Photo
Archives (NMHM/DCA), 136510

Francisco Street solidly lined with dwellings; and plots of farmland encircling
town. Gilmer also delineated house shapes: some are simple rectangles, many are
U-shaped or L-shaped with placitas, and most of the houses close to or bordering
the plaza are square and have totally enclosed placitas.

Lieutenant John James Abert (1788–1863), assigned in 1846 by General
Stephen Watts Kearny to survey the newly conquered territory of New Mexico,
wrote a lengthy report that provides us with additional information on mid-
nineteenth-century Santa Fe. Published by Congress in 1848, Abert's report
includes lithographs based on his field sketches, including one of the earliest
known views of Santa Fe.[3] A stylized, simplified bird's-eye view, "La Ciudad de
Santa Fé" shows small, rectangular adobes dotting the landscape as far as the eye
can see. Like in the Gilmer map, there is a concentration of houses near the plaza.
Some have placitas in the center, corrals enclosed by latilla fences, and smoke
emanating from the chimneys. The old parroquia can be seen (center, left) with
tiny crosses atop the towers. Excessively large American flags wave from poles situated in the center of the plaza and on a distant hilltop.[4] In the distance are the
much exaggerated Sangre de Cristo Mountains and in the foreground are figures
wearing the local dress and portrayals of native plants (prickly pear cactus and
yucca) that give a sense of place to the scene.

In the text of his report Abert provides a lively account of the plaza, then
surrounded by the stores of merchants and traders on three sides and the palace on
the north side: "There all the country people congregate to sell their marketing
and one constantly sees objects to amuse. Trains of 'burros' are continually enter-
ing the city, laden with kegs of Taos whiskey or immense packs of fodder, melons,
wood, or grapes. Our own soldiers, too, are constantly passing and repassing, or
mingling with the motley groups of Mexicans and Pueblo Indians."[5] Elsewhere he
describes the appearance of New Mexico residents he encountered: "señoras with
their heads enveloped in their 'rebosas,' the men with their pantaloons . . . Indians

La Parroquia, ca. 1867

Photograph by Nicholas Brown, courtesy Palace of the Governors Photo Archives (NMHM/DCA), 055484

[with] pack mules laden with buffalo robes and meat. Their jet black hair . . . tied up . . . with some light colored ribbon."[6]

At that time Santa Fe had about twenty-five stores, including a printing shop, many saloons, two tailor shops, two shoemaker's stalls, one apothecary, a bakery, and two blacksmiths.[7] A large number of the businesses were owned by German Jews, such as Solomon Jacob Spiegelberg, who opened his mercantile house in 1846. The tallest building was still the parroquia, at the head of San Francisco Street—a humble mud-brick edifice with twin crenellated towers that loomed above all the flat-roofed houses in town. Lieutenant Abert was somewhat impressed by the church. "Although mud walls are not generally remarkable, still, the great size of the [parroquia], compared with those around, produces an imposing effect."[8]

The governor's residence, called the "Adobe Palace" by the Anglo-Americans, was the only building in town with glass windows.[9] When U.S. agents visited the palace in 1846 they found a modest governor's office furnished only with homespun rugs on the dirt floor and two calico-covered sofas.[10] The first governor to live in the palace under territorial rule was Charles Bent. Besides the palace and the ruins of the presidio attached to it, no other casas reales remained. Abert recalled seeing at least one impressive residence: "The house of Padre Ortiz, on the right side of the church, has a fine portail [portal] in front, being one of the best dwelling houses in the city."[11]

Santa Fe citizens' greatest concern at mid-century was the unpredictable threat of raids by various tribes of American Indians, who were searching for horses, mules, cattle, and sheep. Although reports of violence were often grossly exaggerated by the press, the Indians did cause the citizens of the territory great concern. In the early 1850s the territorial governor established a Volunteer Corps of New Mexican men to "protect their families, property and homes."[12] Not all the American Indians that appeared in the city were a threat. John Watts noted in 1859, "The Navajos and Utahs met here in Santa Fe and made a peace . . . they marched round the plaza singing stopping at intervals and singing firing their guns and dancing."[13] In fact, the sight of Indians in town was not uncommon. For instance, the *New Mexican* reported in 1872 that a small band of Apaches was seen "curiously threading the streets and peering into . . . doors and windows."[14]

With its new designation as a U.S. territory, Santa Fe attracted a steady stream of Americans from the East. Many of these newcomers were surprised by the lack of sophistication in the architecture they saw: mostly single-story, flat-roofed homes built of adobe bricks and mud-plastered with lime, with ceilings of hand-adzed vigas and latillas. Daniel Hastings, a private who marched into Santa Fe with General Kearny, wrote in his diary: "Great indeed was the contrast between the beautiful and magnificent city which my imagination had pictured and the low dirty and inferior place which I then beheld."[15] That same year, Englishman George F. Ruxton wrote in his diary, "The appearance of [Santa Fe] defies description, and I can compare it to nothing but a dilapidated brick kiln or a prairie-dog town."[16] And then a few years later, Anna Maria Morris of Morristown, New Jersey, who accompanied her husband, Lieut. Col. Gouverneur Morris to Fort Marcy in 1850 wrote that Santa Fe was "the most miserable squalid looking place I ever beheld & except the Plaza there is nothing decent about it. The houses are mud, the fences are mud, the churches & courts are mud, in fact it is *all* mud."[17]

Six years later, not much had improved. U.S. Attorney W. W. H. Davis, who wrote an account of his tenure in Santa Fe in 1856, explained: "The first sight of Santa Fé is by no means prepossessing. Viewed from the adjacent hills as you descend into the valley, whence it falls the first time under your glance, it has more the appearance of a colony of brick-kilns than a collection of human habitations. You see stretching before you, on both sides of the littler river of the same name, a cluster of flat-roofed mud houses, which, in the distance, you can hardly distinguish from the earth itself."[18]

Roofs during the Territorial period continued to be constructed primarily of tree branches and packed dirt. As Davis observed, "Sometimes a single roof will weigh several tons, the load of dirt accumulating from year to year."[19] Sometimes the weight would cause a roof to tumble down upon a home's occupants; such was the case with merchant Elias Spiegelberg, who died in 1855 when a dirt roof collapsed on him while he was sleeping.

A few Americans from the States, such as Marian Russell, whose mother ran a boarding house on the northwest corner of the plaza from 1854 to 1856, actually found the Mexican adobes of Santa Fe comfortable and cozy. She described the interior of the large home where she lived with her mother and the military personnel who boarded there: "The uneven adobe walls were whitewashed; the window embrasures were deep as divans. Folded Indian blankets covered the wooden settees that flanked the fireplace. The fireplace, Mexican made, was of adobe and rather small. The fires that burned there were of fragrant cedar and piñon. The candles on the mantle were home-made of sheep's tallow and very large. . . . The candlelight in the evenings flickered over the dark beams of the ceiling and over mother's great pottery jar."[20]

To dress up and disguise the plain facades of adobe houses, the Anglo-Americans transported wagonloads of whitewashed milled lumber and window glass from the States along the Santa Fe Trail. Newspaper reports and early photographs illustrate how the streets leading to the plaza and the plaza itself were lined with wagons bringing building materials and goods to the city. "Three large trains came in this morning from the east. One for Seligman & Bro., another for the Messrs. Delgado, and the other for Pures & Co. All of these trains come heavily loaded with dry goods, groceries, etc.," announced the *New Mexican* in 1868.

Structures around the plaza were refurbished by replacing the tree trunk columns and rough beams of the Mexican portals with imported whitewashed milled posts and trim. Merchants expanded the size of their establishments, and doors and windows were cut into the walls of existing adobe buildings. Skilled carpenters and good sawmills in the region also resulted in larger windows with sliding sash and paneled doors. Carpenter and builder Calvin Scofield was busy in the early 1850s with the adobe walls and portals of the Webb & Kingsbury store and home, as well as building projects for Bishop Jean-Baptiste Lamy.[21]

Even the Palace of the Governors, once again in need of repairs, received a makeover in the late 1850s with the addition of a modest front portal of slender milled columns. In the following decade, double front doors with recessed panels, overlights, and exterior wood trim with a pedimented lintel were added and today

TOP

Wagon Trains, San Francisco Street at Plaza, ca. 1869

Photograph by Nicholas Brown, courtesy Palace of the Governors Photo Archives (NMHM/DCA), 070437

BOTTOM

West Side of Plaza, Lincoln Avenue, ca. 1866

Photograph by U.S. Army Signal Corps, courtesy Palace of the Governors Photo Archives (NMHM/DCA), 011177

TOP

Palace of the Governors, ca. 1855

Photograph by William Henry Brown, courtesy Palace of
the Governors Photo Archives (NMHM/DCA), 009099

BOTTOM

Kaune-Bandelier House, ca. 1890

Photograph by Charles F. Lummis, courtesy Palace of
the Governors Photo Archives (NMHM/DCA), 009167

remain one of the few vestiges of this Victorian-era facade. In 1858 the Santa Fe *Gazette* reported on the many changes it observed in the city: "There seems to be considerable improvement in progress in Santa Fe at this time. We took a ride around the city a few evenings since and [were] surprised to see the number of adobes that are being made. In every direction there seems to be preparation for building of some kind. . . . The city looks lively and prosperous."[22]

For their building and renovation projects, the easterners preferred a simplified provincial Greek Revival design, referred to locally today as the Territorial style. Old handmade window frames surrounding sheets of translucent selenite were replaced with mill-made, double-hung sash windows of glass with triangular pediments. Doors were also framed in milled lumber and sometimes adorned with triangular pediments. The round, hand-carved posts and corbels of the portals were replaced with slender rectangular porch posts with molding on the top and sometimes on the bottom, to resemble the capitals and bases of classical columns.

The facade of the house known today as "Kaune-Bandelier," on East De Vargas Street, has a Territorial-style portal of this type, with square, unpainted posts topped with small strips of molding suggesting Doric capitals.[23] Additionally, the facade has the pedimented lintels over doors and windows typical of the style.

On the interiors of Territorial-style houses, ceilings were often supported by rectangular milled beams instead of vigas, and doorways received transoms and milled molding in the simplified Greek Revival manner. The officer's quarters constructed at Fort Marcy in 1870, in accordance with army regulations, were adorned with simple Greek Revival details and helped establish the popularity of the Territorial style of architecture.[24]

Fired red bricks were brought into the area for the first time but were expensive due to freighting costs. They were used sparingly in fireplaces and as protective cornices at the top of adobe walls. These brick cornices were laid by American masons in patterns that evoked classical Greek dentils and entablatures—and are the most noticeable feature of the Territorial style.

The Greek Revival style, a visual statement of democratic principles, flourished in America from about 1830 to 1850. The style spread through carpenters' guides and pattern books, and in the case of Santa Fe, through Americans who settled in the new territory. Although its popularity had waned in the East by the 1840s, it remained fashionable in Santa Fe for several more decades. The manner persisted in part because of the city's distance from the eastern style centers and the fact that Greek Revival elements blended so easily with the simple forms of Spanish architecture.[25]

Improvement efforts slowed during the Civil War. Several significant battles occurred in New Mexico, but Santa Fe's role in the war was brief. The primary event consisted of the Confederate flag being flown over the plaza for a few weeks. In general Santa Feans were reluctant to take part. As the editor of the Santa Fe *Gazette* explained, "What is the position of New Mexico? The answer is a short one. She desires to be left alone."[26] During the war, building materials were at a premium. According to one eyewitness, when Union troops were ordered to withdraw from Santa Fe, a group of local residents descended upon a building that had housed Union soldiers and "tore from there everything made of either wood, iron or glass . . . like so many famishing wolves."[27]

After the Civil War, the first professional architects, who offered a variety of skills from masonry to carpentry to design work, arrived in Santa Fe. Among the earliest were John and M. McGee who advertised in 1868: "Plans and specifications furnished for all kinks [sic] of public and private buildings. Contracts...taken in either brick or stone."[28] And the following year "Dofflemeyer and Grace" were listed as the architects for the remodeling of the Speigelberg store on the plaza.[29]

Around this same time, improvements were made to the plaza, still the heart of the city. Trees were planted, walkways and a fence were constructed, and in 1866 a bandstand was built. Under the shade of the cottonwood trees, butchers, bakers, and fruit vendors sold their products and women cooked meals they set out on tables for customers.[30] Sometimes American Indians performed dances there, and the infantry band of Fort Marcy frequently played concerts.

Agriculture continued to provide sustenance and a livelihood for many of the village's citizens. "More land is being plowed and planted this year around Santa Fe than has ever before been put under cultivation in this vicinity," reported the *New Mexican* in 1869.[31]

By the early 1870s some of the materials for the Territorial-style buildings in Santa Fe were provided by local businesses. Lumber was sold at sawmills operated by Louis W. Leroux in Las Gallinas on the Las Vegas River and Bachman and Provencher on the Pecos River.[32] The latter had a machine that made "any quantity of [wood] shingles on demand." James L. Johnson's store advertised in 1872 that they sold hardware, paints, and oils, and "a full assortment of all articles necessary for Carpenters and all classes of mechanics [builders]."[33]

Some Americans from the East found the mud-plaster finish of adobe homes untidy, and when cement plaster became available in Santa Fe in the 1870s, merchants and the wealthy rushed to stucco their adobe buildings.[34] In some instances the smooth, gray, plaster finish was then scored and painted to imitate stone or red brickwork. The practice was known as tattooing or stenciling, and today is known as faux-brick or faux-stone finish.

Attempts were made by Santa Feans to improve the stark, plain adobe and plaster-walled interiors, as well. In 1850 Anna Maria Morris had the wood planks and walls of her home whitewashed. To prevent the whitewash from rubbing off on people's clothing, calico was tacked to the walls, reaching well above the height of backs and shoulders. After visiting a fellow army wife's home, Anna Maria Morris noted in her diary, "I know now exactly how to fix a Mexican house, a width of paper or [calico] is indispensable around the wall."[35] In 1856 Santa Fe trader John M. Kingsbury describes "getting sufficient white lead to paint all the rooms & portals" of his buildings.[36] Apparently, paint was difficult to come by; just the year before, Kingsbury had written to his business partner that it was "impossible to get a keg of White Lead in the Territory."[37]

As early as 1859, American merchants ordered wallpaper from the States to decorate interiors. Kingsbury wrote to his business partner in St. Louis: "send One Case or about 200 rolls paper hangings . . . get good Satin Wall paper to cost from 30 cents to 50 cents. Select light & flashy patterns, also send plenty of border paper to match."[38] Hispano residents further decorated their interiors by hanging "images, pictures of Saints, crosses, looking glasses and rosettes made of paper" on the walls.[39]

H. B. Baca Mercancias Generales,
Agua Fria Street, ca. 1895
Courtesy Palace of the Governors Photo
Archives (NMHM/DCA), 028905

The mud floors were covered with wood planks, or with buffalo or other animal skins, or with locally woven black and white wool carpets known as *jerga*.
Morris wrote that she "cut" and "sewed on" the carpets she purchased for her
Santa Fe home.[40] For heating and cooking, small, hive-shaped fireplaces were built
in the corners of the rooms, in which aromatic piñon logs burned and emitted an
intense heat. Sometimes bleached muslin was tacked to the overhead beams to
prevent the packed earthen roofs from sifting down between the wooden beams
onto the room's occupants.

Santa Feans could also improve the interiors of their homes by purchasing
some of the fancy goods hauled over the Trail. In 1868 Staab & Brothers advertised
the sale of foreign and domestic carpets, and trader Peter Connelly advertised
"sets of fine oiled walnut bed room Furniture complete with marble top bureau
and washstand. A tea sett [*sic*] of forty-five pieces . . . Dining and toilet setts [*sic*].
All of which goods have just been received from the states."[41] In 1872 Johnson and
Koch advertised the sale of "carpets and oil cloths of the very latest patterns" and
Z. Stabb & Co. sold "carpets—brussels, piles, etc. of the most beautiful patterns"
and "handsome parlor and bedroom sets, rocking chairs, camp chairs" and "silk,
satin, cotton, woolen and linen goods."[42]

However, not everyone could afford these luxuries, and many adobes remained
unembellished. Sister Blandina Segale wrote an evocative description of the accommodations provided for the Sisters of Charity, who arrived in Santa Fe in 1865.

Imagine the surprise of persons coming from places where houses are built with
every convenience and sanitary devices, suddenly to find themselves introduced
into several oblong walls of adobes, looking like piled brick ready to burn, to
enter which, instead of stepping up, you step down onto a mud floor; rafters sup-

porting roof made of trunks of trees, the roof itself of earth which they were told had to be carefully attended, else the rain would pour in; door openings covered with blankets; the whole giving you a prison feeling; a few chairs, handmade and painted red; a large quantity of wool which they were assured was clean and for their use; no stoves, square openings in corners where fires could be built—all those things were to constitute their future home.[43]

Plenty of other residents also grumbled about the lack of modern building materials used in Santa Fe. After a particularly rainy summer in 1868, the *New Mexican* ran the following front-page story:

> During the past two days the outpouring of rain from the skies has been nearly incessant. The consequence is nearly every roof in the town has [leaked] like a sieve, to the utter disgust of all who have been affected. . . . Health is injured, furniture destroyed, homes are made uncomfortable, housewives without good humor, and all because our people persist in the antiquated custom of piling *dirt* upon their roofs instead of building good shingle or board roofs to their houses.
>
> The adobe house is the most comfortable tenement in the world when well roofed. Nor do we object to the dirt roof—but it is this sort of roof *alone*, to which we take exceptions. A good dirt roof, and this covered by planks, is nothing but excellent both in summer and winter. . . .
>
> It is not difficult at this time to procure lumber of every description, anywhere in the Territory, for building purposes, and we hope ere another season of rain rolls around, to witness a decided improvement in the roofing of houses—one that shall evince some progress of our people in the simple style of architecture now in use amongst us.[44]

Progress was slow. Four years later the *New Mexican* declared, "All the burros and wagons about town seem to be busy bringing timbers for roofing and pallisading from the mountains. There is more building going on this year than ever before. But it's all mud! mud!"[45] The newspaper advocated the use of "Tin, or some other 19th century material" to replace the dirt roofs that leaked badly during rainstorms. "There are more goods damaged and destroyed during the year here, than would pay for decent roofs on every house about the plaza," suggested the editor. "But then it is so refreshing to be awakened out of a sound sleep by a stream of muddy water playing all the way from the roof into your face! [So,] dirt by all means."[46]

Santa Fe's houses of worship were equally rustic, until the arrival of the French Bishop Jean-Baptiste Lamy, who organized the building of a Romanesque-style cathedral (1869–86) and other religious structures in the architectural styles of his homeland. Through his building projects he brought one of the first major sources of aesthetic change to the city—a tangible sign of progress for the dusty frontier town. This and the increase in commerce meant that Santa Fe in the early 1870s was "no longer a mere trading post for Indians and trappers, it is a city in business importance and appearance."[47]

RAFAEL AND MARÍA BORREGO HOUSE

724 CANYON ROAD

ca. 1842 (addition 1860/renovation 1928–30)

I n 1930 Margretta Stewart Dietrich, as the owner of the Rafael and María Borrego House, was awarded $100 in an annual architectural competition for the best "correct" restoration of a house in the "Santa Fe Style."[48] When she purchased the old adobe in September 1928, Dietrich had found it was "in very shabby condition" and immediately hired Katherine "Kate" Muller Chapman to return it "to its original beauty."[49] Dietrich, an extraordinary woman who was responsible for restoring several important Santa Fe houses, was a wealthy widow whose late husband had been a governor of Nebraska and a U.S. senator. An ardent activist for women's rights and American Indian rights, Dietrich also helped establish the Spanish Colonial Arts Society in Santa Fe.

During Kate Chapman's almost two-year-long meticulous remodeling of the house, she updated it with modern conveniences

LEFT

Rafael and María Borrego House

ABOVE

Rafael and María Borrego House, Canyon Road, August 1936

Photograph by Frederick D. Nichols.
Library of Congress, Prints & Photographs
Division, HABS NM, 25-SANFE, 4

like plumbing and replaced rotten wood in the floors and windows, but was careful to retain the integrity of the original structure.[50] In a pamphlet published in 1930, entitled *Adobe Notes*, Chapman described the techniques she used in restoring adobe homes like the Borrego House. For instance, she used "a smallish, primitive trowel" to create the "uneven or hand-made surfaces of indoor walls" and when replastering adobe facades she advised "simply taking from the dooryard the dirt that has washed down the walls, and putting it back on top of the walls again."[51]

Although one portion of the house may have been built in the eighteenth century, most of the structure standing today dates to the mid-nineteenth century.[52] A classic example of the Territorial manner, Borrego House is single-story with a long portal fronting the main sala, brick coping on exterior walls, and triangular pediments over the front door and over windows on the east and west facades. The foundation is fieldstone laid up in adobe, the floors are pine, and exterior walls are adobe brick with adobe mortar. Ceilings consist of pine boards laid across vigas, and the roof, originally earth, was covered by composition in the 1930 renovation. The front portal columns were once painted a color up to the height of the surrounding picket fence. Although it has housed many families and businesses and currently hosts a gourmet restaurant, the house is one of the best-preserved buildings on Canyon Road.

The earliest record concerning this property dates to 1753, when the soldier Ysidro Martín conveyed the land to Gerónimo Lopez. The latter's will of 1769 refers to two houses on the property ("the house where he lived and another newly built house, both houses containing 7 useful rooms") and an orchard of fourteen trees and "farming lands."[53] Sometime between 1769 and 1839 the houses were purchased by Gerónimo Gonzales, who in turn sold them in 1839 to his son-in-law Rafael Borrego. At that time the property consisted of a house of five rooms with a portal, another room and a stable, an orchard with a little room, and adjoining lands. Upon Borrego's death, his children inherited half of the property, and his widow, María Refugio Gonzáles de Borrego, inherited the other half.

When María died, she left her home—the "old house" that contained three rooms, a hall, and a portal—to her son, Pablo, and bequeathed one room on the property to her servant Quirina. It was common for nineteenth-century homeowners in Santa Fe to divide their property this way, deeding individual rooms in one house to different

parties—a practice that complicated property deeds in Santa Fe for generations. Between 1890 and 1903 Pablo and his wife, Beatrice, mortgaged their property four times. By this time the property had a placita and "an orchard of bearing fruit trees and alfalfa." Unable to pay off his mortgage, Pablo Borrego lost the house to the bank in 1906. Over the following years, the house changed hands many times; at some point early on, the main house and two-room adobe were divided and owned separately.

Window detail, Rafael and María Borrego House

During the seventy-five years the property remained in the hands of the Borrego family, the house was the scene of much activity. The Borregos were leaders in the social and political life of Santa Fe and used their sala and extensive portal (added to the house about 1860) for many significant social gatherings.[54]

In her memoirs, Dietrich described the house as she found it in 1928: "Because of its front room, which was fifty feet long, it had been used in the early days for political conventions, *bailes*, and other large gatherings, but later it was turned into a feed store, with two temporary partitions in the front room. The handsome double front doors, made by hand, had been removed to be replaced by glass 'store' doors. It had been built in Territorial style of lime plastered adobe and brick pretil, with a wide portal across the front, its roof supported by slender, tapering handmade columns. The back of the house and west side opened into a typical Santa Fe placita, surrounded on the other sides by other old houses, and with a well in the middle."[55]

In 1939 Dietrich purchased the small dwelling adjacent to the main Borrego House and then sold the two structures together to Agnes Sims, and once again the Borrego family property fell under single ownership. The following year the Historic American Buildings Survey (HABS) recognized the importance of the main structure and sent a field crew to Santa Fe to document it. Founded in 1933 as a federal assistance program and still in existence today, HABS identifies and documents surviving architectural masterpieces of the past, particularly those that might be threatened with demolition or development.

The HABS report referred to the structure as the "McCormick Prize House," after the 1930 award Dietrich received for restoring the building. It documented the house with eight black and white photographs and five large sheets of detailed, measured drawings of the facades and individual features, such as window and door frames and the fireplace in the sala. By comparing the present-day structure with these records, we can see that much of the front facade has remained the same, including the portal columns with chamfered corners and simple capitals. The long, low windows in the front room on the west and east facades are about the same, as is the brick coping along the cornice.[56]

However, the HABS documents do indicate that in recent decades some of the original fabric of the Borrego House has been lost. The double wood front door and Territorial-style fireplace in the sala are noticeably absent, and the rear of the building has been altered significantly (there is no longer a well or placita, for instance). Thus, as intended, the HABS drawings and photographs exist as records of these features.

In 1961, fearing it was endangered with possible demolition, the Old Santa Fe Association (OSFA), using its own funds and substantial contributions from John and Faith Meem, bought the Borrego House. The OSFA renovated it at a considerable cost, and the house became a restaurant and "showplace" for the unique features of nineteenth-century Santa Fe architecture.[57] Eight years later the house became one of the first Santa Fe residences to be listed on the New Mexico State Registry of Historic Buildings (founded in 1966). Agreeing that "commercial use of this fine territorial style building provides the means for its preservation," the OSFA eventually sold the property to a private owner who agreed to continue its preservation.[58] Today it houses the popular restaurant Geronimo, named after Gerónimo Lopez, one of the first owners of the property.

OLIVER AND ISABEL HOVEY HOUSE

136 GRIFFIN STREET

ca. 1858

In John Watts's diary of 1859, concerning the year he spent living in Santa Fe, he makes several references to "Hovey's 'brick' house."[59] He was correct to put quotes around the word brick, for the exterior was actually mud plaster painted with a brick pattern. Today it stands as a rare and unusual example of a faux technique applied to adobe—an elaborate and time-consuming process. The painting and scoring of earthen buildings goes back to antiquity, with many examples in the Middle East, but instances in the U.S. are less common. In the Southwest faux-brick buildings were generally erected by people with eastern U.S. sensibilities using the technique to dress up a humble adobe home.[60]

Such was the case with the Vermont-born Oliver Perry Hovey. A resident of the territory since 1846, Hovey served as a private under Cerán St. Vrain in his "mountain men militia company" and helped Colonel Sterling Price defeat the Taos Rebellion of 1847.

LEFT
Oliver and Isabel Hovey House

ABOVE
Oliver and Isabel Hovey House, Griffin Street, ca. 1880–81

Courtesy of the Historic Preservation Division, Department of Cultural Affairs, Santa Fe, SF.1605

....

Following this he engaged in various ventures: with Edward T. Davies he established New Mexico's first English-language newspaper in 1847; he supplied food stuffs to the Army; and he was involved in the American Indian and Utah trade. He also dabbled in politics, serving as Santa Fe's representative in the territorial legislative assembly in 1858–59 and 1861–62.

In December 1856 Hovey married Isabel Conklin, the daughter of Juana and James Conklin—James was a French-Canadian trader who came to Santa Fe in the 1820s, shortly after the Santa Fe Trail opened. By February of the following year, James had deeded a portion of his property on Griffin Street to Oliver.[61] And within a year Oliver had built a grand, seven-room residence for himself and his bride on the land across from the Presbyterian Church, in the heart of Santa Fe. As red-fired bricks were hard to come by in 1850s Santa Fe, Oliver hired workmen to cover the adobe walls with a smooth, brick-colored plaster and paint white lines in a pattern simulating brick.[62]

Evidence exists suggesting that Hovey added on (both in width and height) to a pre-existing adobe house on the property. The Urrutia map (see page 4) shows that in circa 1776, a long, low building was already at the location. During recent work on the house by the Historic Santa Fe Foundation (HSFF), which owns the building, materials were found (such as mud plaster with micaceous clay on an exterior wall) that indicate the house dates to an earlier time.[63] A thick interior wall was likely originally an exterior wall—as it would have been structurally unnecessary for an inside wall to be that thick.

The house has features characteristic of the Territorial style: flat roof, pedimented windows, simplified Doric columns in the porches on the east and south facades, and a brick-capped parapet in a pattern resembling Greek Revival dentils. Shortly after it was built, the stylish house attracted the attention of the Santa Fe *Weekly Gazette*. The newspaper noted when trees were planted in front of the residence in early 1858, and in May of that year, a short article on the progress of Santa Fe architecture noted: "Lord Hovey is adding still other conveniences to his already handsome property."[64]

Oliver and Isabel furnished their house with expensive commodities, most of which had to be hauled out west to Santa Fe in wagons. Among the items they purchased were a wardrobe, a bedstead, a settee, a sofa, a table, book-

Territorial-style fireplace surround, Oliver and Isabel Hovey House

cases, a writing desk, iron safes, paintings, card tables, eight looking glasses (including a large gilt glass), numerous chairs, and a vast library called the "best in town" and consisting of 892 volumes.[65] They also purchased two carriages and mules. The 1860 census lists Hovey, at age thirty-three, as a "commission agent" who owned real property in Santa Fe valued at $18,000 and personal property at $35,000—remarkable sums for the time period.[66]

Called "General" by Kearny's men and the "Great Lord Hovey" by others in town, Oliver Hovey was a generous man who loaned out books, money, his mules, and even a bathtub.[67] But he was also famous for "spend[ing] money fast & foolishly" and was constantly in debt.[68] As Santa Fe trader John M. Kingsbury noted in November 1859, "Hovey still keeps up his extravigance [sic] but is pushed to the utermost [sic] to get money [and] is in hot water all the time. He appears to owe everybody, cannot appear on the plaza without being dunned on all sides, for my part I cannot see how he can keep going much longer."[69]

The lavish lifestyle of the Hoveys did finally catch up with them. By summer 1859, John Watts and his brother Joshua had moved into the Hoveys' brick mansion on Griffin Street, and Oliver and Isabel had moved to a house nearby that was owned by James Conklin. By November 1860, Oliver had mortgaged the property for $1,612 and leased it to a Major Fry. When he died just two years later, Oliver left a widow, three young children, expensive possessions, extensive debts, and the brick mansion appraised at a value of $6,000.[70] Isabel's father sold the house to J. Howe Watts, the son of one of Hovey's business partners, for $4,000 in February 1863.

In the following decades, new owners made various alterations to the house. The most drastic changes occurred in the early twentieth century, when the false brick facade was covered under stucco in the then-popular pebble-dash texture. Owners and business partners Grace Bowman and Jennie Avery divided the house into four apartments and heavily renovated the building for the new use.

Although it was one of the first historic structures in Santa Fe to be placed in the State Register and was listed in the National Register, the Hovey House was almost razed in 1972 by a Santa Fe attorney who wanted to sell the land for a four-million-dollar commercial development. Fortunately, Santa Fe's Historic Styles Committee denied the demolition permit, and in March 1974 the HSFF borrowed funds to purchase the house at market value. To pay off the loan, HSFF launched a fund-raising campaign led by architect John Gaw Meem.

In 1976–78, with generous funds from the Santa Fe Community Development Program and the National Park Service, HSFF had the building restored to its earliest documented appearance. A photograph of the house from the early 1880s, owned by the granddaughter of Colonel William Breeden, who had lived in the house from 1871 to 1881, was used as a guide.[71] The biggest challenges for the local crew were the removal of the exterior stucco down to the adobe brick and the replastering and repainting of the false brick facade. Remarkably, during the restoration a small section of the original wall finish was discovered over the doorway in the south porch and used as a guide to restore the rest of the walls.[72] The original section, preserved under glass, shows that the nineteenth-century artisans painted a faux brick flat arch over the doorway, and during the 1970s restoration this feature was repeated above all the exterior doors and windows.

The present seven-room configuration resembles the original floor plan of the Hovey House.[73] Other original interior features are the simple Territorial-style wood fireplace surrounds, high ceilings, tall window frames, and varying height of floors and doorjambs.[74] Some of the doors appear to have their original Victorian-era molding and overlights (or gaps where the overlights once existed).

EL ZAGUÁN
(JAMES AND MARIA JOHNSON HOUSE)
545 CANYON ROAD
ca. 1854 (additions 1860s–70s/renovation 1928)

Described in 1875 as "one of the finest villas on the edge of the city, with very neat and attractive surroundings built without regard to expense," El Zaguán is one of Santa Fe's finest historic houses built on one of the city's oldest streets.[75]

Named for its covered passageway running lengthwise through the building, with doors opening onto various rooms, this long, low adobe was built on Canyon Road in 1854 by James L. Johnson and his wife, Maria Jesusita Montoya of Chihuahua, Mexico. From a prominent Maryland family, James first arrived in Santa Fe in 1845, the year before General Kearny claimed New Mexico for the U.S. He soon became a prosperous merchant and trader, purchasing stock that he shipped to Santa Fe along the Old Santa Fe Trail.

Johnson eventually became the owner of a business block on the northeast corner of the plaza. By the 1870s he was involved in real estate, banking, and mining, as well as his retail business. Notices of his activities, whether receiving wagonloads of merchandise from

ABOVE

El Zaguán, ca. 1900

Courtesy Palace of the Governors
Photo Archives (NMHM/DCA), 031821

RIGHT

*Artist apartments,
east end of El Zaguán*

the States or making improvements to his plaza store, were often reported in the *New Mexican*.[76] For instance, in 1872 the newspaper noted that Johnson had "the handsomest store building in the Territory" and in 1875: "James L. Johnson, Esq. . . . left on yesterday's eastern coach, for St. Louis and New York. He goes thus early to lay in the fall stock of this well known and popular firm."[77]

In keeping with his respected standing in the community, it was important for Johnson to own a stylish home. In 1854 he took the first step by acquiring property on the north side of Canyon Road from Juan Bautista Moya.[78] At that time Canyon Road ran through a sparsely populated area amid fields cultivated by Spanish families. Already existing on Johnson's land was a house of unspecified size and a corral. Over the following decades, as his household grew to include seven children and a number of servants, he purchased adjacent plots of land and enlarged the house with a Territorial-style portal facing the garden, an exterior entry corridor, and new rooms stretching along Canyon Road. It was certainly around that time that the *New Mexican* declared there was "None more inviting on the whole range of the Rocky mountain section" than the Johnson home.[79]

Early photographs of the house show the Canyon Road facade before the 1920s restoration: a relatively simple mud-plastered adobe surface with exposed vigas and simple Territorial-style window frames. In 1881, due to a financial crisis, Johnson lost his home and everything else, including his business block and other properties, to Thomas B. Catron, a powerful lawyer and politician in Santa Fe.[80]

Owned by the Historic Santa Fe Foundation (HSFF) since 1979, El Zaguán today is almost 180 feet long and approximately 50 feet wide at the widest point. Although most of the building dates from the mid- to late-1800s and early 1900s, one section may date as early as 1815. Den-

drochronology testing of some of the vigas in the ceiling of that section indicates a cutting date of between 1813 and 1815, predating the Moya ownership.[81]

El Zaguán combines features of the Territorial style—brick coping at the parapet and Greek Revival–style wood trim around doors and windows—with features of the Spanish Pueblo style: flat roof, linear floor plan, and adobe walls with softly rounded contours. The interior, reconfigured over the years, includes a spacious sala. At the west end of the zaguán is a long, brick-floored porch that looks out onto the formal gardens. A 1928 article suggests, "The garden was planted by the late Mrs. Johnson and contained many Madonna lilies, peonies, and the wonderful horse chestnut trees which provided what looked like an oasis in the desert."[82] In the early 1990s it was redesigned to give the appearance of a "genteel turn-of-the-century" garden. Along and east of the zaguán are rooms that the HSFF uses for offices and apartments for the artists-in-residence program—providing artists and writers housing at an affordable rate.

During the Historic Santa Fe Foundation's recent restoration of the house, layers of old cement stucco and paint were painstakingly removed from the walls and then the walls were refinished with coats of mud plaster and lime wash.[83] The project started with the walls of the zaguán being taken all the way down to the adobe bricks. The oldest wall finish discovered during the process was mud plaster with a lime wash and a *tierra amarilla* wainscot. Tierra amarilla is a term used in northern New Mexico for a wash of micaceous clay that is employed as a wainscot finish because it repels water. The zaguán walls were restored by replicating this original, historically accurate finish.

Among the exciting discoveries made during the restoration was *rajuelar* under the cement plaster in one section. Rajuelar is an anchoring system in which mud-mortar

joints in the adobe are replaced with stones set in lime mortar, a technique commonly used in Mexico but almost unknown in New Mexico.[84]

El Zaguán has been home to a distinguished list of guests and residents over the centuries, including the Swiss-born anthropologist and ethnographer Adolph Bandelier, who rented it in 1891–92. The last private owner was Margretta Stewart Dietrich (see page 64), who purchased the house in 1928 after discovering that it was about to be sold to a developer and "cut up into small lots."[85] Known around town as the "old Baca place" (after James Baca, Johnson's grandson, who owned the house from 1916 to 1926), the house was renamed El Zaguán by Dietrich.

With plans to turn the property into an "elite summer hotel, small but fashionable,"[86] Dietrich hired her friend Kate Chapman to restore and expand the house. On Dietrich's orders, she did not alter the exterior, and on the interior only made the necessary adjustments to turn the building into small apartments. Margretta later recalled, "Like all old houses, the wiring [in El Zaguán] had been done by the owner, the plumbing was far from sanitary, and the floors were almost worn out. . . . It cost as much to put the property into rentable condition as it had to buy it."[87] Chapman added three cottages, garages, and the zaguán's brick walkways and west porch floor. From the beginning, the small apartments with "attractive surroundings and furnishings" were rented out to artists and other visitors for around $50 a month.[88]

Dietrich's sister, Dorothy N. Stewart, a nationally prominent painter, muralist, and printmaker who often added an artistic touch to Margretta's restoration projects, more than likely painted the elaborate, colorful floral still life in the panels of paired exterior doors.

Dietrich and Chapman's sensitive restoration of El Zaguán was praised by the local press: "Walls three feet in thickness; mellow old beamed ceilings; carved and paneled doors, many-paned windows, tin lanterns, nichos, Indian rugs, arched passages, paved portales have had their ancient allure heightened by artistic and understanding treatment. . . . The most gratifying thing about the deal is that it saves from the modernizer such a large section of that part of the city . . . the quaintest and most Spanish thoroughfare of Santa Fe."[89]

ABOVE
Floral mural attributed to Dorothy N. Stewart, ca. 1928, El Zaguán

OPPOSITE TOP
The sala, one of the oldest rooms in El Zaguán

OPPOSITE BOTTOM
The gardens at El Zaguán

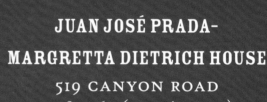

JUAN JOSÉ PRADA–
MARGRETTA DIETRICH HOUSE
519 CANYON ROAD
ca. 1820s–60s (renovations 1920s)

Like so many Santa Fe residences, the style and shape of the Juan José Prada–Margretta Dietrich House has evolved over the centuries. Since the house was named for Juan José Prada, a laborer who lived there during the Territorial period, and many features of the property relate to that time, this house is being placed in this chapter.

There is no disputing the fact that the Prada family owned land and buildings at this spot on Canyon Road for more than one hundred years. During renovations of the buildings in 1986, archaeologists were called to determine the nature of artifacts unearthed, and at that time an in-depth study of the property was begun. The results of the study, published in 1990, help unravel the threads of the house's intricate and multifaceted history.[90]

Juan José Prada (born ca. 1842) grew up in the first house built on the land and eventually inherited a portion of the complex. Juan was the son of Guadalupe Ortega Prada and Francisco Prada, a farmer who served in the New Mexican Army from 1838 to 1841. Property deeds indicate that by 1854, Juan's father had died and his

LEFT

West section of the Juan José Prada–Margretta Dietrich House

ABOVE

Territorial-style window detail, Juan José Prada–Margretta Dietrich House

mother had inherited the house and land. The 1860 census lists eighteen-year-old Juan as a laborer still living at home with his mother and sister. By the 1870 census there were two dwellings on the property and Juan was living in his own, new house to the west of the original house with his wife, Feliciana Chávez, and their two children. By then Juan was a "farm laborer," and his duties likely included tending to the family's sheep and goats. Among the remarkable features of the Prada complex today is the small barn, situated against a stone wall at the northern end of the property. It is one of the finest remaining examples of jacal construction—squared-off cedar logs set into the ground vertically and chinked with adobe.

Sometime after 1865, stylish improvements were made to the Prada adobe home, suggesting that the family's financial position improved over time. Brick coping was added to the roofline, and double-hung sash windows, framed with milled wood in the Greek Revival style, were installed.[91] Both were features of mid-nineteenth-century New Mexico Territorial-design homes.

When Juan's mother died in 1884, the house or compound was divided into three sections, running north-south. Juan's family lived in the west end; Juan's daughter, Juana, and son-in-law, Miguel Gorman, lived across the passageway in a separate dwelling; and Guadalupe lived in the east wing, which adjoined the Gormans' dwelling. Guadalupe's space contained a kitchen, a *portalito*, and a room for her grandson Gregorio López. Upon her death, Guadalupe's rooms were inherited by the grandson.

In the deeds for each section, Guadalupe Prada specified that no obstacle or hindrance was to be placed in any passageway that might bar access to quarters. Because of the typical adobe house construction of the day, in which each room was generally reached by an exterior door only, this "right of passage," or *entradas y salidas libres*, was a convention written into deeds.[92] Today the Prada house has seven exterior doors, several of which date back to the time when the Prada family's access to their rooms had to be guaranteed through these deeds.[93]

The Prada family lived together in the complex of adobe buildings until the end of 1886, when some of them began to leave. In 1925 Juan's son-in-law, Miguel Gorman, by then a widower, sold the house and remaining property to Margretta Stewart Dietrich, who lived in the house until her death in 1961. By this date Anglo-Americans were buying up and modernizing the old adobes in the Canyon Road area, which was gradually turning from a farming community into a residential neighborhood.

Dietrich added other rooms to the house, built of the same adobe walls covered in lime plaster, and modernized the whole interior with plumbing and electricity. She covered the hard-packed earthen floors with red bricks made at the state penitentiary, and a new, waterproof roof was added. Dietrich hired local, Spanish-speaking workmen, and the house retains the touch of their handcraftsmanship. At the suggestion of Kate Chapman she hired women from Tesuque and Cochiti pueblos to hand-build traditional, corner, adobe brick and mud-plaster fireplaces.

In 1934 Dietrich acquired the west section of the Prada family complex and joined the two together. When renovating the new addition, Dietrich wanted to enhance the rooms with "really handsome ceilings."[94] On a horseback ride to Cow Springs Mesa, she discovered a "tumbled-down house which had a beautiful ceiling of heavy spruce limbs about 20 inches in circumference." She purchased the vigas for the bargain price of ten dollars, but when it was discovered that the beams had to be dragged out a few at a time by horses from their original site to the main road a good distance away, her ceilings turned out to be very expensive.

The Prada house has several unique, artistic features, including handcrafted wood radiator covers made by WPA artisans and decorations inspired by Dietrich and her sister Dorothy N. Stewart's many trips to Mexico. There is a tile mural by famed Mexican artist Diego Rivera inset in a garden wall; an inscription on the tiles suggests it was either made at, or sold at, a pottery shop in San Luisito, Mexico. On the walls of the breezeway, an addition to the rear of the house, is a fantastic mural created by Stewart, painted in the style of Rivera. The subject is the interior of a crowded second-class Mexican railway car.

Listed on the State Register of Cultural Properties in 1972 and the following year on the National Register of Historic Places, the Juan José Prada–Margretta Dietrich House has been owned and carefully preserved by gallery owner Nedra Matteucci.

· ·

OPPOSITE, TOP
East section of the Juan José Prada–Margretta Dietrich House

OPPOSITE, BOTTOM
Jacal, Juan José Prada–Margretta Dietrich House

Decorative radiator covers made by WPA artisans, west
sitting room, Juan José Prada–Margretta Dietrich House

Diego Rivera tile mural, garden wall,
Juan José Prada–Margretta Dietrich House

Dorothy N. Stewart mural, Juan José Prada–Margretta Dietrich House

CHAPTER 4

"MODERN" VICTORIAN ARCHITECTURE ARRIVES VIA RAILROAD

1875–1900

"On the hillsides are cottages with green lawns and thrifty fruit trees; on the avenues more stately mansions. Everywhere the thick foliage of fruit gardens rises above adobe walls. Occasionally, groves of cottonwoods with darker hues, and shade trees on the streets more completely each year hide the shapeless adobe houses that must give way gradually to modern buildings."

—Santa Fe *Daily New Mexican*, 8 October 1889

THE ARCHITECTURAL TRANSFORMATION of the city in the late nineteenth century can largely be attributed to the arrival of the iron horse, which reached Raton Pass, New Mexico, in December 1878 and Santa Fe in February 1880. The railroad not only brought a multitude of new building materials to the territory, but also new ideas concerning aesthetics. Although bypassed by the main Chicago-to–Los Angeles line because of the difficulty of laying tracks through surrounding mountains, Santa Fe constructed a spur line to the Atchison, Topeka and Santa Fe Railroad stop at Galisteo Junction (later Lamy), eighteen miles to the east. The railroad energized city leaders into launching major projects of modernization. In October 1880 a new gasworks was established, and when the pipes were laid in town a large crowd gathered to watch the momentous occasion.[1] The following year the telephone reached Santa Fe, and after a water storage reservoir was built in 1880–81, water mains were laid along the principal streets, and by March of 1882 the water began to flow.

Beginning in the 1870s, well before the railroad reached Santa Fe, the business community sought to transform the city into a modern "Americanized" city. The large adobe commercial buildings around the plaza were remodeled into even larger Italianate-style business blocks. Large windows were installed on the facades of businesses owned by the Staabs, Spiegelbergs, and others. Concerning this improvement the *New Mexican* reported, "The days for crawling through dark holes in a mud wall have passed, and show and advertising have taken place."[2]

Around this time, three-story adobe brick civic structures in the French Second Empire style, with mansard roofs and heavy ornamentation, began appearing in Santa Fe. These and other modes of the Victorian era reached the southwest through architectural plan books and taste-making journals, from trained architects and builders who settled on the frontier, and via the transcontinental railroad. Among the earliest Second Empire structures in Santa Fe were St. Michael's

OPPOSITE

*Hayt-Wientge House,
built in 1882, Paseo de la Cuma*

College (1879) and Loretto Academy (1881). As photographs of this era attest, these new, large, "modern" Victorian structures contrasted sharply with the simpler, older, diminutive mud structures so long a part of Santa Fe's streetscape. For example, William Henry Jackson took a photo of the old San Miguel Church and the new St. Michael's College. Built by the Christian Brothers, the three-story ornate college building was praised for its "unusually handsome style with porticoes, galleries, veranda, and Mansard roof."[3]

One of the most important early building innovations in Santa Fe was the use of tin roofing. As the Santa Fe *New Mexican* declared in late 1877, "Tin roofs are becoming popular in our city and whenever the money can be spared are taking the place of the proverbial dirt roofs in the business centres because of their durable and fire-proof qualities."[4] Santa Fe homeowners, however, were slow to use the new material. After a particularly rainy July in 1875 a reporter exclaimed, "The heavy rains have so increased the weight of dirt roofs that almost daily we hear of houses caving in, to the danger and infinite disgust of the occupants. Fortunately, we have thus far no loss of life to record."[5]

Among the first to sell and install tin roofs in Santa Fe were Alexander G. Irvine and William A. McKenzie of the "Irvine & McKenzie Hardware" store, and in later years E. D. Franz.[6] In autumn 1872 Irvine was busy selling tin, as well as cast-iron heating and cooking stoves, fire shovels, tongs, and other items, at his

San Miguel Church and Saint Michael's College, Santa Fe, 1881

Photograph by W. H. Jackson & Co., courtesy Palace of the Governors Photo Archives (NMHM/DCA), 001403

Overall view and detail of the Alexander G. Irvine–Henry McKenzie House, built in 1881

"Pioneer Tin Shop" and installing a tin roof on James L. Johnson's plaza store.[7] When he installed tin roofs the following year on the Staab and E. Andrews stores, the *New Mexican* reported: "Irvine is an old hand at the business and knows just how to do it. It is warm work however, if we are to judge by the red hot hands and faces of himself and workmen. They are literally sandwiched between two fires—the dazzling glare of the tin in front and the roasting rays of the sun behind. Tin roofing may well be called a 'cooked up job.'"[8]

The Scotland-born Irvine, who served for a time as an Indian agent, built a two-story home in 1881 on Irvine Street (today called McKenzie), which naturally boasts a tin roof. The house, with its steeply pitched roof and ornamental wood-work (jigsawed bargeboard and porch with decorative wood brackets), is a rare instance of Gothic Revival influence in Santa Fe. The house was sold to Henry McKenzie, Irvine's father-in-law, in December 1881 for $900. Threatened with demolition in 1984 to make room for a massive three-story Spanish Pueblo Revival office building, the imperiled structure was saved through the efforts of the Old Santa Fe Association and other historic preservationists in the city.[9] The engineers who examined the structure to determine its stability found Alexander Irvine's name painted on several ceiling joists.[10] After a three-year restoration project, the house was designated a "contributing structure" in the Santa Fe Historic District in 1986.

Viewed by many as old-fashioned and unsightly, the facade of the Palace of the Governors received a Victorian face-lift. In 1877 the exterior was plastered, whitewashed, and painted by a "Mr. La Cassagne" with a pattern imitating blocks of granite, and a plank sidewalk was laid in front. The following year contractor George H. Thompson built a Victorian-style portal with substantial pillars topped by capitals and a classical balustrade. Irvine installed a modern tin roof. The *New Mexican* reported that the new design was "elegant" and reflected "credit on the taste displayed by [William] Ritch, and the workmen employed."[11] One of the portal pillars from this period can be seen on display in the Palace of Governors museum today.

Visitors to Santa Fe marked the progress in the capital city's architecture. A writer for *Harper's Weekly* described Santa Fe in 1879 as "by no means a picturesque or imposing town. . . . The city residences and other buildings are almost universally of the Mexican style, built of adobes, or sun-dried brick, one story high." But by the following year, when Ernest Ingersoll wrote an article on the city's attractions for *Harper's New Monthly*, he observed that many of the residences had become "large and ornamental, their doors are broad and well cased, their windows often of large size, and set with place-glass instead of scraped sheep-skin."[12]

In his speech celebrating the 1880 arrival of the railroad in New Mexico, General William T. Sherman told the crowd gathered in the Santa Fe plaza: "I hope that ten years hence there won't be an adobe house in the Territory. I want to see you learn to make them of brick, with slanting roofs. Yankees don't like flat roofs, or roofs of dirt."[13] His desires were almost achieved, in the capital at least, for in 1881, one visitor reported, "Numbers of private houses are finished with tin roofs & painted, plastered and decorated in such a beautiful manner that they would be an addition to any young city."[14] That same year, the *New Mexican* announced, "Two-story houses are superseding the old Mexican style of

Charles Graham, "The Governor's Palace," 1890

Engraving published in *Harper's Weekly*, 19 July 1890. Collection of the author

architecture."[15] And years later it was observed that Santa Fe's "quaint, old, Mexican, one-story adobes have given way to a considerable extent to brick blocks and residences of modern style."[16]

By this time the railroad had brought new and varied building materials, such as planed lumber, brick, shingles, cast-iron decorative elements, and metal roofing, as well as new architectural styles. The availability of machine-made ornament meant that Santa Feans could build homes in the eclectic and elaborate Victorian styles then popular in the Midwest and East, including the Italianate, French Second Empire, and Queen Anne. With varying degrees of success, Santa Fe residents duplicated as best they could the aesthetic quality and building traditions of an eastern rather than a western home.

Two- and three-story mansions of the Second Empire style, with the ubiquitous mansard roofs and heavy ornament, began to appear in Santa Fe during this period. This was due in part to Archbishop Lamy, who had brought French styles of architecture to Santa Fe earlier in the century. Additionally, this style remained the first choice of wealthy homebuilders and their architects because it was considered thoroughly modern and fashionably flashy.[17] Again, photographs of the era show the sharp contrast between humble adobe homes and the exuberant detail of these multistory Victorian mansions (see page 102).

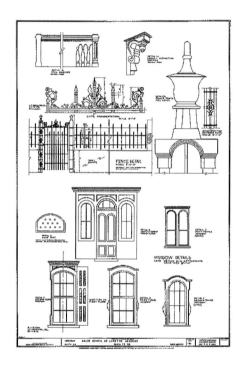

Example of architectural details brought to Santa Fe via the railroad. Grade School at Loretto Academy, Don Gaspar Avenue, Santa Fe, NM

Library of Congress, Prints & Photographs Division, HABS NM, 25-SANFE, 9

Builders and homeowners specially ordered new supplies that were shipped from the States via the railroad. In 1881 the Spiegelberg brothers replaced their store on the plaza with a "modern" building featuring the first cast-iron facade in Santa Fe.[18] Architect F. H. Brigham "ordered from Chicago the trimmings for a handsome new residence" he was building, noted the *New Mexican* in 1886.[19] A new roofing type appeared around this time, as well. As local builder John Hampel advertised in the late 1880s, "The Dirt Roof Must Go. Keep out the Rain, Snow and Sleet by ordering a Composition and Gravel Roof."[20]

In addition to cast-iron facades, new adobe and brick buildings were embellished with popular architectural details like pressed-tin ceilings, pressed-metal cornices, factory-made window sashes and doors, and ornate brackets. Eventually local artisans began providing these new details. By 1882 Phillip Hesch had a planning mill by the Santa Fe River, and five years later "Hesch and Sons" advertised a shutter and sash mill near the Santuario de Guadalupe for "turning out all sorts of mouldings, fancy castings, stair railing, etc."[21]

Spiegelberg Brothers Store, ca. 1885

Courtesy Palace of the Governors Photo
Archives (NMHM/DCA), 150156

Unlike the single-story, linear arrangement of earlier adobes, most of these "modern" residences had a central entrance passage that led into a hall with rooms off to the sides, and a grand staircase leading to a second story. The interiors typically featured elaborate wood trim, inlaid wood floors, stained glass, ornate fireplace surrounds of marble or wood or tile, and patterned wallpaper imported from the East. Public edifices were likewise lavishly appointed. When Santa Fe businessman J. W. Akers was fitting up his "finest saloon in the west," he traveled to Denver to purchase the interior furnishings and fittings, including expensive tile flooring, "trimmings" of red wood, and polished marble.[22]

These new styles and more complex structures warranted the services of professionally trained architects and builders. Beginning in the early 1880s, architects were increasingly listed in the New Mexico business directories and placed advertisements in the newspaper. Among them were D. D. Cobleigh and W. G. Gibson, Antonio Windsor, F. H. Brigham, and the firm of Wheeler & Randell.[23]

Some early Victorian-era buildings are visible in the 1882 bird's-eye view of Santa Fe, prepared and published by Joseph J. Stoner of Wisconsin. Although not drawn to scale, the map shows the large commercial, religious, and public buildings on the main streets in town. In the distance are the Sangre de Cristo Mountains. Numerous signs of progress and prosperity are highlighted in the scene: at lower right is a train pulling into the depot; the city's new gasworks and four hotels are depicted; and the recently built planning mill appears near the Santa Fe River. A legend below the map lists the principal buildings and includes historic sites such as the "Oldest building." When examined closely there are some inaccuracies; for example Stoner shows St. Francis Cathedral with two tall spires, which it did not have. Still, the map expresses the optimism and bustling enterprise of 1882 Santa Fe.

Another interesting description of the city around the same time was written by Captain John G. Bourke. He noted in his diary, "From my rambles around Santa Fé, I have seen much to impress me with the great changes wrought within the past decade. The newspapers are no longer issued in Spanish, and with the advertisements, store signs etc. are printed entirely in English."[24] However, Bourke was quick to add that the new innovations "jostle against and contrast strangely with the medieval rookeries of adobe, the narrow streets, still lit at night with camphine [sic] torches [and] filled by day with a motley crew of . . . blue-coated soldiers, curious tourists, señoritas wrapped . . . in rebosas, muchachos enfolded in bright colored serapes, Pueblo Indians . . . marching alongside their patient burros, upon whose backs are tied great bundles of wood or hay."[25] Indeed, Santa Fe had a rural feeling for many more decades; in 1889 straggling cows, sheep, and other animals still wandered about the plaza unattended.[26]

Many predicted that when the railroad reached Santa Fe, the town would become a popular tourist destination. "[T]he wealthy, who possess leisure, will seek our mountain scenery for the preservation of that greatest of all boons—health,"[27] wrote the *New Mexican* years earlier. The railway did indeed bring an increased number of visitors to the city, including miners, capitalists, workers, and tourists. To accommodate the influx of visitors, the elaborate, eighty-five-room Palace Hotel was built in 1881 (it was destroyed by fire in 1922). A quintessential

BIRD'S EYE VIEW OF THE CITY OF
SANTA FÉ, N.M.
1882.

1. Palace.
2. H'd Qra. Dist. N. M.
3. Post of Fort Marcy.
4. Government Corral.
5. First National Bank of Santa-Fe.
6. Second National Bank of New Mexico.
7. Cathedral.
8. St. Vincent Hospital.
9. Academy,
10. Chapel, } Sisters of Loretto.
12. Convent, }
13. St. Michaels College.
14. San Miguel Church. Erected in 1582, distroyed by
    Indians 1680, rebuilt 1710 by the Marquis de la Penuela
15. Congregational Church.

16. Guadalupe Church.
17. M. E. Church.
18. Presbyterian Church.
19. Episcopal Church.
20. Oldest Building in Santa-Fe.
21. Palace Hotel, P. Rumsey & Son.
22. Exchange Hotel, Reed & Bishop.
23. Capitol Hotel, Gray & Bailey.
24. Herlow's Hotel, P. F. Herlow.
25. Santa-Fe Planing Mill, P. Hesch.
26. Cracker Factory, D. L. Miller & Co.
27. Post Office.
28. Depot.
29. Gas Works.
30. Fisher Brewing Co.'s Brewery.

Victorian-style structure with iron columns, balconies, filigree-topped towers, and mansard roofs, it reportedly cost $60,000 to build—but room rates in 1882 were a mere $3.00 per day.[28]

By the late nineteenth century New Mexico was advertising itself as the "Land of Sunshine" and its capital city was seeking to establish itself as a health resort. The region gained notice because of its seven-thousand-foot altitude— many believed in the curative value of thin air for relief from respiratory diseases. In addition, the nearby mineral springs of Ojo Caliente made Santa Fe the ideal and natural health resort. St. Vincent's Hospital, founded in 1865, was already caring for patients suffering from tuberculosis, and beginning in the early 1880s the hospital began a building program to enlarge its facilities.[29]

As part of their effort to attract tourists and health seekers, the citizens of Santa Fe in 1883 staged a grand "Tertio Millennial"—or 333-year celebration of its founding. However, it was a "fake" event, for it was sixty years too early for the anniversary. It was also that year when city leaders fashioned myths that Santa Fe was the "Oldest City in North America" and home to the "Oldest Church" and "Oldest House." Photographer W. Henry Brown contributed to the spreading of these myths by taking stereoscopic images of the landmarks and printing the names and short histories of the buildings on the verso. Other photographers did the same.

Bird's Eye View of the City of Santa Fé, N.M., 1882. Lithograph by Joseph J. Stoner, Madison, Wisconsin

Photograph courtesy Palace of the Governors Photo Archives (NMHM/DCA), 023306

In 1889 the *New Mexican* noted that "[Dana B.] Chase has turned out a set of hand-some views for the Santa Fe Southern [railway], showing many attractive scenes along its line. . . . These views are to be grouped . . . for advertising purposes."[30]

Advertisements in newspapers and journals referred to Santa Fe as an "old Spanish City."[31] By 1886 a regular feature in the Santa Fe *Daily New Mexican* was an article that described the city's virtues and "points of interest," which of course included the "oldest dwelling house," the "Adobe Palace," the "grand modern stone" cathedral, and other sites. Residents and visitors could buy pottery made by Pueblo Indians on the plaza or at Jake Gold's, or Navajo blankets and Apache sad-dlebags at L. Fisher's store.[32] They could enjoy fresh oysters that arrived by "express" at W. W. Tate's City Bakery. They could take excursions to dances and other festivities at local pueblos. In August 1889 the *Daily New Mexican* reported, "Large posters announcing an excursion for Sunday over the Santa Fe Southern [railway] to San Ildefonso, and thence five miles in spring wagons to the historic cliff houses of the Pueblo Indians, were placed about town yesterday. The trip will prove a pleasant and interesting one, especially for those who are inclined to archaeological research."[33]

Newcomers to Santa Fe filled their homes with treasured heirlooms from homes in the States and decorative objects made locally. The 1891 inventory for easterner Eva Scott Muse Fényes's home on Hillside Avenue includes antiques she brought to Santa Fe, as well as: Mexican-made portieres, cups, and water bot-tle; coyote, bear, and sheep skin rugs; Moqui Indian baskets; a cross inlaid with straw; an Acoma olla and other American Indian pottery; and quiver, bow and arrows, and "eagle feather war bonnet."[34]

While wealthy Santa Feans and newcomers from the East were erecting houses in modern styles, local residents of modest means also sought improvements to their buildings. The *New Mexican* noted in May of 1886, "The native citizens about town are hard at work manufacturing thousands of adobes. They have caught the new spirit of improvement and evidently intend to build extensively this summer and fall."[35] The newspaper periodically ran a column called "Notes of Progress," which listed the various building and renovation projects going on in town. One such column in October 1886 noted, "The model cottage idea bids fair to take well in Santa Fe. Some twenty or more parties are thinking of erecting such cosy [*sic*] institutions here."[36]

In the mid- to late 1800s kiln-fired brick was the favored building material in Santa Fe. In 1889 the *New Mexican* exclaimed: "Six Millions of Brick to Go into New Buildings in Santa Fe this Spring," and "Speaking of brick, why, the capital city is having a regular brick boom."[37] The bricks were hand-molded and burned in a kiln on or near the construction site, or they were pressed by machine and transported to the site. Roughly the same size as machine-pressed brick, hand-molded brick has noticeably uneven edges and is generally less smooth than the pressed bricks. If Santa Feans wanted "press brick," they ordered it and had it shipped from manufacturers in the East or Midwest. For instance, in 1881 Walter V. Hayt had pressed brick shipped from Philadelphia for his new storefront on San Francisco Street, though he used locally made, hand-molded brick for his own home.[38]

Brick making became quite an extensive and competitive business in Santa Fe. In October 1882 contractor, builder, and brick maker Florence Donoghue burned a large number of bricks that he claimed were "equal to any manufactured west of St. Louis." As the *New Mexican* explained, this "demonstrated satisfactorily that in time Santa Fe's houses may be constructed of as fine brick as the residences of Philadelphia or any other eastern city."

Inmates at the New Mexico state penitentiary in Santa Fe, using clay in close proximity to the prison yard and eventually a "horse power brick machine," became excellent brick makers as well.[39] "The daily output [at the penitentiary] has now reached 15,000. . . . The clay is said to be of extra good quality," the *New Mexican* announced.[40] By 1894 the penitentiary was making close to two million bricks a year. To draw attention away from the prison-made bricks, the firm of Donoghue and Monier boasted that they made the "best grade of Pressed Brick" and used "No Convict Labor!"[41]

Mud-brick homes, however, did not lose favor with Santa Feans completely. As the *New Mexican* reported in the late 1880s, "A large number of new adobe cottages are being built in the suburbs. When properly treated this material makes, after all, the most comfortable dwellings."[42]

In the spring and summer of 1886, the city seemed to be experiencing a building boom. A prominent builder stated, "The brightest times in the history of our city are dawning upon us. . . . [T]he way business is filling up at present we expect to have our hands full till cold weather comes."[43] And a reporter for the *New Mexican* exclaimed, "It has been many a year since the builders here were so busy. . . . The brick and stone masons and the carpenters . . . the iron workers, plasterers and painters can not meet the demands upon them."[44] With Santa Fe's sawmills unable to supply the constant demand for lumber, mills in nearby Pecos Valley, Las Vegas, and Glorieta were overrun with orders for loads of lumber for the boom. Under

Details, Italianate-style Catron Building, built in 1891

construction in summer 1886 were the St. Catherine Indian School, additions to St. Vincent's Hospital and St. Michael's College, a new public school on the south side, a new capitol building, and numerous stores and homes.

Improvements continued to be made to businesses around the plaza. In 1891 Thomas B. Catron, a lawyer, politician, and financier, built a $40,000 Italianate building on the east side, with large windows overlooking the plaza.[45] Today it stands as the last remaining example of the Victorian architecture that once dominated Santa Fe's commercial center. Designed by architect F. H. Brigham, it was built of red brick by the firm of Palladino and Berardinelli, Italian stonemasons whom Archbishop Lamy had brought to Santa Fe to complete the St. Francis Cathedral. The brick (now painted beige to harmonize with the other plaza architecture) was manufactured at the state penitentiary. The facade was decorated with eyebrow lintels over the windows and an elaborate pressed-metal roof cornice that was shipped out from the East. As the Santa Fe *Daily New Mexican* reported, "The interior iron work, stair-cases, gratings, etc., arrived from Denver last night over the A.T. & S.F. for the Catron block."[46]

Anglo-Americans successfully transformed Santa Fe's native New Mexican architecture, and by 1900, much of the new construction in Santa Fe resembled that of small towns in midwestern and eastern America. Some found the changes disagreeable. One visitor commented, "The plaza, in the broad light of day, lacked charm. . . . Brick buildings of an ugly, utilitarian type have replaced the old portals that once surrounded it."[47] To others, the Spanish portals that were still remaining were unsightly, old-fashioned, and "unhealthy." In 1891 the Santa Fe *Daily New Mexican* ran numerous complaints about them in its "Round About Town" column. For example, on October 9: "The portals must go; they are a nuisance and an eye sore," and on October 23: "Down with the 16th century portals; this is the nineteenth century and the latter part of it. Get a move on yourselves."[48] The writer of the column urged that the portals be replaced by modern fabric awnings.

In the late nineteenth century Santa Fe citizens were encouraged by the wealth of building projects in progress, and yet, in reality, the disadvantage of being off the main rail line caused the city's economy and population to begin a steady and serious decline. One result was a lowering of the property values. As the *New Mexican* noted, the real-estate market favored the buyer, and "rare bargains" could be had throughout the city.[49] A further blow to the city was the closing of Fort Marcy by the U.S. government, which ended a significant payroll and considerable purchasing power in Santa Fe. The military reservation's almost seventeen acres of land and buildings in the heart of the city were auctioned off in 1891. Hopeful of a brighter future, Santa Feans placed their faith in tourism at the end of the century. "As a summer resort Santa Fe takes the cake, the whole cake and the biggest cake," declared the *New Mexican*.[50]

PEYTON
WRIGHT
GALLERY

WILLI AND FLORA
SPIEGELBERG HOUSE
237 EAST PALACE AVENUE
1880

I n the mid-nineteenth century many young, adventurous immi-
grants, including German Jews, began arriving in Santa Fe to try
their luck in the new U.S. territory. Among them was Willi Spiegelberg, who emigrated from Prussia in 1859 to join his brothers' mercantile business in Santa Fe. After becoming one of the city's most
prominent businessmen, he and his wife, Flora, built an impressive
European-style house on Palace Avenue, where most of the city's
wealthiest merchants lived.[51]

Willi ran the enormously successful family retail firm with his
brother Lehman. "Messrs. Spiegelberg Bros. sent out yesterday one
of the largest shipments of goods ever made from Santa Fe," stated
the New Mexican in 1873.[52] By the early 1880s they had two retail
stores on the south side of the plaza—two-story brick buildings
adorned with elaborate Victorian ornamentation (see page 93). With
all five of his brothers, Willi invested in mining, land speculation,
insurance, and construction. The brothers also served as sutlers and

LEFT

Willi and Flora Spiegelberg House

ABOVE

*Flora Spiegelberg and daughters Betty
and Rose at the Spiegelberg House, 1888*

Courtesy of Susan (Spiegelberg) Warburg
and Felix M. Warburg

TOP LEFT
*Territorial-style detailing over window,
Willi and Flora Spiegelberg House*

TOP RIGHT
Dormer window detail, Willi and Flora Spiegelberg House

BOTTOM
Parlor fireplace, Willi and Flora Spiegelberg House

mail route contractors for New Mexico Territory military posts and Indian agencies. In July 1868, for instance, the *New Mexican* reported: "Mr. Willie [*sic*] Spiegelberg . . . left today for new Fort Wingate, where he has been appointed post trader. We learn that he will open up there a large and selected stock of goods suitable to the location."[53]

A cofounder of the Second National Bank of Santa Fe, Willi acted as bank treasurer. Involved in local politics, he was elected probate judge in 1884 and served as mayor of Santa Fe. Willi, who spoke three languages and four Indian dialects and was known as an expert with the lariat and whip, was clearly much admired in his adopted city.[54] After he took a vacation at the Las Vegas hot springs, the *New Mexican* commented: "We are glad to see Willie [*sic*] Spiegelberg's merry good looking face on the street again."[55]

During a visit to Germany in 1874, Willi met and married eighteen-year-old Flora Langermann, a well-educated and highly accomplished young woman who spoke three languages. Born in New York, Flora was the daughter of Colonel William Langermann, who had migrated to San Francisco during the gold rush of 1849. After his death, Flora returned to Germany with her mother and siblings. Following an elaborate wedding and extensive honeymoon in Munich, Vienna, Paris, and London, Flora and Willi settled in Santa Fe in 1875.[56] In her memoirs, Flora recorded that she was one of only eight American women then living in the territorial capital, and the only source of entertainment was "a buggy ride every Sunday to visit the nearby Indian Pueblos and watch them mould pottery and make gold and silver jewelry."[57]

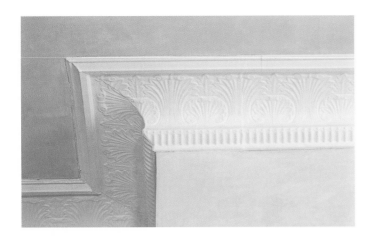

Stamped-metal molding, Willi and Flora Spiegelberg House

Five years later Willi had the house of fourteen rooms (ten on the first floor and four on the second) built for his wife and their two young girls, Betty and Rose. Like the Spiegelberg brothers' store on the plaza, Willi's home was fashionable in style and equipped with all the latest conveniences, including water and gas. In September 1880 the *Daily New Mexican* observed: "The first house in Santa Fe to have gas pipes is the residence of Mr. Willi Spiegelberg on Palace Avenue. Mssrs. Irvine and McKenzie have just finished supplying this building with appliances for affording it gas as soon as the works are finished."[58] In fact, Willi was one of a group of backers of the gasworks, which were incorporated in April 1880.

Flora played an important role in designing their homestead. On the verso of an 1888 photograph taken of the house she proudly wrote: "My first home planned by me & built under my direction, the first house to have gas & water in Santa Fe, New Mexico." To realize her design, Flora and Willi hired European artisans, who had initially come to New Mexico to work on Archbishop Lamy's building projects.[59] Constructed of adobe walls and a steeply pitched roof clad in wood shingles, the Spiebelberg house displays the European detailing and overall massing of the Victorian era, as well as local architectural traditions. The windows and doors, for instance, have the triangular molding typical of the New Mexico Territorial style. The unusual wood-stick capitals on the porch columns match those in the Palace Hotel porch, constructed about the same time.

Most of the Victorian details visible in the 1888 photograph were later removed (or covered by stucco), including the cresting along the roof line, the quoins (scored and painted to simulate stone); the decorative bargeboards, finial, and crossbracing in the gables; and the slender porch columns. Not visible in the photograph are the pressed-tin tiles that sheathe the pediment and pilasters of the front dormer window—likely added later in the nineteenth century by either the Spiegelbergs or subsequent owners.

During a six-month-long restoration project in 1998, interior details were restored and the rooms reconfigured to house an art gallery.[60] The hardwood floors, grand staircase, and shallow fireplaces (intended for coal burning) were all carefully refurbished. The front-parlor fireplace has a particularly ornate, hand-carved wood surround that may be of English origin. The twelve-foot-high ceilings in the front rooms have retained their stamped-metal molding in designs that resemble decorative plaster. Some portions of the molding had to be replaced with replicas. Stamped sheet metal such as this was popular in the Victorian era and used for ceilings, walls, and exteriors in homes and commercial buildings.

Known for their hospitality, the Spiegelbergs entertained many of Santa Fe's most illustrious citizens and most famous visitors during their years in the house. "In those good old days wines and champagne flowed freely, toasts and speeches were made, thrilling war and pioneer stories related, and the real western spirit of good-will and fellowship prevailed," recalled Flora in her memoirs.[61] A gracious host with cosmopolitan airs, Flora was known for holding musical evenings during which she played Chopin on the piano.[62] Among the Spiegelbergs' close friends were New Mexico Governor Lew Wallace, who lived just down the street, and Archbishop Lamy. Flora recalled that one day she glanced out her front window and saw the Archbishop planting a pair of willow trees near the wrought-iron front gate.

In the early 1890s, desiring better educational, social, and religious opportunities for his daughters, Willi liquidated the Spiegelberg business concerns in Santa Fe and moved to New York, where his brother Lehman already lived. He sold the Palace Avenue mansion for $3,000 to Teresa Symington, wife of New Mexico doctor John Symington. In 1900 Teresa sold the house to another well-known Jewish merchant family in Santa Fe: Solomon and Emilie Spitz. Solomon was founder and owner of the S. Spitz Jewelry and Manufacturing Company.[63] The Spitz family owned the house until 1963, and since 1973, it has been listed on the National Register of Historic Places.

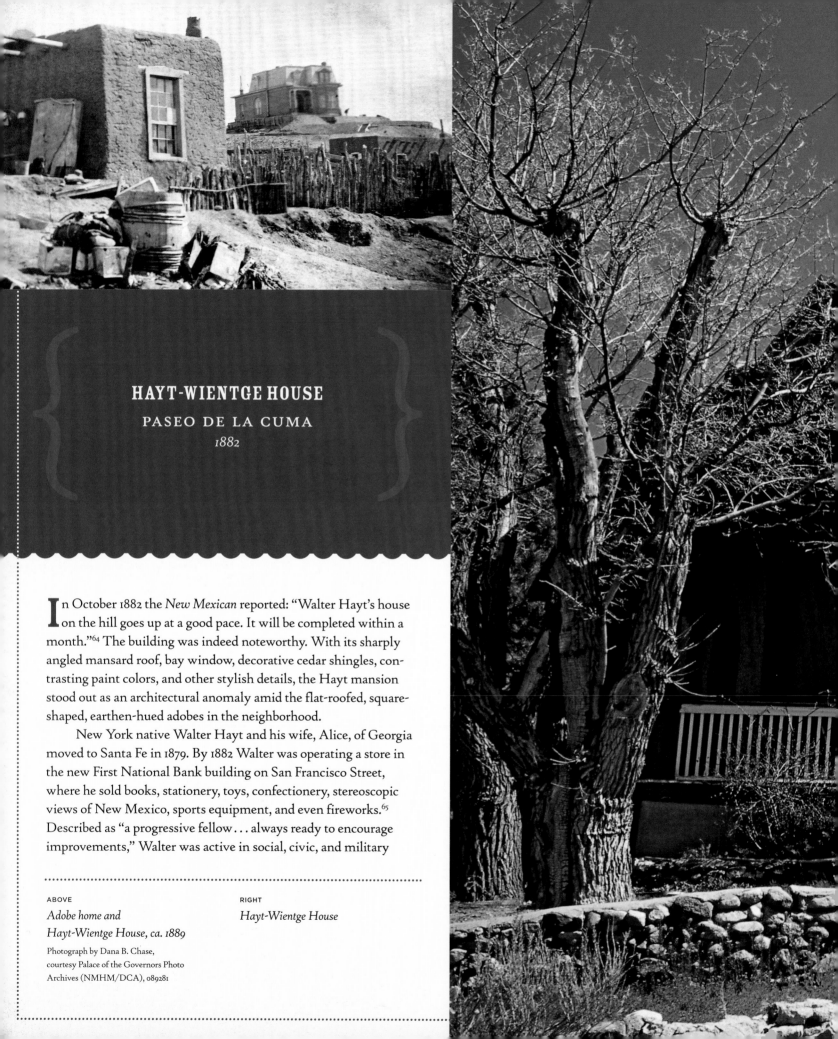

HAYT-WIENTGE HOUSE
PASEO DE LA CUMA
1882

I n October 1882 the *New Mexican* reported: "Walter Hayt's house on the hill goes up at a good pace. It will be completed within a month."[64] The building was indeed noteworthy. With its sharply angled mansard roof, bay window, decorative cedar shingles, contrasting paint colors, and other stylish details, the Hayt mansion stood out as an architectural anomaly amid the flat-roofed, square-shaped, earthen-hued adobes in the neighborhood.

New York native Walter Hayt and his wife, Alice, of Georgia moved to Santa Fe in 1879. By 1882 Walter was operating a store in the new First National Bank building on San Francisco Street, where he sold books, stationery, toys, confectionery, stereoscopic views of New Mexico, sports equipment, and even fireworks.[65] Described as "a progressive fellow... always ready to encourage improvements," Walter was active in social, civic, and military

ABOVE

*Adobe home and
Hayt-Wientge House, ca. 1889*

Photograph by Dana B. Chase,
courtesy Palace of the Governors Photo
Archives (NMHM/DCA), 089281

RIGHT

Hayt-Wientge House

Living room fireplace, Hayt-Wientge House

Detail of faux-marble slate fireplace, Hayt-Wientge House

Curving staircase, Hayt-Wientge House

affairs of the city.[66] He was a member of the New Mexico Territorial Militia, served on the board of trade, and was county clerk for several years. When running for the latter position, the newspaper remarked: Walter V. Hayt "is an active young man, eminently qualified and very obliging."[67]

The elegant new Victorian house he built for his young family on a hill just north of the plaza, though not as sizable or ornate as the Staab mansion built the same year, was befitting of Walter Hayt's position in Santa Fe society. The two-story house was constructed of double, hand-molded, fired bricks made on land south of the house near an acequia. The house reflects traditional Southwest architecture in the thickness of the walls and the less elaborate decorative trim on the exterior, as compared to similar Victorian houses in the eastern and midwestern U.S.

Overall the house is an eclectic mix of Italian- and French-inspired design. The main facade is asymmetrical, with a bay window on the right and the entranceway on the left. There are segmental-arched windows on the second floor and full arched and framed windows on the first floor. The paired entry doors have glass in the upper segments and middle arched portions, with solid square panels on the bottom. The sharply angled, patterned mansard roof, which gives both distinction and extra living space to the house, has different-shaped cedar shingles placed in rows to form distinctive patterns. Victorian architects and builders were notorious for using common wood shingles, sometimes painted in contrasting hues, for decorative effect. The paired arched windows on the bay and side elevations have an equally distinctive curved wood element in the spandrel.

On the first floor (where ceilings are eleven feet high) are the parlor, study, dining room, kitchen, and bedroom. Upstairs is a landing hall and three bedrooms. Numerous architectural details, such as the six-foot-high pine first-floor windows, paired entry doors, remarkable curving staircase banister, and elaborate brass door hardware, were likely purchased from mail-order catalogs and shipped via railway to Santa Fe.

The three fireplaces on the first floor are excellent examples of faux-marble painting on black slate, a popular and cheap replacement for real marble fireplace surrounds in the Victorian era. The faux-marble panels are further decorated with geometric designs carved and painted in gold. Remarkably similar fireplaces graced the historic Bergere House at 135 Grant Avenue.[68] The fireplace in the living

room of the Hayt house has a cast-iron "Washington" coal-burning stove with mica panels made by B. C. Bibb & Son in Baltimore, Maryland.

Many other Victorian-era details remain in the interior, including the entryway with a fantastic curving staircase with spindle decoration and the arched paired doors; a cast-iron light fixture in the dining room; decorative plaster ceiling medallions; and elaborate door hardware. Among the unusual features in the house is a small mirror set into the baluster at the base of the staircase.

The Hayts sold their house in 1888 for $3,000 to Christina F. Wientge, who co-owned a millinery shop on the plaza with her sister Anna Mugler. Shortly after she moved into the house with her husband, Frederick, the Wientges had a small adobe structure built just north of the residence where Frederick made and sold his filigree jewelry. By September 1889 Frederick had opened a shop in the Griffin block, where he sold his jewelry, as well as clocks, silverware, and optical goods.[69] He had stiff competition, for fine filigree jewelry was sold at numerous shops in late-nineteenth-century Santa Fe.[70]

After serving as one of Teddy Roosevelt's Rough Riders during the Spanish American War, Frederick died in 1898. Christina is listed in the 1900 census as a "farmer," but she primarily supported her four daughters by renting rooms to boarders.[71] The Wientge family owned the house until 1972.

By examining photographs taken of the house over the years we can trace the various changes made by the different owners. A photograph dated 1898 shows the red-brick facade, the dark trim, and only a simple front porch.[72] A 1920s-era shot shows that the front porch was extended along the west side of the house and the lighting was converted from gas to electric.[73] It was also around this time that the stone terracing in front of the house was built by Dave Steele, who had married Christina and Frederick Wientge's daughter Freda. Yet another photo shows that by 1935, like so many of Santa Fe's Victorian buildings, the bricks on the front facade had been stuccoed over.

After serving as a daycare center for several years, the house was purchased in about 1976 by Susan and Mike

OPPOSITE
Paired, arched doors and detail of spindle decoration in staircase, Hayt-Wientge House

LEFT
Front-door knob, Hayt-Wientge House

Weber, who spent approximately $100,000 and six years on a carefully researched and meticulously executed restoration.[74] Mike was the associate director of the Museum of New Mexico and curator of the Palace of the Governors. Having worked with architect John Conron on the restoration of the palace, Mike hired Conron to restore the Hayt-Wientge House. The Webers had Conron remove layer after layer of paint, linoleum, and other later additions to reveal the original surfaces throughout the house. The roofing was peeled back until the original cedar shingles of different shapes were found; they were replaced with new ones in the same pattern. The milled trim was stripped and repainted in maroon and two shades of green, which the owners considered to be the original colors.[75]

Originally surrounded by orchards and acres of open land, the Victorian mansion is now enveloped by condominium developments. However, from its perch on the steep hill on Paseo de la Cuma, it still has spectacular views of the city.[76]

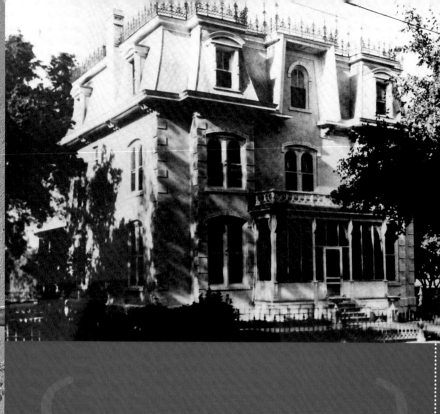

ABRAHAM AND JULIA STAAB HOUSE
(LA POSADA DE SANTA FE)
EAST PALACE AVENUE
1882

The three-story, fashionably ornate Staab mansion appears on Stoner's 1882 lithograph that features only the prominent buildings of Santa Fe (see page 94). A stylized engraving of the house also appeared in the 1885 book *Illustrated New Mexico* as an example of the modern and refined architecture of the city. Today, nearly swallowed up by the faux-adobe La Posada resort complex, this house barely survives as one of the few remaining vestiges of Santa Fe's Victorian past.

Like many of the other German Jewish pioneers who settled in Santa Fe, Abraham Staab (1839–1913) left his homeland of Lüdge, Westphalia, to seek new opportunities on the Western frontier. He arrived in Santa Fe in 1858, joining his brother Zoldoc, who was then working for their cousins, the Spiegelbergs. The following year the

LEFT
Window and door detail, rear section of Abraham and Julia Staab House (La Posada de Santa Fe)

ABOVE
Abraham and Julia Staab House, ca. 1900
Courtesy of La Posada de Santa Fe

Abraham and Julia Staab House entrance, inside La Posada lobby

Staabs established their own retail store on San Francisco Street (Z. Staab & Bro.) and became post traders at Fort Marcy. Eventually their enterprise became known as "one of the largest and most influential wholesale establishments in the west" and served New Mexico territory, Texas, Mexico, Arizona, and southern Colorado.[77] At the plaza store they sold dry goods, silks, clothing, and shoes they had specially manufactured in the East; wines and liquors; cigars and tobacco; and "miners' goods of every description."[78]

Described as a shrewd and keen businessman, and "one of the most affable of gentlemen," Abraham was one of Santa Fe's most important merchants.[79] He became sole owner of the business (after the death of his brother in the mid-1880s), as well as a director of the First National Bank; one of the founders and first presidents of the Santa Fe Chamber of Commerce; and a member of the "Santa Fe Ring," a dominant political group in New Mexico headed by Thomas Benton Catron. Abraham was also instrumental in bringing the Denver and Rio Grande Railroad (known as the Chile Line) from Denver into Santa Fe in 1889, and he and his associates became financiers behind the construction of St. Francis Cathedral. According to family tradition, Archbishop Lamy put the Hebrew inscription "YHWH"—meaning Jehovah—on the arch over the cathedral doors in gratitude for Staab's financial support of the church.[80] By 1890 Staab & Bro. had a monopoly on sales of supplies, including striped material for prison uniforms, to the state penitentiary.

On a return visit to his hometown in Germany in 1865, Abraham married Julia Schuster (1844–1896). After returning to Santa Fe they settled into an adobe house on Burro Alley, where they raised seven children.[81] Abraham purchased land from the Baca family on East Palace Avenue in 1876 and six years later built a new home on the property. The style he chose for his three-story mansion was French Second Empire—a popular building type in Santa Fe since 1880. The Staab brothers' store on the plaza was described as a "handsome two-story building" that was "fitted up in the latest and most attractive style."[82] Therefore, it is not surprising that Abraham desired a similarly fashionable and handsome home for his family.

Characteristic of the Second Empire manner, the Staab house originally had a third story featuring a dominant mansard roof with dormer windows, molded cornices, and elaborate iron cresting along the roofline. An early photograph that now hangs in the Julia Staab suite at La Posada shows the original configuration. The overall exterior design and specific details match those seen in various pattern books of the era, including *Cummings' Architectural Details* of 1873.[83] For example, plate 16, a design for a dwelling with a "French roof" and exterior wood details "of a bold and effective character," has similar features (except for the central tower) as the Staab house.

In building his house, Abraham Staab may have hired the architectural firm of Wheeler and Randell, which was then building new storefronts for Z. Staab & Bro., or possibly the French and Italian builders of Archbishop Lamy's French Romanesque Cathedral.[84] The *New Mexican* followed the building of the mansion closely. For instance, it reported on February 3, 1882, "Mr. Staab's new dwelling will be enclosed by a handsome stone wall." And one day later, "Mr. Staab is provident. He has provided his new residence with a tank, pipes for using water from the water works and a well. He intends to suffer no inconvenience from dry weather."

The third story of the Staab house was destroyed by fire sometime after 1913, and today the two-story house is

The Staab house facade rises above the entrance to La Posada resort on Palace Avenue

capped by a heavy cornice with decorative brackets in the eaves. The elaborate entranceway, with paired doors and the entwined initials "A S" exists within the lobby of La Posada. Other remaining exterior details, such as the decorative molding over the arched paired windows, can be viewed best from the back courtyard of the resort. The grounds around the Staab house were originally planted with a large orchard and lush gardens, where Julia raised her prized roses. She was an invalid for much of her life due to the difficulties of childbirth, and gardening was one of her few pleasures.

In February 1882 the *New Mexican* announced, "Mr. Staab has decided to have a portion of his new dwelling trimmed on the inside with highly finished walnut. It will be exceedingly handsome."[85] Indeed, the interior was appointed with the most luxurious of details and most expensive of materials. Still remaining today are the grand staircase with elaborately carved newel post, ornate marble fireplaces, and intricate wood inlay floors.

The Staabs and the family mansion on Palace played a significant role in Santa Fe social life. Among the guests who were lavishly entertained at the Staab home were members of the old Spanish families, Army officers and their wives, Archbishop Lamy (who was a special friend), and members of the city's large Jewish community, many of whom lived on upper East Palace Avenue.

Not surprisingly, the Staabs and their activities were constantly in the news. Everything from morning horseback rides to trips to Europe ended up in the *New Mexican* society column. "Mr. and Mrs. A. Staab and their three charming daughters, Misses Anna, Adele, and Bertha, are at the Las Vegas springs," the newspaper wrote in 1886.[86]

Julia Staab died in 1896, and following Abraham's death in 1913, the mansion of the millionaire and pioneer merchant of Santa Fe was sold by the remaining six Staab children. In 1936 the house was purchased by R. H. and Eulala Nason, who gave it the name La Posada.[87] After purchasing additional land surrounding the home from the Baca family, the Nasons turned the house into a hotel with cottages built where the fruit trees once stood. Since 1974 La Posada has been owned and operated as a hotel by private concerns.

Two details of inlay wood floor patterns, Abraham and Julia Staab House (La Posada de Santa Fe)

Staircase, Abraham and Julia Staab House (La Posada de Santa Fe)

Fireplace, Abraham and Julia Staab House (La Posada de Santa Fe)

GEORGE AND MARGARET PRESTON HOUSE
106 FAITHWAY
1886

I n August 1886, the Santa Fe *New Mexican* declared, "Palace avenue property is in demand. Several palatial homes will be built on this thoroughfare this fall."[88] One of the palatial homes built off Palace that year was for George Cuyler Preston, an easterner and a successful law partner of Charles H. Gildersleeve. Among the buildings already erected near his property on Palace was the stone Gothic Revival–style Church of the Holy Faith (1882).

The George and Margaret Preston mansion is the finest example of Victorian architecture extant in Santa Fe today and one of only two known Queen Anne–style buildings in New Mexico.[89] This style, loosely based on the red-brick, half-timbered buildings of Queen Anne's reign in Great Britain (1701–14), was embraced by Americans from the 1870s until the turn of the century as a symbol of prosperity, community, and family. It was an especially popular style for sprawling seaside estates.

In addition to being a lawyer, George was a notary of the public and a highly visible member of the community. When a grand

ABOVE

Tile detail of parlor (or study) fireplace,
George and Margaret Preston House

OPPOSITE

Front facade with garden,
George and Margaret Preston House

RIGHT

Staircase, George and Margaret Preston House

BELOW

Staircase Hall, Design No. 18. From Henry Hudson
Holly, Modern Dwellings in Town and Country
(New York: Harper & Brothers, Publishers, 1878)

OPPOSITE

George and Margaret Preston House

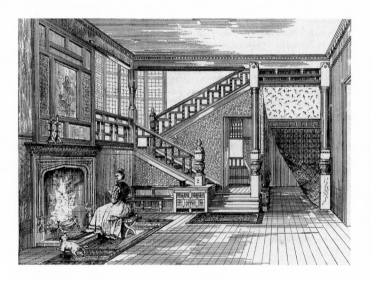

parade and celebration was planned for the arrival of newly elected Governor L. Bradford Prince in April 1889, Preston served on the reception committee. George and Margaret's names appeared frequently in the social column of the *New Mexican*. For example, the newspaper noted in 1886, "Mr. and Mrs. G. C. Preston returned last night from a very delightful visit to the Zuni country."[90] And later that summer: "Mr. and Mrs. Geo. Cuyler Preston go east next month to select furniture for their elegant new home on Palace avenue."[91] The latter is particularly interesting, as it suggests that the Prestons were not pleased with the choice of furniture in Santa Fe at the time. There were certainly stores on the plaza that offered furnishings, but apparently none that matched the Prestons' tastes.

After purchasing land in November 1885 for $3,250, George Preston hired Michael Berardinelli and Gaetano Pal-

ladino to oversee the construction of the house, which began in May 1886.[92] As the *New Mexican* explained, these Italian "hewers of stone and layers of brick" had the reputation of "first class workmen as the many, fine buildings they have erected in New Mexico prove."[93] Periodically, the newspaper reported on the progress of the Preston mansion. That May the paper announced: "The costly mansion of Mr. G. C. Preston will be finished with red sand stone from Las Vegas," and in October: "Painter Rhyman's men are doing a handsome job on the Preston mansion."[94] The latter, A. L. Rhyman, was a house, sign, and carriage painter who advertised "calsomining and paper hanging done in quick order."[95]

Like most Queen Anne–style houses, the Preston home is distinguished by its use of multiple gables, porches, window types (including half-round, oriel, and multi-paned), rooflines, and other elements that produce

ABOVE

Parlor (or study) fireplace, George and Margaret Preston House

OPPOSITE

Porch detail, George and Margaret Preston House

a striking, asymmetrical silhouette. Even the upper-story dormer window (with metal barrel-tiled gable and sunburst-pattern wood decoration) and the porch (with fanciful turned columns and unique circle-patterned brackets) were used as an opportunity for ornamental expression. Another characteristic of the style is the variety of surfaces—wood, stone, brick, tin, stained glass, and ceramic tile—seen throughout the facade.

The two-and-a-half-story house was built on a stone foundation and is constructed of fired brick and frame. The first-floor walls were covered with stucco and the second story was covered with sheets of metal embossed with a design that simulates cedar-wood shingles. The latter cladding was typically used in Queen Anne–style homes in the eastern U.S. The metal sheets were lighter, less costly, and easier to install than individual wood shingles. Additionally, these metal sheets are rot-proof and fireproof.

The steeply pitched roofs were sheathed in metal, red-barrel tiles that add yet another layer of texture and ornament. The letter "P" on the brick chimney has been attributed to the house's first owner, but it may actually refer to the last name of Dr. Louis E. Polhemus, an herbalist and dietician who owned the house in the 1940s and 1950s. During his tenure the house was known as the "Palace of Health."

In 1963 New Mexico architectural historian and professor Bainbridge Bunting assigned three of his students the task of making drawings of the exterior and floor plans of the Preston house.[96] The floor plans are particularly important, for they show the house arrangement before it was transformed into a bed and breakfast. As the drawings indicate, the first floor was originally fluid and open, providing a large space for entertaining. There was a small, narrow back staircase that led to the second floor, where there was a small bedroom for a servant and two larger rooms for family members.

The overall massing and details of the Preston house are similar to designs found in Henry Hudson Holly's 1878 *Modern Dwellings in Town and Country*, a popular pattern book of the era featuring mostly Queen Anne–style homes. The Oriental-style staircase with turned banisters and spindles, painted black and gold, is remarkably similar to design number eighteen in the book. Holly explained that this staircase "has somewhat of a Japanese effect" and the "Japanese joinery is of a thoroughly honest construction."[97]

Fireplaces in Queen Anne homes tend to have mantelpieces with a dizzying array of ornaments—towers, columns, brackets, beveled mirrors, glazed tiles, and shelves for trinkets. The three original fireplaces on the first floor of the Preston house are fine examples of these High Victorian designs. All the decorative features draw attention to the fireplace—a symbol of family and prosperity in late-nineteenth-century America.

Ornamental wood friezes and a decorative column frame the openings to the living room and parlor (or study), providing a visual separation from the entrance hall. Typical of the Victorian era, examples of vibrantly colored stained glass can be found throughout the house, including the living room and the original dining room (now a guest suite). The latter has a spectacular curved wall of clear and stained glass.

Using their Queen Anne–style mansion as collateral, the Prestons speculated in building lots in Santa Fe.[98] In the 1890s, after they defaulted on a bank loan, the Second National Bank took possession of the house. By this time the Prestons had moved to Denver. After changing hands many times and being modernized in the early 1970s with new plumbing and electrical systems, as well as baths and a kitchen, the house became an inn in 1980 and operates today as the Madeleine B&B.

PHILLIP AND CATHERINE HESCH HOUSE

324–326 READ STREET
1888

I n March 1888 Phillip August Hesch (1828–1914) purchased for the sum of $1,200 two lots of land, and the remains of a building partially destroyed by fire, from Annie H. Hull on Read Street. Shortly thereafter the *New Mexican* noted, "Mr. Hesch is now perfecting plans and will erect a very pretty French roof upon the old building which will make an attractive looking and useful dwelling." One month later the newspaper reported on the progress: "P. Hesch . . . has added a second story that is as full of shapely beauty as the symmetrical curves on the neck of a champaign [*sic*] bottle."[99]

Hesch, a highly religious man, may have chosen the location for his new home because it was within walking distance of the Santuario de Guadalupe, where he attended daily mass.[100] The property was also a valuable building lot because of its proximity to the terminus of the railroad.[101] Today the Hesch house is one of the few remaining in Santa Fe that has a French mansard roof and carpenter-Gothic-style ornament.

ABOVE

Phillip and Catherine Hesch House,
February 20, 1893

Photo courtesy of Connie Hesch

RIGHT

Phillip and Catherine Hesch House

Phillip and Catherine Hesch, ca. 1890s
Photo courtesy of Connie Hesch

Phillip and Catherine Hesch and their daughters at the Read Street home, ca. 1890
Photo courtesy of Connie Hesch

An accomplished carpenter and woodworker, Hesch built this large, wood-frame home for his wife, Catherine (1834–1929), and their twelve children. Born in Bavaria, Germany, Phillip was brought by his parents to Ontario, Canada, when he was two years old. He learned the carpentry trade, and in 1852 married Catherine Maier. Together they moved to Titusville, Pennsylvania, where oil had been discovered in 1864. Twenty years later, seeking a healthful place to live, the Hesches traveled to Santa Fe where Phillip "at once took an important part in the upbuilding of the city."[102] His two-story, wood-frame planning mill, located between Agua Fria Street and the river, was featured in Stoner's 1882 bird's-eye-view lithograph of Santa Fe, as a sign of the city's progress (see page 94). Several of Hesch's sons also became skilled woodworkers and together they worked with their father on many buildings in the city. In 1887 Hesch and Sons placed advertisements in the *Daily New Mexican* for their "shutter and sash mill" near the Santuario de Guadalupe, where they manufactured "all sorts of mouldings, fancy castings, stair railing, etc."[103]

In the years following the 1880 arrival of the railroad in Santa Fe, there was an abundance of work and excellent wages available for master carpenters like the Hesches. Carpenters could earn up to $4.00 per day (as compared to $4.00 per week for a "common laborer").[104] Phillip's name appeared numerous times in the *New Mexican*'s "Improvement Notes" column concerning building projects in the city. For instance, in April 1888 it was noted that "Hesch is erecting a beautiful pavilion on the spacious grounds of the Catron homestead. It is to be of the Japanese pattern."[105] In addition to his own home, Phillip built other residences, including the 1890 Eugenie Shonnard House on Paseo de Peralta, named after the sculptor who lived there for forty years. He is also credited with working on the Catron block on the east side of the plaza, various storefronts on San Francisco Street, and St. Catherine's Indian School. Concerning the latter, the Santa Fe *Daily New Mexican* reported in November 1889: "Hesch & Sons have the wood work contract [for the Indian school] and it will keep them pretty busy to finish it before March 1."[106] It is believed that Phillip and his son John built the balusters and hand railing on the renowned and miraculous spiral staircase in the Loretto Chapel.[107] Phillip traded his labor at the chapel for the 1886 or 1887 tuition of his five daughters at the Academy of Our Lady of Light.

An 1893 photograph of the Hesch House, owned by Phillip and Catherine's great-granddaughter, shows that the homestead originally boasted a dazzling array of decorative millwork. The entire facade was sheathed in courses of square-cut wood shingles, and rows of scallop- and diamond-

Detail of dormer window, Phillip and Catherine Hesch House

shaped shingles graced the mansard roof. The elaborate veranda consisted of clusters of slender columns with fanciful brackets and pendants supporting the roof. The trim was all painted a dark hue. In another early photograph of the Hesch family sitting on the veranda, details of the paired entry doors with triangular molding and the pointed-picket fence that enclosed the yard can clearly be seen. The triangular molding, also used over the windows throughout the facade, is a distinctly New Mexico Territorial-style feature.

Like most of Santa Fe's Victorian houses, the Hesch house facade was later stuccoed over, and the fanciful shingles and woodwork were removed. Even the porch is supported by stuccoed piers and has a much simpler cornice with brackets and dentils. Remaining features of the original design include the first-story bracketed cornice, triangular-shaped moldings over the windows, outwardly curving

mansard roof, and effusive Victorian decoration in the projecting central dormer window.

The last time the house was surveyed by the New Mexico State Register of Cultural Properties, much of the interior woodwork—including an impressive curving staircase and intricately carved newel post, the work of Phillip Hesch and his sons—was extant in the western portion of the house.[108] At that time it was also noted that the east side of the house had been remodeled into an apartment.

In 1912 Phillip and Catherine Hesch moved to California and sold their Santa Fe home to Arthur G. Whittier. The house changed hands many times. After owners Mr. and Mrs. Eloy Ulibarri restored the house in 1970, the Historic Santa Fe Foundation awarded them a plaque indicating the house was deemed worthy of preservation. In 1972 it was added to the State Registry of Historic Places.

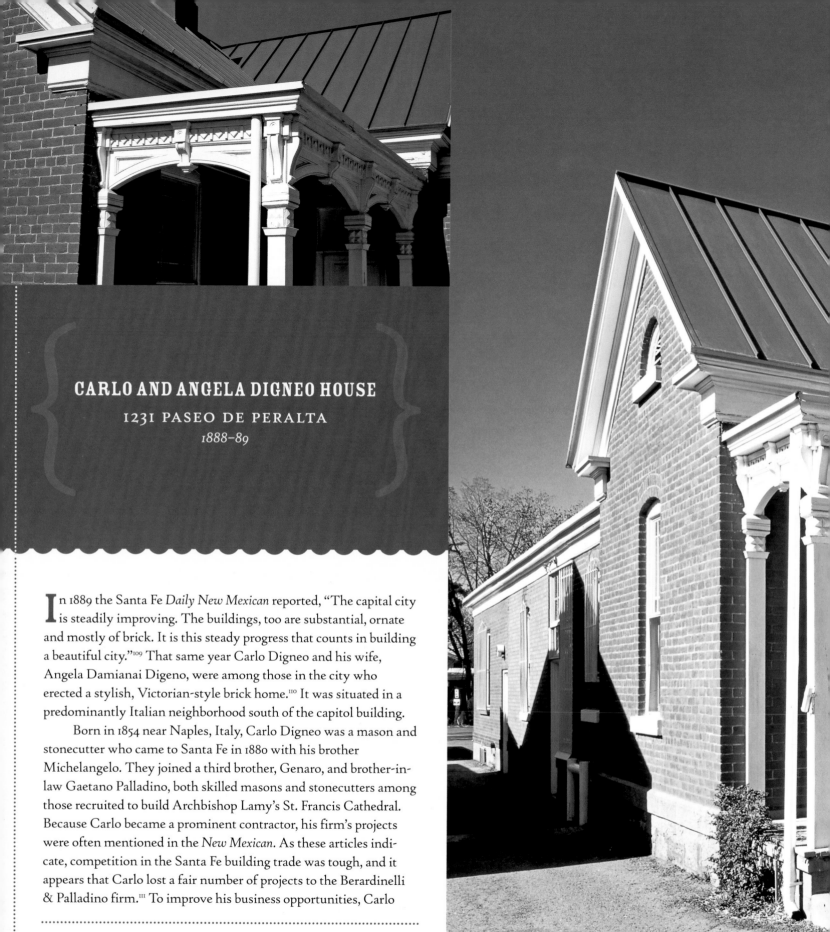

CARLO AND ANGELA DIGNEO HOUSE

1231 PASEO DE PERALTA
1888–89

I n 1889 the Santa Fe *Daily New Mexican* reported, "The capital city is steadily improving. The buildings, too are substantial, ornate and mostly of brick. It is this steady progress that counts in building a beautiful city."[109] That same year Carlo Digneo and his wife, Angela Damianai Digeno, were among those in the city who erected a stylish, Victorian-style brick home.[110] It was situated in a predominantly Italian neighborhood south of the capitol building.

Born in 1854 near Naples, Italy, Carlo Digneo was a mason and stonecutter who came to Santa Fe in 1880 with his brother Michelangelo. They joined a third brother, Genaro, and brother-in-law Gaetano Palladino, both skilled masons and stonecutters among those recruited to build Archbishop Lamy's St. Francis Cathedral. Because Carlo became a prominent contractor, his firm's projects were often mentioned in the *New Mexican*. As these articles indicate, competition in the Santa Fe building trade was tough, and it appears that Carlo lost a fair number of projects to the Berardinelli & Palladino firm.[111] To improve his business opportunities, Carlo

ABOVE

Porch detail, Carlo and Angela Digneo House

RIGHT

Carlo and Angela Digneo House

Portrait of Carlo Digneo

SRC Miscellaneous Collections; Courtesy New
Mexico State Records Center & Archives; 24450

and his siblings formed partnerships with various builders
in the city to erect residences and public buildings throughout the territory. For instance, in 1889 Digneo Brothers
teamed up with Florence Donoghue to build the new brick
and stone Indian school building. Generally speaking,
stonemasons and stonecutters earned high wages for their
work ($3 to $4 a day and $4 to $5 a day, respectively).[112]

In July 1889 the *New Mexican* reported, "Brick masons
are still in demand here. . . . Digneo Bros. want half a dozen
more of this class of mechanics at $5 a day."[113] Perhaps the
masons who responded to this notice helped build Carlo
and Angela's fashionable four-room, one-and-a-half-story
house on East Manhattan Avenue (now Paseo de Peralta) in
1889. That year many buildings were being erected or renovated in the neighborhood.[114] Carlo and Angela raised six
children in the house, and as the younger Digneos began

families of their own, they built brick houses for themselves
nearby.[115] Around the corner from his own home, Carlo
built a brick house at 512 Weber Street for his sister Jennie
Britton, and later his son Charles bought the house.

The Carlo and Angela Digneo House rests on a sandstone foundation over a full basement. The walls are hand-
molded red brick, made and fired in a kiln on or close to the
building site. Later painted an orangey-red color, the bricks
have irregular, rounded corners and striations typical of
handmade sand bricks.[116] Characteristic of Victorian-era
architecture, the house has a cross-gabled roof (clad in red-
tin tiles), corbeled brick chimneys, a large bay window, and
an Eastlake-style porch. The latter mode is named after
English architect and interior designer Charles L. Eastlake
and is distinguished by ornate carved and turned-wood decoration. Similar to Queen Anne houses, the front windows
of the Digneo house have multi-paned windows with blue-
glass panes in the four corners.

Now reconfigured into offices, the main floor formerly consisted of a parlor, dining room, bedroom, and sitting room, with a kitchen and additional bedrooms in the
basement. When the first addition was built at the rear
sometime after 1900, the kitchen and bedrooms were
moved there.[117] Some rooms still retain original details typical of the late nineteenth century. There are two shallow,
coal-burning fireplaces with elaborately carved wood man-
tels, decorative embossed brass hardware (heavily painted
over) on the doors, and finely detailed trim around doorways and windows. The fancy woodwork and hardware
may have been ordered from a company like Sears, Roe-
buck & Co., which published catalogs by this time, or perhaps the woodwork was manufactured locally by craftsmen
such as Hesch and Sons.

Fireplace, Carlo and Angela Digneo House

Trim details, Carlo and Angela Digneo House

JEAN-BAPTISTE LAMY
BRINGS A EUROPEAN AESTHETIC TO SANTA FE

LEFT *Bishop Jean-Baptiste Lamy, ca. 1870*
Photograph by William Henry Brown, courtesy Palace of
the Governors Photo Archives (NMHM/DCA), 009970

ABOVE *St. Francis Cathedral under construction, ca. 1880*
Courtesy Palace of the Governors Photo Archives (NMHM/DCA), 131794

When the French Bishop Jean-Baptiste Lamy arrived in Santa Fe in the early 1850s, he complained that the crumbling earthen churches reminded him of the "stable of Bethlehem."[118] A native of the Clermont-Ferrand region of France, where grand stone cathedrals graced the countryside, Lamy was not impressed with the stark mud walls and roofs of Santa Fe's humble houses of worship. He complained to his French peers that New Mexico's churches were "of moderate dimensions with no architectural character, and as poor in the interior as the exterior."[119] With great enthusiasm and zeal, the bishop changed all that by introducing the architectural styles, building techniques, and skilled artisans of his homeland to nineteenth-century Santa Fe.

Appointed by the Vatican in 1850 to reinstate Roman Catholic orthodoxy to the region, Bishop Lamy quickly organized the building of a French Romanesque Revival–style cathedral at the head of San Francisco Street. Begun in 1869, the structure was built around the walls of the old parroquia. Construction moved at a snail's pace, often delayed because of a lack of building funds. Over the years the *New Mexican* reported on its progress. On November 20, 1872: "The new stone cathedral . . . is slowly but surely progressing. One of the southwest entrances is already beginning to indicate the fine and massive style of architecture. It makes us impatient to see the whole imposing plan completed." When it was finally close to completion in the summer of 1882, the newspaper claimed it was "the finest church edifice west of St. Louis."[120]

To design and build the rounded arches and polychromatic stonework of his cathedral, Lamy recruited architects from France and stonemasons from France and Italy. The pink- and yellow-hued sandstone used to build the walls

Lamy house and chapel

was quarried on the summit of Cerro Colorado near the present-day village of Lamy and hauled to Santa Fe on wagons. The cathedral was finally completed in 1886, but without the twin spires of the original design.

Significantly, many of the French and Italian stonemasons who were brought by Lamy to work on the cathedral settled in Santa Fe and became independent builders and contractors. Their accomplished stonework and European-inspired designs can be seen in many of the prominent civic, educational, and religious buildings of the era. Among Lamy's recruits was Projectus Mouly of Volvic, France, who designed the Gothic Revival Loretto Chapel (inspired by Sainte-Chapelle in Paris) built in Santa Fe between 1873 and 1878. Italian-born Michael Berardinelli and Gaetano Palladino, who were also brought to town for the cathedral construction, formed their own firm and built many homes in Santa Fe, including the Queen Anne–style Preston mansion on Faithway Street.

In the early 1860s, in need of peace and refuge from his official duties, Lamy bought a piece of land along the Little Tesuque brook in the foothills outside Santa Fe. By 1875, the year he was elevated to archbishop, Lamy had erected a modest retreat on the land consisting of a bedroom, sitting room, and tiny chapel with an altar. He called his house *La Villa Pintoresca* (the picturesque villa) after the entrancing vistas of the Sangre de Cristo Mountains and Rio Grande Valley.

Combining New Mexican Territorial features with European conventions, the house was constructed of mud-plastered adobe walls atop a stone foundation, with steeply pitched shingled roofs, wood gable ends, and a steeple.[121] A portal was installed on the west and south facades, and Lamy surrounded the house with lush gardens and orchards. When he made improvements to his property in the summer of 1875, the *New Mexican* found it noteworthy: "Bishop Lamy has been painting and kalsomining his residence in a very tasteful manner. . . . It gives a most pleasing relief to the primitive adobe."[122]

Archbishop Lamy died on February 13, 1888. Through his building projects he brought one of the first major sources of aesthetic change to the city—a tangible sign of progress for the rustic frontier town. Today his grand cathedral is one of the most visited sites in the city, and his humble home with its magnificent views is lovingly preserved by the owners of the resort in which it proudly stands.

CHAPTER 5

CALIFORNIA INFLUENCE

Spanish Mission Revival

TOP

Postcard of the Alamo Chapel,
San Antonio, Texas, ca. 1909

Collection of the author

BOTTOM

Postcard of Castañeda Harvey House,
Las Vegas, New Mexico, ca. 1908

Collection of the author

OPPOSITE

329 Sena Street, ca. 1934

WHILE THE VICTORIAN STYLES came via the railroad from the Midwest and the East, the next major architectural trend to reach Santa Fe in the early 1900s hailed from the West. Adapted from the white-stuccoed and arcaded Spanish Colonial missions that dotted the California landscape, it became known as the California Mission Revival style. Interest in the manner was spurred by California's campaign in the late nineteenth century to restore these buildings, many of which were in ruins. In addition, the California Building at the 1893 Chicago World's Fair and the Bertram and Goodhue Spanish Revival designs at the 1915 Panama California Exposition in San Diego contributed to the national craze for Spanish Mission Revival homes.

Illustrations and descriptions of the California missions in magazines, including the short-lived but influential *Architecture News* and Charles Lummis's *Land of Sunshine*, helped spread the style to the southwest. In addition, books about historic Spanish and Mexican architecture by Rexford Newcomb, Arthur and Mildred Byne, Sylvester Baxter, and other architects, designers, and writers inspired revivals of the Spanish Mission style. Postcards of famous missions sent across the country by tourists helped disseminate the style, too. The facade of the Alamo Chapel in San Antonio, Texas, with its distinctive *espadaña* (curvilinear gable parapet) inspired countless Mission Revival designs throughout the country.

Builders, architects, and homeowners in Santa Fe and elsewhere in the southwest copied the California Mission features on domestic architecture in varying degrees of faithfulness. Prominent characteristics of the style are white stucco or buff brick walls, round-arched windows, quatrefoil windows, verandas enclosed with round arches, espadañas, wrought-iron grillwork, and corner towers. Red barrel-tile roofs were also common. As architect Rexford Newcomb explained, "The crowning glories of many a Spanish [Revival] house are its . . . wealth of red tiles with which the roof is covered."[1]

The California Mission style officially became established in New Mexico in the late 1890s, when the Atchison, Topeka and Santa Fe Railroad (A.T. & S.F.) adopted the style for its new depots and hotels. In *Old-New Santa Fe and Round-about*, a promotional brochure that the railroad published in 1912, photographs of Mission-style residences in Santa Fe were featured.[2] The first railroad hotel built in the style was the Castañeda Harvey House at Las Vegas (built 1897–99), designed by California architect Frederick L. Roehrig, followed by the grand Alvarado Hotel in Albuquerque (built 1901–04; demolished 1970), designed by

A.T. & S. F. Santa Fe Railroad Depot, Santa Fe, New Mexico, ca. 1912

Photograph by Jesse Nusbaum, courtesy Palace of the Governors Photo Archives (NMHM/DCA), 066658

Chicago architect Charles F. Wittlesey. The Alvarado, a rough-stuccoed building with towers and round-arched arcades, was a particularly influential example of the Mission Revival style. Several years later the El Ortiz Hotel was built at the depot in Lamy, New Mexico, just south of Santa Fe (built 1910; demolished 1943). Designed by Kansas City architect Louis Curtiss, the eclectic California Mission–style El Ortiz also had a few distinctly New Mexican aspects: flat roofs, projecting vigas, hand-carved zapata capitals, and exposed adobe on the sides.

The A.T. & S.F. built a modest-sized California Mission depot in Santa Fe in 1909. Constructed of brick, with a plaster and pebble-dash finish, it has a red tile roof, round-arched openings, and a curvilinear cornice. Shortly after its completion, the depot was hailed by the *New Mexican* as "a beauty from the architectural standpoint" and "modern and convenient in every respect."[3] It stands today as one of the few remaining unaltered buildings in the railroad yard district of Santa Fe.

As early as 1904, New Mexico leaders and boosters considered the California Mission style appropriate for the state because of its evocation of a Spanish Colonial past. When architect Isaac Hamilton Rapp was commissioned to design the New Mexico Building for the 1904 Louisiana Purchase Centennial Exposition in St. Louis, Missouri, he created a Mission Revival design. Rapp and the New Mexico Commission responsible for the building identified the style romantically and morally with the Spanish friars who introduced European culture to the area in the seventeenth and eighteenth centuries.[4] Therefore, it was considered appropriate for a building that was meant to enhance the reputation of New Mexico and illustrate the territory's culture and history to thousands of fair visitors.

Concurrently, Classical Revival–designed public buildings were erected in Santa Fe. The architect I. H. Rapp was responsible for many of these Italian Renaissance–inspired buildings, including the Territorial Capitol (1900), Executive Mansion (1908), County Courthouse (1910), and First National Bank (1911). Most of Rapp's neoclassical buildings, distinguished by their massive classical columns and porticoes, were later destroyed or drastically remodeled.

In June 1909 the Santa Fe *New Mexican* ran an editorial called "Architectural
Unity," in which the Mission style was encouraged for new edifices. "Some time
ago, the New Mexican expressed the desire, or rather the hope that architects in the
future will seek to plan buildings for Santa Fe in harmony with its unique traditions, history, location, and surroundings. The Moorish or Mission style . . . is
especially adapted to this country, is in harmony with its unique traditions and
location. . . . Santa Fe can not be a city beautiful if its people persist in rearing architectural dissonances out of tune with the genius of the city which has put a stamp
of charm and individuality upon it that attracts hundreds of people annually."[5]

A number of Mission-style public buildings were erected in Santa Fe during
the early 1900s, including the brick Women's Board of Trade Library on Washington (1907; remodeled 1932) and the Elks Club on Lincoln (1911, later demolished).
Designed by I. H. Rapp, and an adaptation of his World's Fair building, the Elks
Club with its arched veranda, barrel-tile roofs, miniature towers, and curvilinear
parapets, received much praise from the press when it was built. The *New Mexican*
exclaimed that it was "one of the most beautiful mission style buildings in the
southwest" and "peculiarly suited to the Ancient City."[6] One of the finer examples of the style that exists in Santa Fe today is the 1912 Scottish Rite Temple on
Paseo de Peralta. Designed by the Los Angeles firm of Hunt and Burns, which
had championed the California Mission style since the 1890s, the temple exhibits
a Moorish variant of the style, modeled after the Alhambra's Gate of Justice in
Granada, Spain.[7]

Despite passionate advocates of the style, such as the architect Rapp and
writer Lummis, the popularity of this revival was short-lived and ultimately failed
to capture the public's favor. It was superseded by a new trend—the "New-Old
Santa Fe" style. In 1912, the year New Mexico finally achieved statehood, the
Santa Fe Chamber of Commerce held a competition for house designs in the new
manner, and Sylvanus Morley warned contestants that "The California Mission
style is not regarded for the purposes of this competition. . . . Nothing can retard

the development of Santa Fe style more than to confuse it with the California Mission Style."[8] Later he wrote that "The Roman arch of California Mission Architecture is fatal to the artistic success" of the Santa Fe style.[9]

In August 1913 a writer for the *New Mexican* further explained: "A great boost has been given for the New-Old Santa Fe style of architecture in the acceptance of this style for the building of a house for a prominent eastern lady. The enthusiasts for this style will be pleased to hear that the southern California Mission style was at first thought of and then the New-Old Santa Fe style proved so alluring that it was substituted for the California Mission."[10] A decade later, Eva Scott Fényes and her daughter Leonora S. M. Curtin considered building a house designed by famed California architect Wallace Neff—a two-story Mediterranean-style home with a barrel-tile roof, many round arches, and wrought-iron details—but changed their minds after deciding it was no longer the appropriate style for Santa Fe. Instead, they designed a house in the New Mexico Territorial manner with a few Spanish-Pueblo touches.

Annoyed that the Mission Revival style persisted in the city, artist Carlos Vierra wrote a booklet defining what he considered to be the true Santa Fe style and said, "There is room here for the simpler type of building from old Spain. There is no room here for the silly hybrid California [architecture] now being discarded by that state."[11]

Despite Vierra's diatribe and the increasing popularity of the New-Old Santa Fe style, the Mission Revival manner continued to be chosen by residents desiring a picturesque southwestern building. Bungalows, apartment complexes, and a few public buildings with California Mission–inspired details were built well into the 1930s. When the Santuario de Guadalupe was renovated in the 1920s after an electrical fire destroyed much of the church, the archbishop decided to rebuild in California Mission Revival. Many of the features of that restoration, including the curvilinear parapets and pitched roof clad in red tile, remain visible in the church today.

TOP
Scottish Rite Temple, Paseo de Peralta, built in 1912

BOTTOM
The Elks Club, Lincoln Avenue, 1912
Photograph by Jesse Nusbaum, courtesy Palace of the Governors Photo Archives (NMHM/DCA), 061366

OPPOSITE
Santuario de Guadalupe, on Guadalupe Street, exhibiting features from the 1920s renovation

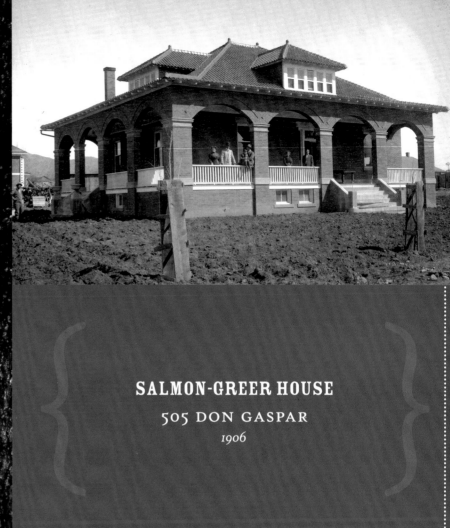

SALMON-GREER HOUSE
505 DON GASPAR
1906

When the A.T. & S.F. Railway Company produced its 1912 promotional brochure, *Old-New Santa Fe and Roundabout*, the Nathan and Petra Salmon House was featured as one of the city's most appealing, modern residences.[12] Considering that the company had adopted the California Mission Revival for its depots and hotels, it is not surprising that it chose to illustrate the Mission-style Salmon residence.

Born in Syria, Nathan Salmon arrived at Ellis Island, New York, in 1888.[13] On a trip to New Orleans in 1891 he met and married Petra Mahboub Elhage, who was also of Syrian descent.[14] On their way to Colorado, the couple was stranded in Santa Fe during a blinding snowstorm and decided to make their home in the ancient city. With a small amount of cash and merchandise, Nathan began his career selling goods out of the back of a wagon. In 1894 he had saved enough to buy a small establishment, and by the early 1900s he had become a successful, prominent businessman, owning a large

LEFT

Salmon-Greer House

ABOVE

Salmon-Greer House, ca. 1909

Courtesy Palace of the Governors Photo Archives (NMHM/DCA), 053118

building on the plaza and operating a retail store. In 1913 he
became a founding member and first president of the Santa
Fe Retail Merchants' Association. After selling his large
department store in 1925, he entered the movie theater business, building first the Paris and later the Lensic cinemas.

Known for their generosity and charitable work,
Nathan, Petra, and their daughter, Salome, were leading
members of Santa Fe society. Their names appeared frequently in the *New Mexican*'s gossip columns. For example, on
June 13, 1913, the paper reported: "Mrs. Nathan Salmon accompanied by her daughter, Salome, will arrive in Lamy this
evening after spending nine weeks touring the eastern states.
Mr. Salmon . . . will go to Lamy in his new car, the 'Pilot'
which arrived in the city a few days ago." When Salome
Salmon married Elias John Greer, vice president of Nathan
Salmon's real estate management firm, the 1919 wedding and
reception were featured on the newspaper's society page.[15]

By 1906 Salmon had purchased a lot at the corner of
Don Gaspar and College Street (now Paseo de Peralta),
where he built a house for $7,000.[16] Naturally, Salmon
needed a home that reflected his hard-earned success.
When purchasing merchandise for his store he traveled to
the fashion centers to study the latest styles and then advertised his business as "The largest and the only up-to-date
store in Santa Fe."[17] No doubt he did the same research
when considering the choice of home design, for he chose
the then-popular Mission Revival style for his mansion.
Nathan was assisted by Petra in all aspects of the house
plans and furnishings, and his home was declared "one of
the most luxurious homes in Santa Fe," notable for its
"many beautiful rugs from the orient."[18]

Originally surrounded by spacious grounds with
extensive flower and vegetable gardens, the two-story mansion was built of red brick on a high sandstone foundation.
Typical of the California Mission Revival style, the house
has a deep, arcaded veranda around two sides and a hipped
roof with closely spaced brackets supporting the broad
eaves. The roof is sheathed in red-tin shingles that simulate
Spanish ceramic tiles. Much lighter, cheaper, and easier to
install, tin roof shingles became available in America just
after 1900.[19] Double-hung windows on the facade are sym-
metrically placed and have minimal framing. The entrance
door is enhanced with rectangular sidelights and a transom.
In the 1920s a garden room with carved beams was added to
the rear of the house, as was a large fireplace with a mantel
supported by brackets.

A photograph of the house probably taken in the early
1920s shows that sometime after it was built the Salmons had
the red brick facade stuccoed and painted white, a finish that
accentuates the Mission Revival arched forms of the design.

The interior of the house was designed with a typically
Victorian layout: a spacious central entrance hall, with the
living room on the right side and the dining room on the left
side. The stairway rises to the eight former bedrooms on the
second floor. Now divided into office space, the interior does
retain some of the original woodwork, including the square,
fluted newel post at the base of the stairs and a handsome
built-in sideboard in the dining room. When a writer toured
the house in 1985, he reported: "Interior detail throughout is
not ornate, but neither does it allude to the rustication of
some Mission Revival models."[20] The house has a full basement, an unusual feature in New Mexican houses of this
period that was apparently built to provide room for a pool
table (Nathan Salmon's favorite pastime was billiards).[21]

One of the unique features of the Salmon home is the
elaborate stucco and wrought-iron wall enclosing the yard.
Built in the 1920s and inspired by a wall Nathan Salmon saw
during a visit to Chapultepec Heights in Mexico City,[22] the
wall is decorated with colorful hand-painted ceramic *azulejos*
(tiles) and iron gates and arabesques with curlicue patterns.
A perfectionist, Salmon had the tiles and ironwork produced
in Mexico and imported to Santa Fe.[23] Originally there were
many more azulejos in the wall than exist today (see above).

OPPOSITE

Detail of inset tile work in the wall enclosing the Salmon-Greer House

ABOVE

Detail of stucco and wrought-iron wall enclosing the Salmon-Greer House

After Petra Salmon died in 1931, Salome, Elias John Greer, and their six children left their mansion and moved in with Nathan Salmon.[24] After Nathan's death in 1941, the Greer family continued to reside there. Later owned by Greer Enterprises and leased to various companies over the years, the building is now owned by a private business. The flat-roofed, two-story addition to the rear of the house was added in recent years for office space. In 1988 the house was renovated extensively, but no structural changes occurred.[25]

In addition to his own home, Salmon made a major contribution to Santa Fe's cityscape when he built the Lensic Theatre in 1931 on West San Francisco Street. Not surprisingly, Salmon and his business partner, son-in-law Elias John Greer, chose the eclectic Spanish Revival style for the facade instead of the Spanish Pueblo Revival manner then popular in Santa Fe. Inspired by the Spanish-style architecture he had seen in Southern California,[26] Salmon chose the famed Boller Brothers firm of Kansas City, who specialized in theater design, to develop plans for the Lensic. The final result is a facade ornamented with terra-cotta tiles of fanciful sea monsters and miniature towers; it carries the Spanish flavor and playfulness of Salmon's own home to the extreme and remains one of the city's most important architectural landmarks.

{ **BRONSON M. CUTTING HOUSE**
908 OLD SANTA FE TRAIL
1911 }

The Santa Fe *New Mexican* reported in September of 1911: "One of the interesting social affairs of the summer will be the 'house warming' tonight at the new residence of Bronson M. Cutting on Buena Vista Heights. The residence, which resembles in design the beautiful Mission style of El Ortiz hotel at Lamy, was recently finished. It contains a fountain in its patio which at night is beautifully illuminated by electric lights."[27]

Originally called "Buena Vista Palace," the Bronson M. Cutting House is one of the few remaining examples of the California Mission Revival style in Santa Fe. Like the Nathan and Petra Salmon house, the Cutting property was featured in the A.T. & S.F. Railway Company's 1912 promotional brochure *Old-New Santa Fe and Roundabout* as a fine example of Santa Fe's appealing, modern residences.[28]

In the summer of 1910, Bronson Murray Cutting (1888–1935), a Harvard University student and member of a wealthy, old New

LEFT

Facade of the Bronson M. Cutting House

ABOVE

Sun Porch, Bronson M. Cutting House, ca. 1930

Courtesy Palace of the Governors
Photo Archives (NMHM/DCA), 047782

Side facade, Bronson M. Cutting House

Living room, Bronson M. Cutting House

York family, traveled to New Mexico seeking a cure for tuberculosis. Not only did he recover, but he remained to become one of the city's major movers and shakers. Cutting's father was a director of the Southern Pacific Railroad and may have secured important contacts for his son in Santa Fe. Bronson served as president of the Chamber of Commerce, was active in the Episcopal Church, owned the Santa Fe *New Mexican* newspaper from 1912 to 1935, and gained national fame as the liberal U.S. senator from New Mexico (1927–35).

Cutting was also active in the city's cultural life. Through his newspaper he supported the art colony that fought vigorously in the 1920s and '30s against threats to Santa Fe's cultural and historical heritage.[29] He was a founding member of the Society for Spanish Colonial Art and a member of the regional committee of the Public Works Art Project. In 1929, when John D. Rockefeller Jr. proposed building an ambitious thirty-eight-building center for anthropological studies in Santa Fe, Cutting was appointed to the jury that chose the final design.[30]

Shortly after arriving in Santa Fe, Cutting and his sister Justine Cutting Ward searched for a home to buy but found none that offered the spaciousness and luxury to which they were accustomed. As a result, Cutting purchased four acres

Door with exposed bolt design, Bronson M. Cutting House

of barren desert land with spectacular views of the mountains and made plans to build a mansion. Situated on Buena Vista Heights (today called Old Santa Fe Trail), two miles south of town, the land was formerly owned by Judge H. Knaebel. The earliest view of Cutting's house shows just how palatial the spread was and also how isolated the property looked in 1911.

Initially desiring "merely an adobe house in Spanish style," Cutting contacted architect Louis Curtiss to design his home.[31] When he and the architect could not reach an agreement over the design, materials, or completion date of the project, Cutting looked elsewhere for a designer.[32] In the end architect Thomas MacLaren (1863–1928), who practiced in Colorado Springs, was hired to design the new residence. Born in Perthsire, Scotland, MacLaren apprenticed with architects in London, studied at the Kensington School of Art and the Royal College of Art, and traveled throughout Europe and Great Britain on sketching tours. Seeking treatment for tuberculosis, he arrived in Colorado Springs in the late 1890s. He remained to establish an architectural practice and over the next two decades received numerous commissions for private residences and public buildings in Colorado.

Bronson and his sister heavily influenced MacLaren's design for their house. The architect was given a drawing that Justine had sketched and was asked to create a Spanish-style house with a placita.[33] A letter by an unknown correspondent states that the final design "was worked out by the owner and based on the façade of a Puerto Rican chapel."[34] As the house on Old Santa Fe Trail indicates, the manner they desired was the California Mission Revival. MacLaren's student sketchbooks illustrate that he already had a strong interest in Spanish missions.[35] One of the more famous Mission-style works he designed was Cragmor Sanatorium, Colorado Springs (1904–14).

Although he was a wealthy man, Cutting was frugal when building his home. He wrote his father, "The cost of our new house, set by Maclaren at 17,000 is rapidly decreasing, as we have got the three local contractors bidding against each other. The lowest bid is at present under $12,000 and it really looks as if we could start in pretty soon."[36] Construction began in October 1910. Anxious that it be completed as soon as possible, Cutting decided against the use of labor-intensive adobe bricks and hard-to-find old timbers.[37] Instead he and MacLaren agreed on a wood-frame structure, heavily plastered on the exterior and interior. The exterior plaster was originally stained a light pink.[38]

Detail of curvilinear parapet, Bronson M. Cutting House

Detail of tile on placita wall,
Bronson M. Cutting House

The house exhibits all the characteristics of the California Spanish Mission Revival style: liberal use of arches around windows and doors, a central courtyard, and a curvilinear gable or espadaña on the principal facade.[39] The same gable appears on the back of the house and is reduced in size on the two sides of the house. The open central courtyard is accessible from all four sides of the house and contains a central octagonal fountain of Moorish influence, and decorative tile panels on the surrounding walls.

For Cutting, who was still recovering from ill health, the plans for his house called for at least three open porches for relaxing and sleeping. Lots of fresh air and sleeping outdoors were considered indispensable for the cure of tuberculosis, and Cutting consulted his doctor on the placement of these all-important porches.[40] Later owners of the house enclosed the sleeping porch in the southeast corner with windows, and the northeast corner porch was converted into a bedroom.[41]

Some of the interior woodwork by local craftsmen has uneven edges or is not symmetrical, suggesting that perhaps the house was a challenge for builders more accustomed to working on adobe structures. Early photographs show that the interior (see page 158) was designed in the Arts and Crafts style, with dark-stained wood trim, many built-ins,

Mission lighting, and heavy dark-wood doors with exposed bolts. The doors and much of the original hardware still exist throughout the house.

The living room was designed with an arched-brick fireplace and arched ceiling that echoes the curves on the exterior windows and doorways. There were also three bedrooms, a spacious kitchen, a butler's pantry, a dining room, a library, and a servant's wing. Among the house's luxuries was a large wine cellar in the basement, which was ironic, considering Cutting's newspaper, the *New Mexican*, advocated prohibition.[42]

The house also had an astounding four bathrooms. In fact, it was big news when a huge metal tank and long sections of black pipe were hauled to the area so that water could be supplied to the Cutting mansion.[43]

Unable to secure everything he needed for the interior in Santa Fe, Cutting asked his parents to forward fixtures and other necessities from New York.[44] He and his sister requested an astonishing eight crates of furniture valued at about $17,000 be sent to furnish the house. Some of those pieces were made by Stickley or other master craftsmen of the American Arts and Crafts movement. After finally moving in, in August 1911, Cutting renamed his mansion *Los Siete Burrows* (the seven burros).

CASA DE ESTRELLAS

300 EAST MARCY STREET

1930s

In the 1930s a Spanish Mission Revival–style complex was built at the corner of East Marcy and Paseo de Peralta. As the *New Mexican* reported, at that time apartments were being constructed in Santa Fe "chiefly to meet the demands of seasonal visitors and persons whose work makes a permanent residence impracticable."[45]

Casa de Estrellas, as it is called today, is a group of bungalows and two-story apartments reminiscent of the Spanish Revival bungalow courtyard and garden apartments that were so popular in Los Angeles, Santa Barbara, and elsewhere in California. Like its West Coast counterparts, Casa de Estrellas once offered its renters economical and pleasant urban housing. *New Mexico Magazine* published a home plan book in 1940 and included plans for a "southwestern ranch home built of skintled brick, whitewashed, with Spanish tile roof" that is remarkably similar to the style of Casa de Estrellas.[46]

LEFT
Spanish Revival–style bungalow,
Casa de Estrellas

ABOVE
Postcard of "Garden Bungalows,
Santa Barbara, California," ca. 1920s
Collection of the author

Front facade of Casa de Estrellas complex

Tile mural detail, Casa de Estrellas

*Stairway with Mexican tiles,
Casa de Estrellas*

The modest-sized buildings of Casa de Estrellas have the hallmarks of the California-inspired revival design: white stucco on the exterior, wrought-iron ornaments, terra-cotta-tile attic vents, and red, barrel-tiled roofs. It is interesting to note that in an effort to save costs, the builder used clay barrel tiles on the roof surfaces facing the street, while the rear portions facing the courtyard were covered with cheaper asphalt shingles.

Glazed-tile accents are also typical of the revival. The stair risers leading to second-floor apartments are decorated with colorful hand-painted Mexican tiles that complement the plain clay-tile treads. More elaborate hand-painted tile murals depicting birds and flowers grace the entrance to each bungalow. As architect Rexford Newcomb noted, by the late 1920s the "fascinating tiles of old Spain" and Mexico were being imported to the U.S. and in some instances replicated by American manufacturers.[47]

The Casa de Estrellas buildings have distinctly New Mexico features as well, including hand-carved wood lintels over windows and doorways, hand-carved doors, and on the interior, exposed wood ceiling beams. The walls were constructed of pentile block made by inmates at the New Mexico state penitentiary. During its recent, eco-friendly renovation, many of the interior walls were refinished using mud and hay from a local farm, and exterior wood details were carved with additional detail.[48]

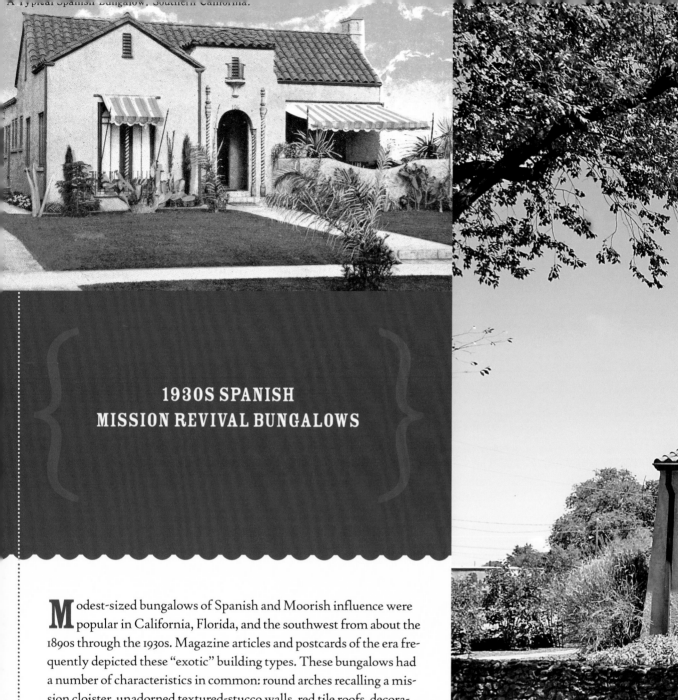

{ 1930S SPANISH MISSION REVIVAL BUNGALOWS }

Modest-sized bungalows of Spanish and Moorish influence were popular in California, Florida, and the southwest from about the 1890s through the 1930s. Magazine articles and postcards of the era frequently depicted these "exotic" building types. These bungalows had a number of characteristics in common: round arches recalling a mission cloister, unadorned textured-stucco walls, red tile roofs, decorative accents of tile or brick around door and window openings, and plain but functional interiors with cozy fireplaces.

A favorite among speculative builders, bungalows of this style were built in the South Capitol District of Santa Fe. The *New Mexican* reported in August 1916 that the Mutual Building and Loan Association had received an application for the "erection of three California bungalows on the south side."[49] The bungalows' small size, attractive style, and low cost appealed to the historically middle-class area.

Three fine examples of California Mission Revival–style bungalows can be seen on Sena Street. The house at 316, built by 1934

ABOVE

Postcard of "A Typical Spanish Bungalow, Southern California," ca. 1916

Collection of the author

RIGHT

333 Sena Street, 1930s

ABOVE

Detail of arched window and tile work, 316 Sena Street

RIGHT

A Spanish Mission Revival house at 843 Don Cubero

• •

and first owned by Gus and Sarah Mitchell, has such note-worthy features as the arched window framed by hand-painted tile. Number 333 Sena is notable for its Spanish arcade of graceful arches and red barrel-tiled shed roofs over the porch and window. Among the earliest owners of this bungalow were José and Mae Martinez.

The tiny bungalow at 329 Sena (see page 132) is an eclectic mix of Spanish-inspired designs: the flat roof and row of "beam ends" marching across the facade are reminis-cent of a New Mexico Spanish Pueblo Revival house. The slightly curving parapet, arched doorway with decorative brickwork, red barrel-tiled shed roof over the window, and white painted stucco exterior are typical of a California Spanish Mission Revival bungalow. The protruding chim-ney wall has a simple decorative brick-and-tile design. Like many houses of this period, its walls were constructed of hollow tile.[50]

In 1926 the *New Mexican* reported that California-style bungalows were "coming more and more into disfavor."[51] However, as the house at 843 Don Cubero Street indicates, bungalows inspired by West Coast fashion continued to be constructed in Santa Fe well into the 1930s.

CHAPTER 6 **BUNGALOW FEVER**

Residences and Retreats for Health Seekers

TOP

A Postcard of "One of California's Cozy Little Bungalows," ca. 1915

Collection of the author

BOTTOM

Marcy Street bungalow, ca. 1910

Courtesy Palace of the Governors Photo Archives (NMHM/DCA), 010520

OPPOSITE

Front facade of Dudrow House, Agua Fria Street

WHEN DISCUSSING WHAT STYLE of architecture best suited early-twentieth-century Santa Fe, archaeologist and City Planning Board member Sylvanus Griswold Morley stated that residents should definitely not consider the "pretty little suburban bungalows, which dot our landscape like the measles."[1] Although he found the diminutive brick houses with their overhanging eaves "charming," Morley said this building type was "as much in place in Santa Fe, as a flea on the back of a well-groomed dog." Other residents, like writer Ruth Laughlin, agreed with Morley, believing wholeheartedly that "native construction" was much "more attractive than the new-fangled red brick bungalows."[2]

Despite their warnings, however, the bungalow epidemic—or "bungle-o fever" as artist Carlos Vierra called it—that swept across America had broken out in Santa Fe by the early 1900s and soon dominated the housing market.[3] Like the Spanish Mission Revival style, this trend hailed from California. The bungalow's appeal was its simplicity, affordability, modest size, and use of natural materials. In the beginning, progressive Santa Fe citizens both Anglo and Hispano embraced the new fad, which they saw as a sign of progress that would transform the city into a distinctly modern "American" community.[4] Small brick and stucco cottages and Craftsman- and Mission-style bungalows, with all the latest modern conveniences, were built in great numbers throughout the city. As the *New Mexican* reported in 1903, "Every carpenter, bricklayer, plumber and contractor in Santa Fe is kept busy these days and can work overtime if he wants to. Santa Fe isn't standing still."[5]

During this era Santa Fe was striving to firmly establish itself as a tourist destination. An 1895 promotional book about New Mexico proclaimed, "As a health resort Santa Fe is unrivalled."[6] Americans suffering from tuberculosis and other lung ailments migrated to the city seeking relief. The city's altitude of seven thousand feet offered the pure, dry mountain air and sunny days thought essential to the cure. By the early 1900s there were many sanitariums in Santa Fe, including Sunmount, Dr. Diaz' Sanitarium, and Nora Summers' Home for Health-seekers.

Bungalows, with their sleeping porches, banks of windows, and emphasis on healthful qualities (like good ventilation), were ideally suited to the health seekers flocking to Santa Fe. Doctors prescribed a regimen that included getting maximum exposure to sun by day, and by night sleeping outdoors in the dry, healing climate. "Dr. Mera at Sunmount, and several local physicians have used sunlight in the treatment of disease and it is reported with marked success," explained the *New Mexican*.[7]

157

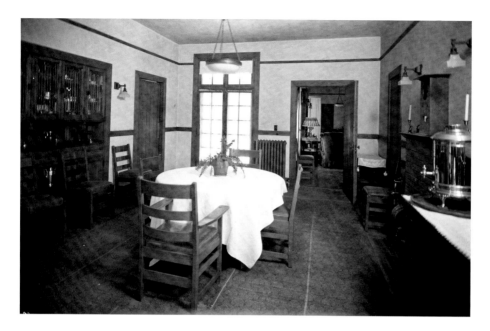

Dining Room, Bronson L. Cutting House, ca. 1930

Photograph by T. Harmon Parkhurst, courtesy Palace of the Governors Photo Archives (NMHM/DCA), 054295

At one point the Santa Fe Chamber of Commerce discussed the possibility of financing the building of bungalows for health-conscious visitors.[8] The *New Mexican* constantly reported on the need for such cottages. In 1900 a journalist explained, "The average healthseeker is a person of some means. He probably never has seen an adobe house before. . . . He wouldn't think of moving into what looks to him like a burrow of frozen mud with a few small windows and doors. As he is generally willing to pay . . . there should be more dwelling houses built in cottage style with modern improvements, large windows and plenty of ground around them. . . . [I]t costs comparatively but a trifle more to build a house that has an artistic exterior and is modern in its interior, than it does to put up an ugly looking dwelling."[9]

A few years later, the paper reported, "Cottages with modern improvements, electric lights and water are greatly in demand. There is not an empty house fit for residence in the city. Dozens of cottages, containing from four to five rooms, with modern improvements, could be rented at a good rate. There are many healthseekers and tourists here who desire to spend a few months in the city who would rent cottages were they to be had."[10]

The *New Mexican* also ran articles on subjects they thought would attract visitors to the area, such as the discovery of gold, copper, and zinc in the Sangre de Cristo mountain range. "A veritable treasure-house of mineral wealth is at the very door of this city," exclaimed the newspaper.[11] Archaeological discoveries made at nearby ancient American Indian ruins were also discussed at length. "Professor [Jesse] Nusbaum is certain the knowledge of the discoveries made [at Frijoles canyon] will ultimately bring thousands of tourists and many scientists to Santa Fe from which the cliff dwellings are so easily accessible," it was reported in 1908.[12] Indians living in the nearby pueblos came to Santa Fe frequently to sell their pottery and other crafts. "Their presence is exciting the interest of sightseers and visitors in Santa Fe," exclaimed one reporter.[13]

Interior, Sylvanus G. Morley House, ca. 1912

Courtesy Palace of the Governors Photo
Archives (NMHM/DCA), 061504

While the city continued to advertise its unique historic qualities, it also sought more modern features such as wider, standard roadways for the new-fangled automobiles. "Now is the time to widen and straighten some of Santa Fe's crooked and narrow streets," a writer suggested. "Enough of these will remain to preserve quaintness sufficient to delight the tourist, but the main residential streets should have the kinks taken out of them. While some . . . are wide enough for two burros to pass, this is the day of automobiles which require a little more elbow room."[14]

IN THE LATE NINETEENTH CENTURY there was a backlash against the ornamental excess of Victorian architecture in America and a renewed interest in nature and handcraftsmanship that was inspired by the Arts and Crafts movement in England. Simpler floor plans and natural materials such as stained wood and rough stone replaced the impractical floor plans and the painted, applied ornamental millwork of the Victorian era. At the forefront of this change was the Craftsman bungalow, a mode inspired by Gustav Stickley's *Craftsman Magazine*. In addition to essays on Arts and Crafts movement–related subjects, he printed architectural sketches of low-cost bungalows, which he called "Craftsman Homes." A disciple of English designer William Morris, whose essays he published in his magazine, Stickley was the leading figure in the American Arts and Crafts movement. He became known for his plain, functional, solid oak furniture with handcrafted joints and a natural finish that enhanced the beauty of the wood.

Arts and Crafts pieces made by Stickley or his competitors, as well as architectural features of the movement, made their way to early-twentieth-century Santa Fe. This fact is illustrated in the photographs of Santa Fe interiors taken by Jesse Nusbaum in the 1910s. Bronson Cutting's California Mission home on

College Avenue and Sylvanus Griswold Morley's Spanish Pueblo Revival home on Washington Street were chock full of Arts and Crafts furniture and interior designs. In his 1915 article in *Old Santa Fe* highlighting the features of Santa Fe–style architecture, Morley wrote that "the tendency in interior furnishings should be toward simplicity," which he felt was best attained by the "Mission" manner.[15] (In this case, the term Mission refers to the Arts and Crafts furniture and designs of Stickley and others.) Some public spaces in Santa Fe, like the reception room at St. Vincent's Sanatorium, designed by I. H. Rapp and built in 1910 on Palace Avenue, also had distinctly Arts and Crafts architectural design elements.[16]

In America the typical "woodsy" bungalow—with its low-pitched, widely overhanging roofs, extensive porches, open plan extending the house outdoors, and natural materials, including shingles, wood, brick, and stone—was largely the invention of Charles S. and Henry M. Greene, architects practicing in California in the 1890s and early 1900s.[17]

The word *bungalow*, however, derives from the Indian word *banglà*, meaning house, and was first used in connection with barracks of the British army in Colonial India. In America it came to mean a single-story house with a low-pitched roof and eventually merged with the tenets of the Arts and Crafts movement to produce the "Craftsman Bungalow." E. W. Stillwells's 1915 pamphlet *Western Bungalows* described the Craftsman traditions of simplicity, economy, and harmony with the outdoors.[18]

In some instances the Santa Fe bungalow was adapted to local building techniques. For instance, the house at 205 Delgado, built in circa 1911–12, has all the hallmarks of a California-style bungalow but was constructed from locally made adobe bricks.[19] When it was remodeled in the 1980s, the house lost its Arts and Crafts–style interior, but much of the original fabric of the exterior was retained. The Japanese pagoda-like facade consists of an impressive overhanging porch roof with exposed rafters and oversized trusses supported by trapezoidal river-rock piers. Little is known about the first owner of the house, but among the earliest to reside there was Clinton J. Crandall, superintendent of the Santa Fe Indian School and agent for the Northern Pueblos.

In the early twentieth century homeownership became available to more
Americans than ever before, and the modest-sized bungalow was very affordable.
O. C. Watson & Co. advertised an eight-room bungalow rental in Santa Fe, completely furnished, for sixty dollars a month.[20] These homes were largely purchased
by members of Santa Fe's growing professional middle class. Some railway employ-
ees, for instance, lived in the small brick bungalows built within walking distance of
the railroad terminus for the spur line and the Denver & Rio Grande line.

Brick bungalows in downtown Santa Fe

A large concentration of bungalows exhibiting a variety of stylistic influ-
ences, including Mission Revival, California, Territorial, and Spanish Pueblo
Revival, can be found in the South Capital District of Santa Fe, as well as on East
Marcy, on San Antonio Street, and tucked into neighborhoods elsewhere in the
city. Quite a few, for instance, were built on Agua Fria Street. An example of an
early-1900s frame-construction bungalow, with low-peaked gable roof and a front
porch supported by masonry columns with river-rock bases, can be seen at 548
Agua Fria (see page 156) . It was built by Charles William Dudrow, who owned a
lumber and builder-supply business that sold window sashes, doors, blinds, and
other products on what is now Dudrow Street.[21] Advertisements in the *New Mexican* indicate that he built several "modern" brick bungalows on Agua Fria.[22]

Built from plans offered in magazines and catalogs and then adapted by individual builders, bungalows in Santa Fe employed the compact floor plan, built-in
furniture, and lighting fixtures typical of the style. By using natural materials, such
as wood and stone, and including generous-sized windows and multiple porches,
the builders of these bungalows were following the tenets of the American Arts
and Crafts movement, which advocated linking outdoor and indoor living spaces.

Mail-order bungalows were purchased by some Santa Feans, though generally this practice was discouraged by city leaders. In June 1934, when the Chamber
of Commerce sponsored a "Buy-It-in-Santa Fe Week" to encourage citizens to
spend their paychecks at businesses in the city, chamber president Henry Dendahl
told his constituents they were "under a civic obligation" to buy locally and must
not buy "a mail order house" from the "here-today-gone-tomorrow peddler."[23]

Some businesses catered to bungalow owners: the Beacham-Mignardot
Company in the Catron Building advertised "superb paint" for making a bunga-

low "cheerful," and Zook's Pharmacy sold "Mrs. Stover's Bungalow Candies."[24] In 1913 W. Lindhardt operated a store on Palace Avenue that sold Arts and Crafts–style hand-hammered brass or copper lamps, desk sets, trays, and other items.[25]

In spite of the proliferation of bungalows, the style was not accepted by everyone. A Denver resident wrote to the *New Mexican* newspaper in 1909 that he "deplored the passing away of the picturesque adobe [in Santa Fe] and the pushing into prominence of brick construction of exotic origin."[26] Artist Carlos Vierra complained in his journal in 1917 that eastern styles—especially the bungalow— were unsuited to Santa Fe because the town had an architectural heritage of its own based on Pueblo and Spanish Colonial adobe buildings. And when the new Spanish Pueblo Revival–style New Mexico Museum of Art was nearing completion in 1917, renowned artist Robert Henri wrote to a fellow artist: "The new museum is a wonder. . . . It looks as though it were a precious child of the Santa Fe sky and the Santa Fe mountains. . . . My hope is that it will shame away the bungalow with which a few mistaken tastes have tried to make Los Angeles of Santa Fe. . . . Santa Fe may do the rare thing and become *Itself*."[27]

It seems, however, that the bungalow style hung around for quite a while longer. When the Santa Fe Chamber of Commerce and its members put a full-page advertisement in a 1920 issue of the *New Mexican* encouraging residents to participate in a "clean-up and paint-up campaign" to improve the appearance of their neighborhoods, it featured a photograph of a bungalow-style house with overhanging eaves, dormer windows, a bay window, and an expansive porch.[28] Beside the photo is a floor plan and description of the design, which came from *American Homes*, a book of 120 house plans. The ad explains that the purpose of the campaign is "to help you Acquire a Home, to better our citizenship, and elevate our city's attractiveness by building more and better homes."

Just six years later, advocates of the new-old Santa Fe style (based on regional vernacular architecture) appeared to be fed up with the presence of the bungalow in the city. At a meeting held to discuss the possibilities of a "community type" of architecture, Sylvanus Morley complained once again that the little brick bungalows were "bungalowing all over the place, clashing with the mellow brown of the soil."[29]

Although today the movement to preserve this building type in America is growing, Santa Fe has lost many of its bungalows in recent decades due to development. One of them—a little red-brick bungalow with four slender white pillars built by well-known Santa Fe contractor August Reingardt[30] at 207 Lincoln Avenue—played an important role in the historic preservation movement in Santa Fe. Sold in 1910 to Annastacia "Anna" Mugler, one of the first successful milliners and businesswomen in Santa Fe, the bungalow was then purchased in 1955 by architect John Conron, who gutted the interior and remodeled the exterior in a wood and glass "ultramodern" style. His actions so shocked the city's historic preservationists that they sought passage of a historic-styles ordinance to avoid such travesties in the future. In 1986 the bungalow was finally demolished and the lot was paved for a law firm's parking lot. More recently, New Mexico state officials demolished a bungalow on Manhattan Avenue to make room for the new court house.[31]

405 PASEO DE PERALTA BUNGALOW

1902

When book publisher Jack Woody purchased the Craftsman bungalow at 405 Paseo de Peralta in 1992, it was in poor condition and had been painted entirely white, both inside and out. Using an old photograph of the exterior as a guide, he spent two years restoring the historic features. In May 1994 he received one of the first "Heritage Preservation Awards" from Santa Fe's Archaeological Review Board and Historic Design Review Board for his successful remodeling efforts.[32]

Built in 1902 by Eugene Frank Wittman at what was originally 173 North Federal Place,[33] this one-and-a-half-story house displays all the characteristics of the Craftsman style: a shingle-covered pitched roof with exposed rafters under the eaves; multi-light wood windows; dormer windows with sharply peaked gables; and a square-columned porch with adjacent enclosed sun porch. Little is known about the history of the house, though we know that one of its earliest owners was Howard L. Bickley, Justice of the New Mexico Supreme Court.[34]

Among the more unusual features of the house are the concrete block columns out front. The lower level of the house is also

ABOVE

405 Paseo de Peralta bungalow

RIGHT

Dining room, 405 Paseo de Peralta

ABOVE

Detail of pergola, 405 Paseo de Peralta

RIGHT

Doors, 405 Paseo de Peralta

OPPOSITE

Living room fireplace detail, 405 Paseo de Peralta

constructed of concrete block, and the upper level is wood frame covered in shingles. Rarely used for houses in Santa Fe, shingle sheathing often appeared on bungalows in American seaside locations. The Oriental influence typical of the Craftsman style can be seen in the slightly upswept gable ends and peaks, as well as in the pergola-style porch.

The compact floor plan places the living room, the dining room, the sun porch, one bedroom, a bathroom, and the kitchen on the first floor, and two small additional bedrooms upstairs. The front doors are solid oak with squared-off corbels under a shelflike projection, below nine-light windows. It is one of the more popular door designs used in early-twentieth-century bungalows and was likely mass produced.[35] The door design echoes the Arts and Crafts–style interior of the bungalow.

Often Craftsman interiors, with wainscoting, built-in cabinetry, and trim stained dark brown, are rather gloomy and dark, but 405 Paseo de Peralta is flooded with light. The walls in the living room and dining room have high wainscoting and plate rails supported by small, squared corbels. The hardwood floors have recently been refinished and were likely stained darker originally. The ceilings in both rooms have dark-stained wood box beams, a favorite treatment of the Craftsman style. The focal point of the living room is the fireplace with terra-cotta matte-glazed tiles, framed by a riveted, hand-hammered iron surround. Centered above the fireplace is a wood mantel.

The dining room is entered through a wide-framed doorway directly opposite the fireplace. French doors lead from the dining room to a small, enclosed sun porch or sleeping porch. Attached to the fireplace in the dining room is the original built-in china cabinet and side-board/cabinet combo. Mirrored panels in the china cabinet doors reflect light.

HARRY AND FLORENCE DORMAN HOUSE

707 OLD SANTA FE TRAIL

1910–11

The Harry and Florence Dorman House is one of the best-preserved examples of the Craftsman manner in northern New Mexico. Since it was built in 1910 on College Street (now Old Santa Fe Trail), the house stands out as an anomaly amid a sea of adobe and stucco homes in the neighborhood.

A native New Yorker and the son of a textile manufacturer, Harry Dorman first came to Santa Fe in 1901 hoping the climate would restore his health. After recovering fully, he married Florence Luckenback in 1908 and settled in Santa Fe, where he became a successful insurance and real-estate businessman. He also was active politically, becoming a member of the New Mexico Progressive Party.[36]

In addition to his own home, Dorman built Craftsman-style bungalows and other types of cottages for the local market. His designs were admired by newcomers to the city. Bronson Cutting, a wealthy friend of Dorman's who was looking for property to buy,

LEFT

View from Camino de Las Animas of Harry and Florence Dorman House

ABOVE

Front facade of the Craftsman-style Harry and Florence Dorman House

remarked in a letter: "This morning we discovered the most attractive pair of houses we have yet seen. They belong to Mr. Dorman, who is out for his health and amuses himself by building houses for rent and sale. One of them is finished. . . . It is a charming adobe house, the only one in Santa Fe that shows any vestige of taste."[37]

A writer for the Albuquerque *Morning Journal* also observed Dorman's talent for building: "He has the eye of an architect, the hand of a master builder and the soul of an artist. He has sprinkled South Santa Fe with new houses, but their style of architecture is not an eyesore to the lover of the Spanish style so befitting of Santa Fe."[38]

Dorman was an early promoter of the "Santa Fe style"—the Spanish-Pueblo Revival manner—and a historic preservationist. Through his efforts with the Civic Center and City Planning Board, and then later with the Chamber of Commerce and Old Santa Fe Association, he promoted Santa Fe as the "Ancient City" and sought to preserve its early adobe architecture. Ironically, Dorman's own home departed markedly from his preaching on the merits of the Santa Fe style. His home was deeply rooted in the Craftsman bungalow tradition.

Florence and Harry Dorman bought the property at 707 College Street in 1910 from the Ortega family. The house has had various incarnations over the decades—as a personal home, an annex for the Unitarian Church, a B&B, and a rental house—and many of these residents made various changes. The most recent owners, artists Francis and Ralph Sanders, have gradually and meticulously restored much of the original charm and Craftsman features to the home. By comparing the photographs taken of the house in 1912 by Jesse Nusbaum, a personal friend of the Dormans, with the present-day structure, one can see how close the house remains to the original design.

The one-and-a-half-story house has a front gable and gabled dormers on each of the side roofs. The sixteen-inch-thick walls of the basement and exposed foundation are ashlar-coursed limestone. The walls are double brick with interior plaster, and the exterior is masonry and decorative half-timbering. Mainly associated with the English Tudor style, half-timbering was originally a process in which the heavy timber structure would be infilled with wattle and daub—thin branches or wood laths combined with mud or clay plastering to form walls.

As one observer wrote in 1912, Dorman "is a believer in putting 'a dash' of pebble in his architecture."[39] Indeed, the masonry on his College Street home was originally pebble dash (made by pressing a thick coat of pebbles into wet stucco). Sometime in the 1950s this finish was covered by a coat of gunite—a mixture of lime-rich cement and sand that is applied through a pressure hose.[40]

The overhanging pitched roof was originally sawn redwood shingles, replaced in the 1950s with asphalt shingles.[41] The exterior is unified by continuous barge boards and panels, which seem to bear the influence of Greene and Greene in their Japanese geometry and proportion. The pergola-style porch is also Oriental in feeling.

The rugged Craftsman aesthetic, which gained prominence in America during the years 1890 to 1910, was firmly rooted in the English Arts and Crafts movement. Like their English counterparts, American builders and architects such as Dorman promoted fine craftsmanship and the forthright use of natural building materials. The handcrafted look of stucco or pebble dash, rustic stone porch supports and fireplaces can be found in his home.

The front rooms on the ground floor have open-beamed ceilings, generous-sized windows with their original panes of glass, and a high wainscot created by vertical battens capped by a plate rail.[42] Battens were often used in modest Craftsman homes as a less-expensive alternative to wood paneling. The living room has a distinctive round-arched, Richardsonian-style brick fireplace (so called after the American architect Henry Hobson Richardson), and the door leading from the living room to the hallway where the bedrooms are located is one of the finest features of the house. The dining room has a built-in china cabinet, typical of the Arts and Crafts style.

....

OPPOSITE, TOP
Living room of the Harry and Florence Dorman House

OPPOSITE, BOTTOM LEFT
Craftsman-style door in the living room of the Harry and Florence Dorman House

OPPOSITE, BOTTOM RIGHT
Dining room with built-in cabinet, plate rail, and battens, Harry and Florence Dorman House

{ SOUTH CAPITOL BUNGALOWS }

After the new sewer system was installed and the road was paved in 1913, Don Gaspar was heavily developed with new homes. The Santa Fe *New Mexican* reported in June of that year, "The boom on the south side still continues, and property values are jumping by leaps and bounds. Don Gaspar avenue cottages cannot be had for love or money."[43] The same writer also stated that "every one of the California bungalows" in the capitol district had already been rented.

At 524 Don Gaspar is a classic one-story California bungalow with a pitched roof, exposed rafters and brackets, an expansive front porch supported by heavy columns, and a low dormer window.

Number 918 Don Gaspar is the Leslie and Pearl Gillett House, built in 1913 and typical of the California bungalow style. Constructed of red brick, the house has a dramatic cross-gable roof with prominent overhanging eaves, nine-light and six-light casement windows, and exposed rafters and braces. The brick is exposed in

LEFT

217 East Santa Fe, built in mid-1920s

ABOVE

Roof detail, Leslie and Pearl Gillett House

the lower part, and shingles sheathe the gables. Although the original veranda with paired wood posts still exists on the east and south sides, a later owner enclosed it with glass.

This property's history can be traced to September 1913, when Michael A. Stanton purchased four lots on Don Gaspar from the Santa Fe Realty Company.[44] In November of that year he sold the property and a house on the land to Margaret E. and Willis Ward of Portsmouth, Ohio, and in April 1914 Margaret sold it to Leslie A. Gillett, a secretary for the Scottish Rite Bodies, and his wife, Pearl. The Gillett family owned the house until 1969.

Many California-style, modest-sized bungalows were built along East Santa Fe Avenue between 1912 and 1928 for the city's growing middle class. City directories for 1928 and 1930 show that a writer for the *New Mexican*, a stenographer, a house painter, a gas station attendant, a grocery store cashier, and a salesman at Moore's clothing store were all residents of this street. Early directories also indicate that many bungalows in the neighborhood were rented and the turnover was frequent.

A builder named Reingardt erected at least two bungalows on Santa Fe Avenue in the summer of 1919, which he sold for around $6,000 each. They were thirty by sixty feet and contained six rooms plus one bathroom, a sleeping porch, and a basement. The *New Mexican* described the houses as "unique" and said they were constructed of "wood, covered or veneered with hollow tile then cemented over."[45] The newspaper also claimed they were the first ever built of these materials and were "cooler in summer and more substantial than either an adobe or an all-tile house."

Number 217 East Santa Fe is one of three modest-sized California-style bungalows in a row that were erected by the same builder, possibly Reingardt, in the mid-1920s. Except for the recently added metal roof, the house retains most of its original features. Typical of the style, it has a street-facing gable, with overhanging eaves, exposed rafters and braces, and a porch with trapezoidal stone piers capped by wood columns. In 1928 Louis C. Mackel, an inspector for the U.S. Geological Survey, and his wife, Eliza, lived at 217 Santa Fe, and by 1930 the house had a new tenant, Isadore Armijo, a clerk for the state highway department, and his wife, Jennie.

OPPOSITE TOP
524 Don Gaspar

OPPOSITE BOTTOM
Leslie and Pearl Gillett House, 1913

MARCY STREET BUNGALOWS

In the early 1910s the north side of Marcy Street was developed with a series of modest, affordable, red-brick, pitched-roof bungalows. Among them is the house at 213, originally owned by Charles McKay, a linotype operator, and his wife, Irene, and then owned by the Berchtold family for eighty-five years. Today it houses the Aaron Payne Fine Art gallery.

In 1912, when Henry Berchtold was diagnosed with tuberculosis, he and his wife, Elizabeth, and their six young children traveled from Siegel, Illinois, to Santa Fe. The family settled into St. Vincent's Sanatorium's new building on Palace Avenue, and two years later Elizabeth purchased the bungalow at 213 East Marcy.[46] Remarkably, the house remained unaltered and in family hands until the death of Clara Berchtold Mabry in December 1999 at the age of 101. Since then the single-story red-brick dwelling has been renovated but retains much of its original character.[47]

Set back from the street on a long, narrow city lot, the Berchtold house is one story with a basement, a raised stone foundation,

LEFT

Elizabeth and Henry Berchtold House, 213 East Marcy Street, built ca. 1911

ABOVE

229 East Marcy Street brick bungalow

and a low, green-shingled roof with overhanging eaves. A raised, open porch spans the facade and is supported by four Tuscan columns. The windows are double-hung and have brick segmental arched lintels. The triple window on the front has decorative glazing in the upper portions consisting of narrow panes and diamonds, a style known in the trade catalogs of the era as "Queen Anne."[48] Similar glazing was installed in the transom over the front door, in the dormer windows, and in an entry-hall window near the south corner of the east facade.

The house originally had an open porch on the rear that was likely used as a sleeping porch by Henry Berchtold during his convalescence. Unfortunately, Santa Fe's fresh air and other healing attributes did not cure Berchtold of his illness, and he died in 1919.

The compact, open floor plan and interior decorative details have altered very little. The house retains the original hardwood floors, flat plastered ceilings, and dark wood trim characteristic of a bungalow, including paneled doors, door and window frames, and picture and plate rails in the main rooms. A pedestal and colonnade divide the living and dining rooms, and the living room has an exposed brick fireplace with a plain wood mantel.

Up the street at 229 East Marcy is another charming brick bungalow, with wood brackets and Arts and Crafts–style door and piers. The date of construction is unknown, but by 1926 Alfred C. and Janet F. Wiley, owners of the Cash and Carry Store (on Don Gaspar Avenue), were living in the home.[49] The Wiley family remained the owners through the mid-1980s.

OPPOSITE
Door detail, 229 East Marcy Street

SUNMOUNT SANATORIUM
HEALTH SEEKERS INFLUENCE ARCHITECTURAL STYLE IN SANTA FE

*by Audra Bellmore, Curator, the John Gaw Meem Archives of Southwestern Architecture,
and Assistant Professor, Center for Southwest Research*

RIGHT *Postcard of Sunmount
Sanatorium, Santa Fe,
New Mexico, ca. 1927*
Collection of the author

FAR RIGHT *Interior of bungalow at
Sunmount Sanatorium, ca. 1912*
Photograph by Jesse Nusbaum, courtesy
Palace of the Governors Photo Archives
(NMHM/DCA), 061398

In the late nineteenth and early twentieth centuries, tuberculosis swept across the country, particularly affecting urban areas where the respiratory form of the virus passed easily from person to person. As a result, thousands of residential clinics, or sanatoriums, developed. In New Mexico, an area with no significant industry but an abundance of fresh air and sunshine, sanatoriums became a big business. TB clinics sprang up across the state. One in particular, Sunmount Sanatorium, located on the outskirts of downtown Santa Fe (near Sun Mountain), helped nurture an arts community that exerted a significant influence on the local built environment.

Sunmount Sanatorium, developed in 1903 by Dr. Frank Mera, first began as Sunmount Tent City, advertised as a destination for both consumptives and tourists. Popular with wealthy Eastern patients who came west to "take the cure," Sunmount grew into a more permanent community with the construction of a main hospital and a surrounding development of stand-alone residential cottages. One of the first converts to the regional architecture, Dr. Mera contracted the local architectural firm of Rapp and Rapp to design his clinic in the Spanish Pueblo Revival manner.

Sunmount's new 1914 clinic possessed all the traditional characteristics of the style, including adobe walls, a smooth, earth-toned finish, vigas, open portals, and courtyards. The grounds were decorated with New England–style perennial gardens. Eastern patients were enticed by the charming imagery, both exotic and familiar.

Patients often took up residence for months, and in some cases years. Staff members tried to create a homelike atmosphere, with an emphasis on regional overtones. Interior spaces at Sunmount featured large Navajo textiles, casually strewn as floor coverings, and Pueblo pottery perched on shelves—decorative objects that capitalized on the popularity of Indian arts and culture. As intended, the picturesque environment at Sunmount delighted and inspired its guests.

Dr. Mera encouraged his patients to engage in social, cultural, and artistic endeavors as a form of therapy. One early patient arriving from Chicago in 1916, writer and editor of *Poetry* magazine Alice Corbin Henderson, organized weekly "Salons," or gatherings for artistic discussion, onsite and open to like-minded Sunmount residents, their family members, and the local Santa Fe artistic set. In the

1920s the Sunmount Salons became a popular platform for views on art, architecture, and socialism, similar to the Arts and Crafts communities on the East and West coasts. The Salons represented the beginning of an organized local art community, which flourishes today.

A common interest shared among Salon participants was a fascination with the local culture and its preservation, including Spanish Pueblo architecture. Alice Corbin Henderson and her husband, artist and architect William Penhallow Henderson, settled in Santa Fe after Alice's stay at Sunmount. They became powerful members of the local community. Interested in promoting and developing the regional style, William designed a number of private residences in Santa Fe and a popular local landmark, the Navajo House of Religion, now the Wheelwright Museum of the American Indian (1937), in the style of a Navajo hogan.

Carlos Vierra, another TB patient and Salon participant, was also instrumental in revitalizing the Spanish Pueblo style. Vierra's paintings and photographs of the local landscape and indigenous architecture can be credited as among the main inspirations in the rebirth of the style. Vierra was a purist, intent upon preserving and re-creating the original architecture of the area. Vierra's own home, designed in 1918, became a model and stimulus for other houses in the area.

However, it was John Gaw Meem, the highly noted New Mexican architect and historic preservationist practicing out of his Santa Fe office from 1924 to 1960, whose work inspired a new wave of Spanish Pueblo design. After contracting tuberculosis, Meem was advised to move from New York City to a dry, western climate to recuperate. Attracted by an advertisement for the Santa Fe Railroad, Meem headed for New Mexico, where he developed an interest in the local indigenous architecture and the early

examples of its revival while recovering at Sunmount Sanatorium. Meem opened his first architectural office on the grounds of Sunmount in 1924.

Unlike the early Spanish Pueblo Revival buildings, with their quality of archaeological reproduction, Meem's designs blended the forms of the traditional Spanish Pueblo buildings with all the requirements of modern living. Meem came from an engineering background and was interested in the application of the latest technologies and modern building methods, while remaining sympathetic to the look, feel, and craftsmanship of the indigenous architecture. It was a happy marriage, resulting in some of the finest examples of the Spanish Pueblo Revival in New Mexico, including a number of homes designed for other Sunmount patients, such as the Cyrus McCormick Estate (1931) and the Mary Vilura Conkey Residence (1928).

Famous aviatrix Katherine Stinson, a friend and fellow Sunmount alum of John Gaw Meem, also became intrigued with the local style. After her sojourn at Sunmount, she stayed on in Santa Fe and married Miguel Otero, the son of the former New Mexico governor. In addition to establishing her own aeronautics company, Stinson Aviation, Stinson Otero became an amateur architect designing homes in the Spanish Pueblo Revival style for herself (the Otero Estate, 1928) and for acquaintances in the area (the Catherine Gay House, 1929).

Spanish Pueblo Revival architecture in Santa Fe may trace some of its roots to the arts community formed by patients who traveled to Sunmount Sanatorium. Indeed, many participants in the Sunmount Salons settled in Santa Fe and formed the stimulus for a unique residential and public design, reflecting the traditional cultures of the Southwest.

CHAPTER 7

"NEW-OLD SANTA FE STYLE"

Spanish Pueblo and Territorial Revivals, 1910s–1940

I N 1912 SANTA FE OFFICIALS, businessmen, and businesswomen devised a plan to revive the city's sagging economy through the development of tourism. Easterners already viewed the southwest as a healthful, restorative place to visit, and were attracted by the railway companies' advertisements of tours to American Indian cliff dwellings and Pueblo dances. By capitalizing on the region's moderate climate, breathtaking scenery, and unique history, the city leaders hoped to attract visitors from across the country.

A major component of the plan was to sweep away the Victorian revivals and "Americanized" building styles, such as the little brick bungalows and Queen Anne mansions, in favor of a new type called the "Santa Fe style." A revival based upon the city's remaining Spanish- and Mexican-era buildings and nearby Pueblo villages, the so-called "new-old" style consisted of earth-toned buildings with protruding vigas, overhanging *canales* (drain spouts), and hand-hewn wooden corbels and lintels. In its austere simplicity, straightforward construction, and use of natural materials, colors, and textures, the manner is a regional manifestation of the Arts and Crafts movement.

The portals that many citizens complained were unsightly and old fashioned in the 1880s and 1890s returned to favor during this time. The Santa Fe *New Mexican* wrote in 1909 that Attorney General Clancy "greatly improved his own property by erecting a well proportioned ornamental portal in front of [his] Palace Avenue residence, affording grateful shade. . . . He has preserved all the features of the characteristic Spanish architecture universal in the best class of residences of the olden times, all of which were built of adobe."[1]

In a later stage of the revival movement, the New Mexican Territorial style—adobe buildings with parapets topped by fired brick, and wooden decorative trim influenced by the Greek Revival movement—was also an accepted manner of building.

During this period many of Santa Fe's Victorian houses and structures were literally stuccoed over. A classic example is the Fort Marcy officers' residence at 116 Lincoln Avenue. The two-story adobe structure, with a cross-gable roof, front porch, and simplified Greek Revival details, was built in the early 1870s and is one of only two army officer residences that survive in Santa Fe today. In 1916 attorney Frank Springer remodeled the house in the Spanish Pueblo Revival mode to serve as a residence for Dr. Edgar Lee Hewett, director of the School of American Research and the Museum of New Mexico.

OPPOSITE

El Delirio, Amelia and Martha White House (now School for Advanced Research administrative offices), Garcia Street

The Spanish Pueblo Revival style was already popular in California, where it first appeared at the turn of the century. Among the earliest proponents of the design were architect Julia Morgan and the journalist and Mission Revival advocate Charles Lummis.[2] The architectural revival made its first appearance in New Mexico in 1905 at the University of New Mexico, where the central heating plant was constructed with a flat roof, terraced profile, corner buttresses, and second-story porticoes typical of the Spanish Pueblo manner.

Vigorously promoted for new structures and the remodeling of existing ones in Santa Fe, the "new-old" style or Spanish Pueblo Revival building trend quickly became popular. As early as 1913 the *New Mexican* reported, "The idea of following the New-Old Santa Fe style is steadily gaining ground." That same year, to raise support for the movement, the Santa Fe Chamber of Commerce launched an architectural contest and listed the features they believed were "essential" to the new style: flat roofs, a single effect ("low and long rather than high and narrow"); exterior walls finished in adobe, lime (rough or smooth), or cement (rough or smooth); light-tint colors (or the natural colors of adobe, lime, and cement plasters); no classical columns, bay windows, tin roofs, or picket fences; and absolutely no attributes of the California Mission style, which would "retard the development of the Santa Fe style."[3]

Edgar Lee Hewett, who helped direct the 1912 city planning effort that defined the new style, noted that between 1912 and 1917 about 90 percent of the old houses remodeled and 50 percent of the new ones erected in Santa Fe were in the approved Spanish Pueblo Revival style.[4] Important public structures were also built or renovated in the manner: the Palace of the Governors (remodeled 1909–13), School for the Deaf (built in 1916), La Fonda Hotel (renovated in 1920), the post office (built in 1920), and Sunmount Sanatorium (built in 1914 and renovated in 1920).

The new Museum of Fine Arts (now the New Mexico Museum of Art), erected in 1916–17 at the corner of Lincoln and Palace Avenue and known as the "Cathedral of the Desert," was a particularly significant building of the Spanish Pueblo Revival. Designed by the architectural firm of Rapp, Rapp and Hendrickson, it was based on Franciscan mission churches at Indian pueblos in New Mexico, as well as on the 1915 New Mexico Building at the Panama Pacific Exposition in San Diego, which the same firm designed. A much romanticized version of missions, the museum is notable for its massive adobe brick walls, projecting vigas, exposed lintels over inset windows and doors, multiple roof lines, and central towers. In addition to spurring the acceptance of the new-old Santa Fe style, the museum played an important role as the center of Santa Fe's burgeoning art colony by featuring exhibitions of work by regional artists.

Artist Carlos Vierra was perhaps the most outspoken figure concerning the vital role Santa Fe's native architecture played in the city's success as a tourist destination. In 1917 he wrote, "Nothing will push Santa Fé off the map, to lie protestingly among the forgotten places, so quickly or so easily as the majestic mansion, the modern cottage, the 'cute' bungalow . . . or the old adobe with the new razorback roof, if we persist in building them until they strangle our own architecture and individuality. We are dangerously near that point of strangulation now."[5] Santa Fe's only salvation, he explained, would be to build "its own characteristic

TOP
Fort Marcy Officers' Quarters,
Lincoln Avenue, Santa Fe, ca. 1880
Photograph by United States Army Signal Corps,
courtesy Palace of the Governors Photo Archives
(NMHM/DCA), 030824

BOTTOM
Edgar Lee Hewett House,
Lincoln Avenue, Santa Fe, 1918
Photograph by Wesley Bradfield, courtesy Palace of the
Governors Photo Archives (NMHM/DCA), 028862

style of original architecture, yet with every modern convenience and comfort" and to build "in the spirit of the old pueblo missions, with their charm and fascinating quality to be found in no other place on earth."[6]

Under the direction of Jesse L. Nusbaum, the Victorian-era facade of the Palace of the Governors received a makeover. At the same time, the building ceased to be the official residence of the governor after nearly three centuries, and the interior was altered to house the newly established Museum of New Mexico. Between 1909 and 1913 the building was "restored" into a picturesque version of the Spanish Pueblo Revival; as the city's most visible landmark, this remodeled building helped encourage the popularity of the mode. The "Spanish portale" was the last phase of the project.[7] No plans or visual images of the palace from the seventeenth or eighteenth centuries existed to use as the basis for the remodel. There were, however, a few clues to work from, including a late-eighteenth-century Spanish Colonial corbel that was embedded in a wall facing the inner patio.

The new-old style was heavily promoted by the Chamber of Commerce, which featured only prominent Santa Fe–style buildings in its 1913 brochure *The City Different*.[8] The brochure boasted that the city "possesses and is cultivating what no other city in America has—a distinctive type of architecture—known far and wide as the 'Santa Fe Type,' the features of which are definitely Southwestern Spanish and Mexican colonial, with a touch of Indian pueblo, producing delightfully artistic results." Likewise, the Santa Fe Railway issued an attractive pamphlet called "Old-New Santa Fe," to advertise the city's new architectural attractions.[9]

Santa Fe realtors also got on board and promoted the style. O. C. Watson & Co.'s advertisement for lots available in the Don Diego Heights declared, "We urge those contemplating to build to adopt the New Old Santa Fe plan."[10] And later it was announced, "Messrs. Bishop and Townsend, owners of the Don Diego addition, have secured the cooperation and promise of the many purchasers of lots in that addition to adopt the Old-New Santa Fe style of architecture in their plans for the new homes to be erected in the near future."[11]

As the Santa Fe *New Mexican* explained in April 1918, Carlos Vierra planned to establish his own architectural district: "The Santa Fe style of architecture—the kind that is so much admired by the artists and people of artistic temperament who come here, will get a big boost in a plan which is to be carried out under the direction of Carlos Vierra, artist and well known resident of this city. In order to see a group of Santa Fe style cottages built, with no discordant architectural note struck nearby, Mr. Vierra has purchased, through H. H. Dorman . . . property along Buena Vista Loma . . . and he has decided to sell lots only to those builders who will erect cottages in this style."[12]

In the same article the writer complained that because of the war the cost of building materials was predicted to rise by 40 percent. But Vierra hoped Santa Feans would build new homes anyway and use materials on hand, including the "unlimited adobe which can be converted into suitable bricks and the forests nearby can supply abundant timber for vigas."

Naturally, builders responded to the new trend, too. All the advertisements for Santa Fe Builders Supply Company included either a Spanish Pueblo Revival or Territorial Revival house exterior or interior. Likewise, Welton Builders on

Manhattan Street advertised "'Santa Fe Type' Architecture" made by master builders "experienced in the modern lines of ancient application," and used illustrations of adobe homes with protruding vigas and other Spanish Pueblo features.

Architectural plan books made life easy for builders and homeowners. In 1936 Santa Fe Builders Supply Company published *Santa Fé Homes, Charming and Practical* with drawings by artist Wilfred H. Stedman, and later *New Mexico Magazine* published a *Home Plan Book* of Santa Fe–style houses also with drawings by Stedman.[13] Articles in *New Mexico Magazine* touted the appropriateness of traditional adobe houses for the city.

Carlos Vierra worried that it would be "hard for workmen whose training has held them down to accuracy and rigid mathematical lines to accept the freedom of . . . free-hand [adobe] architecture."[14] But the local building industry gave a helping hand by providing products such as ready-made decorative details. As early as 1913 the Santa Fe Planing Mill announced that it was making "mulduras or capitals in seven of the old patterns architecturally correct, at one to four dollars each, depending on the complexity of the design."[15] Later the Capital Sash and Door Factory offered their clients doors, windows, molding, and other architectural features made in the "Spanish style" for "Santa Fe Style Homes."[16]

In addition, many architects, builders, and homeowners salvaged hand-carved wood details, such as doors, vigas, window frames, and cupboards (as well as santos, bultos, and furniture) from ruined houses in rural New Mexico for reuse in their new Spanish Pueblo Revival–style residences. Although this practice is frowned upon today, in the 1920s it was seen as a positive preservation method. As the editor of the *New Mexican* explained, "those who are salvaging [the objects] for homes here and are thus preventing their being taken away by tourists are doing a real service."[17]

Others traveled across the state taking photographs of decorative details to later use as models. For instance, in the 1910s and 1920s Carlos Vierra compiled enough photos of Indian pueblos, Franciscan missions, churches, and adobe residences to fill six albums. Beginning in 1909 Jesse Nusbaum, on behalf of the Museum of New Mexico, took shots of the picturesque architecture in Santa Fe

TOP LEFT

*Advertisement for Santa Fe
Builders Supply Company*

From *New Mexico Magazine* (January 1936)

TOP RIGHT

*Advertisement for Santa Fe
Builders Supply Company*

From *New Mexico Magazine* (December 1939)

BOTTOM

*Advertisement for Capital
Sash and Door Factory*

From *New Mexico Magazine* (May 1936)

Jesse Nusbaum, under portal at Penasco house, Trampas, New Mexico, ca. 1915

Courtesy Palace of the Governors Photo
Archives (NMHM/DCA), 013892

and in the nearby pueblos and villages. His images were used to entice visitors to the region and appeared in magazine articles, on postcards, in railroad travel brochures, and in the museum's journal *El Palacio*. Today, all these photographs provide a wealth of valuable information for students, builders, and scholars of New Mexico architecture.

In erecting the new Spanish Pueblo Revival residences, architects and their clients generally preferred to use sun-baked adobe bricks made on the site, in the traditional manner. The hand-made adobes were essential to the authenticity of the style. However, some architects, like John Gaw Meem, preferred to use hollow terra-cotta blocks, finished with a coat of adobe-colored stucco—building materials Meem and others believed were easier to maintain. Meem advised his clients that adobe bricks might cost a little less, but in the long run they were "not as satisfactory as a more permanent material, such as hollow tile."[18] Locally referred to as "pentile," because much of it was made at the state penitentiary in Santa Fe, the hollow tile or blocks were striated, so the mortar adhered to the surface. Beginning in the mid-1920s some builders used earth-color stucco over wood frame, a construction technique that gained popularity in the 1930s when the cost effectiveness of adobe construction receded.[19] One architect reported in 1927 that "many varieties of excellent lime and Portland cement stuccos are now available and the manufacturers supply directions for obtaining the textures and colour effects achieved by the Spanish builders."[20]

No matter what material they used, builders of this style maintained the uneven wall surfaces and undulating forms of old adobe structures, a feature admired by many. As one writer of the era observed, "Irregular wall lines . . . give accent to [the adobes'] primitive charm in a day when the trend of modern builders is toward standardization."[21]

In the early 1920s, when the style came to prominence, the population of Santa Fe was about twelve thousand and the cost of living in the state was among the lowest in the country.[22] A two- or three-room adobe house generally cost less than $10 a month to rent.

During the Great Depression, New Mexico residents were hit hard and as a result built fewer new homes. Tourism in the state was also heavily impacted, although some wealthy worldwide travelers continued to visit and build second homes. Apartments that rented for $65 a month during flush times brought only $35 a month in 1933.[23] Prices for most building materials escalated. The *New Mexican* reported that the price of oak flooring went from $50 per thousand feet in 1932 to $75 in 1933, and the price of cement jumped from $.70 per hundred pounds to $1.10.[24] Despite financial worries, the state participated in Chicago's 1934 "A Century of Progress" exposition by supplying a Spanish Pueblo Revival–style exhibit designed by architect Gordon Street.

As the decade progressed, the situation improved and the city experienced a mini construction boom. In June 1936 a journalist for the *New Mexican* explained: "Choice sites within the city limits are rapidly becoming scarce with the construction on a large scale of the more pretentious type of residence. And in the less expensive tracts, the typical 'dobe huts of one, two, and three rooms are springing up like weeds."[25]

Throughout this time New Mexican women actively participated in the building of the Spanish Pueblo Revival homes. When erecting a vacation home for wealthy businessman Cyrus McCormick Jr. in a village north of Santa Fe, architect John Gaw Meem hired women from the region. "The [nine] fireplaces are being constructed by one of the lady masons of Nambe Valley under Carlos [Vierra's] direction. We are also lining up all the lady plasterers we can get," Meem explained in a letter to his client.[26] Women who specialize in the fine art of building adobe fireplaces are known as *fogoneras* (after *fogóne* or fireplace). Using traditional and modern materials, they slowly build up by hand the softly rounded forms of a corner fireplace (see page 7).

In the 1920s and '30s a network of highly educated, wealthy, middle- and upper-class Anglo-American women from the East and Midwest scooped up loads of property in Santa Fe and built homes that played a crucial role in spreading the interest in regional styles of architecture. They also spearheaded the preservation of historic buildings in the city, and through various philanthropic efforts promoted the indigenous arts of the southwest (both American Indian and Hispano). These women found that early-twentieth-century New Mexico was "a place of freedom from the conventions of gender and class," where they could achieve greater public influence and authority than in their own hometowns.[27]

Alice Clark Myers, the third woman in the U.S. to receive a bachelor's degree in architecture, from the University of Illinois, designed and built a home at 503 Camino del Monte Sol in 1925.[28] Margretta Stewart Dietrich, a Bryn Mawr graduate, former suffragist, and widow of a U.S. senator in Nebraska, invested in Santa Fe real estate, buying several important historic adobe homes and restoring them to their former glory. The Juan José Prada house, El Zaguán, and the Rafael Borrego House, all situated on Canyon Road, were her primary projects. In the early 1920s Kate Chapman, who had no formal training in architecture, began remodeling old adobe houses.[29] She oversaw the restoration of properties owned by Dietrich, who called Chapman "one of the best 'reproducers' of old houses in Santa Fe" who "used true adobe and always employed the oldest men she could find to do the work."[30] Like Chapman, famed aviatrix Katherine Stinson Otero had no formal training but found her niche in 1930s Santa Fe as a designer and builder of traditional adobes.

In 1921 Elizabeth Shepley Sergeant, a New England writer inspired by her friend and fellow author Willa Cather to explore the southwest, purchased land and a crumbling adobe just outside Santa Fe in the small Hispanic village of Tesuque. The following year she wrote a four-part series of articles for *Harper's* magazine entitled "The Journal of a Mud House," in which she described renovating the adobe. Amelia and Martha White, philanthropists from New York and Bryn Mawr classmates of Sergeant, purchased an old adobe and land "with a heavenly view" on Garcia Street in 1923.[31] The sisters hired William Penhallow Henderson to design one of the largest residential complexes in the Santa Fe style. It included a Mayan-influenced swimming pool, indoor theater, and tennis court. The design for the main house (see page 182), dubbed *El Delirio* after a bar the White sisters visited in Spain, is based upon the old Mission chapel at Laguna Pueblo. Often featured in articles of the era as one of the finest examples of the new-old style with the "effect of sun-steeped age," it is now part of the School for Advanced Research.[32]

Kate Chapman, ca. 1915

Photograph by Jesse Nusbaum, courtesy Palace of the Governors Photo Archive (NMHM/DCA), 040927

*Advertisement for Capital
Sash & Door Factory*

From *New Mexico Magazine* (October 1937)

Yet another woman to add to this distinguished list is Mary Cabot Wheelwright, amateur ethnographer and collector, who hired William Penhallow Henderson to build a museum for Navajo art and religion on a hilltop in Santa Fe. Today called the Wheelwright Museum of the American Indian, the building was designed in the shape of a hogan—the traditional home and ceremonial space of Navajo Indians.

In keeping with their interest in the traditional arts of the Southwest, the women and men who built homes in the Spanish Pueblo Revival manner generally decorated their residences with Pueblo pottery, Navajo weavings, and the tinwork and furniture of Spanish and Mexican design picked up during jaunts to the mountain villages of New Mexico. They also purchased items in Santa Fe at such specialty stores as the Native Market, Old Mexico, and Zaraperia Mexicana. Companies like the Capital Sash & Door Factory offered "fine furniture that reflects the charm of old Santa Fe."

With the advent of the "new-old style," Santa Fe was transformed from a dusty, frontier town into a center for anthropology, a health resort, an artists' colony of some renown, and a tourist destination. Visitors were drawn to the city's antique buildings, Hispano and Indian cultures, moderate climate, and beautiful mountain vistas.

However, many residents and newcomers—even those who helped bring about the change—regretted the loss of Santa Fe's unique character and historic architecture that progress brought with it. In a 1924 article called "A City of Change," the poet Witter Bynner expressed what many Santa Feans were feeling at that time. He wrote that until recently the ancient city had remained "different from the rest, had escaped the American cooky-cutter which turns out cities one after another in approximately the same pattern."[33] After the arrival of the tourists, artists, and writers in the 1920s the city changed radically, said Bynner. "We Americans from the outside have quickly made of Santa Fe the city of our discontent. It must be boosted, paved, enlarged, it must be Americanized. The streets which were rough and made us go slowly are smooth now and make us go fast. . . . The little adobe houses near the Plaza have cast down their grassy crowns before a bulk of garages, garages in the Santa Fe style, yes, but inviting blatant vehicles which hurry people's errands and harden their faces."

Bynner knew that in remodeling and expanding his own adobe home on Old Santa Fe Trail and participating in the growth of the artists' colony, he was part of the problem. "We are all doing it. We can not help ourselves. We are attracting people here. We are advertising. We are boosting. We can not care enough that, by professionalizing the apparent difference of Santa Fe, we are killing the real difference. We are crowding out the natives, to make room for improved houses with artificial warpings. We are changing our town from the city different to the city indifferent."

Many living in Santa Fe today probably share Bynner's sentiments of 1924. And yet, there is so much to be proud of and hopeful about. As they grapple with the problems of twenty-first-century life, the city's residents and leaders strive to maintain and recapture the spirit and flavor of the remarkably beautiful architecture of this region.

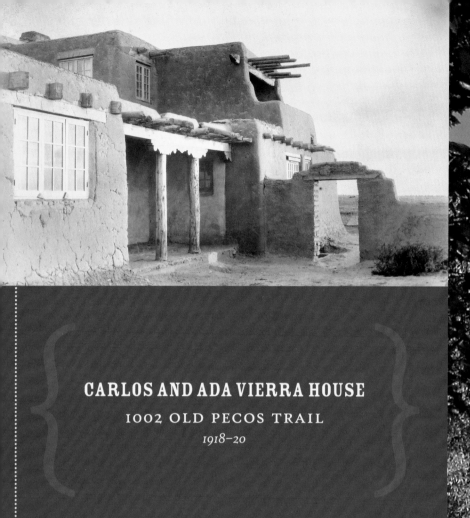

Artist Carlos Vierra (1876–1937) believed that when building a Spanish Pueblo Revival structure, one should "reproduce (instead of merely imitating) the spirit of the original as closely as modern methods and materials will allow."[34] He also believed that while the exterior should "conform to Santa Fé architecture" the interior may reflect one's individual tastes and "express our personality." His home on Old Pecos Trail—which the Santa Fe *New Mexican* dubbed "La Casa Del Indio" because of its similarity to a Pueblo Indian dwelling—fully illustrates Vierra's beliefs.[35]

The son of a Portuguese-American fishing family, Vierra was born in 1876 at Moss Landing, California. After studying art in San Francisco, he sailed around Cape Horn six times and settled in New York, where he worked as a marine illustrator and cartoonist. Diagnosed with tuberculosis, Vierra was advised by his doctors to move to a drier climate. By 1905 he was regaining his health at St.

ABOVE

Carlos and Ada Vierra House, ca. 1920

Courtesy Palace of the Governors Photo Archives (NMHM/DCA), 042066

RIGHT

Facade, Carlos and Ada Vierra House

Photograph by Grant Taylor, courtesy of Plaza Productions, a Webster Enterprises Company, Santa Fe

Carlos Vierra

Courtesy of Plaza Productions,
a Webster Enterprises Company, Santa Fe

Photograph by Carlos Vierra of main plaza at Jemez Pueblo, ca. 1915

Courtesy Palace of the Governors Photo Archives (NMHM/DCA), 042066

Vincent's Sanitorium in Santa Fe and had embarked on a new career as a photographer and painter of New Mexico scenes. He opened a photographic studio on the west side of the plaza. Vierra was one of the first of many artists to come to Santa Fe for his health and make it his permanent home. Many credit him with founding the city's art colony. He gained distinction as a mural painter, and examples of his work can be seen in the St. Francis Auditorium of the New Mexico Museum of Art.

In 1910 Vierra married Ohio native Ada Talbert Ogle, and two years later he joined the staff of the Museum of New Mexico and the School of American Archaeology. He served on the Committee for the Preservation and Restoration of New Mexico Mission Churches in 1924. By the time he built his home, Vierra already had a reputation as a champion of the new-old Santa Fe style. When the Chamber of Commerce held a competition in the fall of 1913 for the "best design of a Santa Fe Style residence not to exceed $3,500," the design Vierra submitted won second place.[36] The design was not, however, the one he would choose for his own residence in the city.

Knowing that Carlos and Ada lacked sufficient funds to build their own home, Frank Springer, an attorney and board member of the Museum of New Mexico and School of American Archaeology, sold the Vierras a lot at the corner of Old Pecos Trail and Coronado Road for $1, with the understanding that they could remain in the house for as long as they lived.[37]

When designing his new home, Carlos consulted his architect-friend Trent Thomas (1889–1951), who was then working with the firm of Rapp, Rapp and Hendrickson on the renovation of La Fonda Hotel. Much of Vierra's inspiration, however, came directly from the Indian pueblos of New Mexico. In comparing the earliest photos of his house to photographs that Vierra himself took at different pueblos, one can see how closely he followed the multistoried buildings of the Indian villages.

Construction began in 1918, and once the roof was completed, Carlos and Ada moved in, shifting from room to room until the work was done. Carlos strove to make his house look "old" and he knew he had achieved his goals when tourists began referring to their home as "the ruins near [Bronson] Cutting's."[38] During the three years his house was under construction, Carlos spent numerous hours a day working on the handcrafted aspects of the adobe.

When completed, the house epitomized the revival style that Vierra advocated for Santa Fe: flat roofs; massive adobe walls and carved porch brackets based on local Span-

Detail of ceiling latillas, beams, and corbels, Carlos and Ada Vierra House
Photograph by Grant Taylor, courtesy of Plaza Productions, a Webster Enterprises Company, Santa Fe

ish Colonial homes; terraced stories reminiscent of old Pueblo villages; and wood casement windows with hewn wooden lintels patterned after historic porch beams. For authenticity, Vierra had the adobe bricks used to construct the walls made at the building site in the traditional manner. Today listed on the National Register of Historic Places and the State of New Mexico Register of Cultural Properties, the house has remained largely unchanged.[39]

In July 1919, when the *New Mexican* reported on "beautiful modern homes being built in Santa Fe," they singled out the Vierra house as a "fine sample of picturesque style." The writer explained: "One of the largest and in many ways most artistic houses is that which Carlos Vierra, the artist, is building south of Don Gaspar avenue, with a superb view of the Sandia Mountains. . . . The construction . . . began many months ago but this spring and summer it has made a mark on the landscape and is much admired. . . . It promises to be 'the last word' on original Santa Fe style houses."[40]

The reporter also noticed that Vierra had included sleeping porches—a common feature in houses built in Santa Fe during this period. Outdoor sleeping in screened-in porches was considered healthy for everyone, and essential for those suffering from lung ailments.

For many years Vierra's house served as a residential prototype for the revival of Spanish Pueblo architecture in Santa Fe. In 1927 it was featured in Rexford Newcomb's *The Spanish House for America* and ten years later in Newcomb's *Spanish-Colonial Architecture in the United States* as one of the best buildings by a contemporary architect who adapted the "indigenous historic spirit" of Spanish Colonial New Mexico in his work.[41]

It was reported that the charm of Carlos and Ada's house could only be appreciated by those who had been inside, where the "proportions reveal the designs of an artist" and "the decorated beams, the carved furniture, the rugs and curtains are [all] in harmony."[42] The rectangular floor plan contains eleven rooms on the ground floor and six rooms on the second floor. In designing the ceilings Vierra used peeled vigas and hand-carved beams that rest on decorative corbels. The carved decoration is painted in vibrant tones of blue, red, and green and is similar to the ceilings of the 1917 St. Francis Auditorium, New Mexico Museum of Art. Throughout the house are wood floors that were laid by artist Josef Bakos and traditional adobe corner fireplaces with stepped shelves.

In the eastern part of the house is Vierra's former two-story studio, illuminated by expansive north-facing

*Hooded fireplace in studio of
Carlos and Ada Vierra House*

Photograph by Grant Taylor, courtesy of Plaza
Productions, a Webster Enterprises Company, Santa Fe

*Pueblo woman sweeping
and hooded fireplace, 1889*

Courtesy of Many Coyotes Photography, Hico, Texas

Living room, Carlos and Ada Vierra House

Photograph by Grant Taylor, courtesy of Plaza Productions, a Webster Enterprises Company, Santa Fe

windows and an unusual adobe fireplace with a wood and adobe hood. It is similar to the hooded fireplaces seen in Zuni Pueblo, New Mexico.

Vierra's influence on Santa Fe architecture can be seen in the work of his protégé, John Gaw Meem. The two met in 1920 at Sunmount Sanatorium, where Meem was a patient. Inspired by Vierra's passion for adobe architecture, Meem soon became an advocate of the revival style and worked toward becoming an architect. Among the sources he studied were the photographs of historic New Mexico Pueblo villages, homes, and missions that Vierra compiled in bound volumes while working for the museum.[43] Meem learned much about construction and style from Vierra; the two collaborated on at least one project: the 1931 Cyrus McCormick estate built in Nambe, New Mexico.

Carlos died of pneumonia at the age of sixty-one in 1937. His widow continued to live in the house until the early 1940s, when she moved to Kansas, and ownership reverted to the Springer family.[44] Carlos's contributions to his adopted city were perhaps summed up best by Paul Walter, who on the day following the artist's death wrote: "It was Vierra's insistence upon purity of style that saved Santa Fe from many an architectural monstrosity. . . . Up to the time of his death he guarded the integrity of the Pueblo and the Spanish colonial architecture with a zeal often leading to heated controversy. That Santa Fe is not only a 'City Different' but also a 'City Beautiful' is more largely owing to him, perhaps, than to any other one individual."[45]

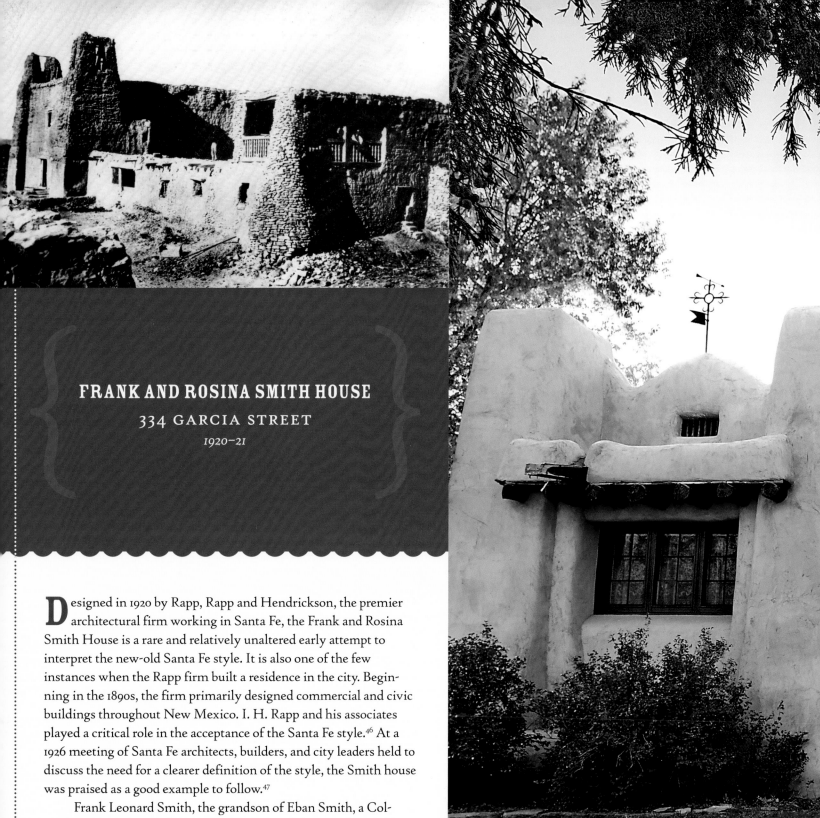

FRANK AND ROSINA SMITH HOUSE
334 GARCIA STREET
1920–21

Designed in 1920 by Rapp, Rapp and Hendrickson, the premier architectural firm working in Santa Fe, the Frank and Rosina Smith House is a rare and relatively unaltered early attempt to interpret the new-old Santa Fe style. It is also one of the few instances when the Rapp firm built a residence in the city. Beginning in the 1890s, the firm primarily designed commercial and civic buildings throughout New Mexico. I. H. Rapp and his associates played a critical role in the acceptance of the Santa Fe style.[46] At a 1926 meeting of Santa Fe architects, builders, and city leaders held to discuss the need for a clearer definition of the style, the Smith house was praised as a good example to follow.[47]

Frank Leonard Smith, the grandson of Eban Smith, a Colorado gold-mining millionaire and founder of the First National Bank of Denver, first came to Santa Fe with his mother and lived in a house on Palace Avenue. In the autumn of 1920, at the age of

ABOVE

*Old Mission Church of Acoma
Pueblo, New Mexico, ca. 1890*

Denver Public Library, Western
History Collection, X-30177

RIGHT

Frank and Rosina Smith House

Courtesy of the Gerald Peters Gallery

The flat roof, projecting vigas and canales (drain spouts), inset windows, and exposed lintels are further characteristic of the early Spanish Pueblo Revival style. One of the house's most distinguishing features is the pink stucco exterior. The color is uncommon in Santa Fe today, but in the 1920s it was considered to be the most appropriate.[49]

Many of Rapp, Rapp and Hendrickson's designs were based on adobe Pueblo Mission buildings in New Mexico. The Smith home, with its exaggerated buttresses and tower-like massing on the east side of the facade, is reminiscent of the Acoma Pueblo Mission Church. Because the Smith house conformed to the "universally acclaimed New Mexican style of architecture," it was featured in architect Rexford Newcomb's 1924 article on "Santa Fe, The Historic and Modern," published in *The Western Architect*.[50]

Further elements of interest in the house are the wood casement windows with divided lights of Arts and Crafts style. The front patio is flagstone, with a three-foot-high stucco wall, an overhang with vigas, and a *nicho* with a tile mural of Christ. The front door opens into the spacious living room, which has a ceiling of hand-adzed beams and intricately carved corbels, and a marvelous stucco fireplace with a wood mantel shelf. There are corner fireplaces in two of the bedrooms. Unusual for that era, the house has a full basement, a built-in vacuum cleaner, copper conduits, and an underground sprinkler system. There is also a two-car garage which was originally equipped with its own gas pump at the request of Frank Smith, who had a passion for automobiles.

After living in the house for only a few short years and having two children, Frank and Rosina divorced in 1924. Rosina was awarded the house in the settlement. Later that spring, twenty-six-year-old Frank died mysteriously of an unknown poison in Denver. The writer of his obituary hinted that his death may have been the result of his lavish lifestyle: "The news of Mr. Smith's sudden death shocked his many friends and acquaintances in Santa Fe, where he was known for several years as a jolly good fellow, who spent money liberally, entertaining in princely style, and buying the latest types of motor cars regardless of price. It is said that Mr. Smith spent a fortune of $100,000 to $300,000 in two or three years, an inherited fortune, his grand-father having been one of the successful mining pioneers of Colorado."[51]

In December 1925 Rosina Bergere Smith married Dr. Robert Osgood Brown, a well-known physician in Santa Fe. Today the Smith House on Garcia Street is still owned and being carefully preserved by a descendant of Rosina.

twenty-one, he bought five undeveloped lots on Garcia Street and hired the most prominent architectural firm in Santa Fe to design a stylish new home. Several months later, in January 1921, Frank married Rosina Bergere, the daughter of Alfred M. Bergere and Eloisa Luna Otero Bergere, who owned a home on Griffin Street. Described as the "prettiest wedding seen here in many winters," the event made the headlines of the *New Mexican*'s society page.

While the couple honeymooned in New York City, their Garcia Street home took shape. The final result impressed the *New Mexican*, which reported that Frank had "built a fine $20,000 or $30,000 house, in Santa Fe style . . . and laid out the grounds artistically. . . . He furnished his home in exquisite taste, with rare paintings, oriental rugs and furniture."[48]

The Smith house was constructed of pentile (hollow tile) with a heavy stucco finish. It is single story, rectangular in overall shape, and divided into three main sections. The buttresses, undulating parapets, and softly rounded corners cleverly imitate the contours of an adobe structure.

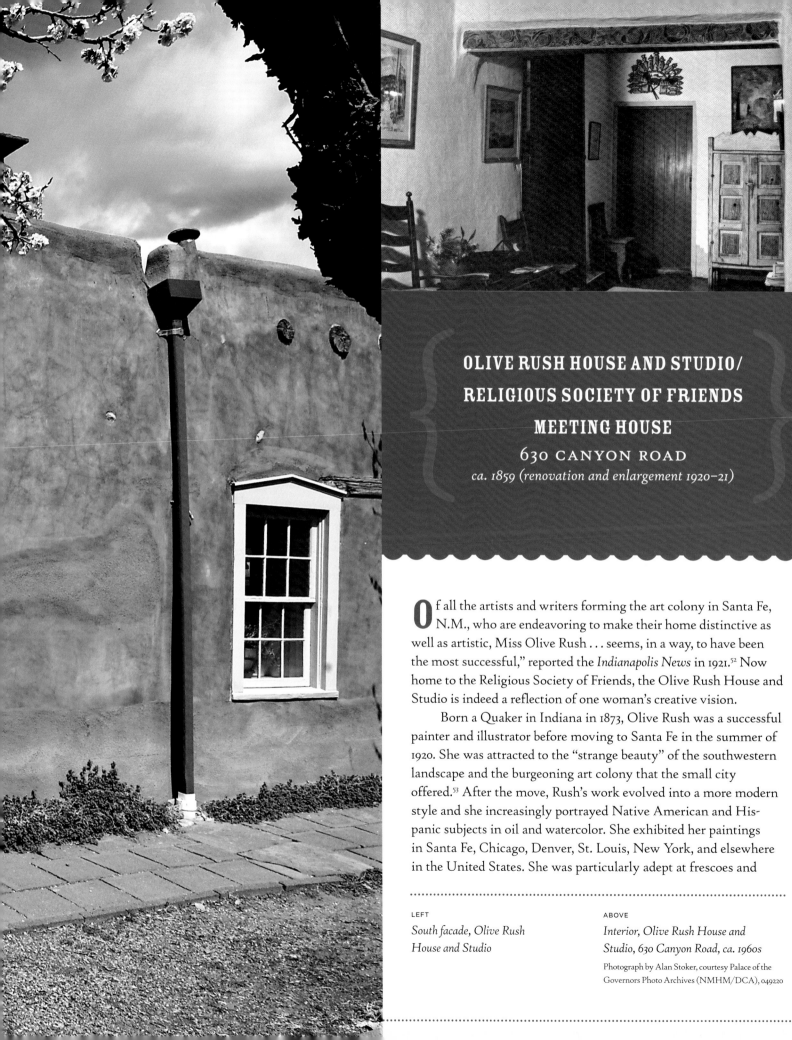

OLIVE RUSH HOUSE AND STUDIO/
RELIGIOUS SOCIETY OF FRIENDS
MEETING HOUSE
630 CANYON ROAD
ca. 1859 (renovation and enlargement 1920–21)

"Of all the artists and writers forming the art colony in Santa Fe, N.M., who are endeavoring to make their home distinctive as well as artistic, Miss Olive Rush . . . seems, in a way, to have been the most successful," reported the *Indianapolis News* in 1921.[52] Now home to the Religious Society of Friends, the Olive Rush House and Studio is indeed a reflection of one woman's creative vision.

Born a Quaker in Indiana in 1873, Olive Rush was a successful painter and illustrator before moving to Santa Fe in the summer of 1920. She was attracted to the "strange beauty" of the southwestern landscape and the burgeoning art colony that the small city offered.[53] After the move, Rush's work evolved into a more modern style and she increasingly portrayed Native American and Hispanic subjects in oil and watercolor. She exhibited her paintings in Santa Fe, Chicago, Denver, St. Louis, New York, and elsewhere in the United States. She was particularly adept at frescoes and

LEFT

South facade, Olive Rush House and Studio

ABOVE

Interior, Olive Rush House and Studio, 630 Canyon Road, ca. 1960s

Photograph by Alan Stoker, courtesy Palace of the Governors Photo Archives (NMHM/DCA), 049220

Canyon Road facade, Olive Rush House and Studio

undertook numerous mural commissions at homes, businesses, and public buildings.

With money earned from portrait commissions in Indianapolis, Rush bought an old adobe on Canyon Road that became her studio and home for the next forty-two years.[54] Little is known about the early history of the structure. County records indicate the house was owned by José Domingo Fernandez in 1859 and belonged to the Sena-Rodriguez families for several generations.[55]

The house is significant, for it is one of the few remaining artist studio-homes in the Canyon Road area, dating from the early twentieth century, that are largely unaltered. It is also a fine example of the Spanish Pueblo Revival style. Rush modernized the house with plumbing and electricity, added a room or two, and adapted the space to her needs, but she was careful not to change the overall historic character and simplicity of construction. As a newspaper reporter of the era explained, "She has retained the flat roof, the thick adobe walls, the deep set windows with their small panes, the means to carry away the waste water from the roof, the porch, with its earthen floor, the heavy double doors with their immense iron hinges and great crossbar for fastening and the outside adobe [horno] characteristic of Mexican and Pueblo homes."[56]

Except for general signs of deterioration from weather and wear and tear, the loss of the horno oven, and the replastering of the mud-plaster walls with cement stucco in the mid-1970s (only a few patches of the original mud finish remain on the west and east sides), the house has changed little from this early description.

Olive Rush in the garden at 630 Canyon Road, ca. 1930s

Courtesy Palace of the Governors Photo Archives (NMHM/DCA), 019270

Detail of alacena and rug in studio of Olive Rush House and Studio

Believing the Rush house to be a significant New Mexico structure, architecture professor Bainbridge Bunting asked his University of New Mexico students to measure and record it as a term project.[57] Bunting believed that such drawings would "be of value as a historic record and of unique interest to those who cherish the old traditions."[58] The east portal of the Rush house was enclosed with removable Lexan plastic walls in 1992, and the student drawing of this elevation (incorrectly titled "north") provides details of the design as it was in Olive Rush's day.

As Bunting's students noted, all the walls in the Rush house are "18 inches or 24 inches adobe."[59] The interior walls were covered with "yeso"—a smooth plaster finish made from gypsum that gives a white-to-golden appearance to the surface. The ceilings were constructed from tablas and hand-hewn pine vigas, and most rooms in the house have a corner fireplace.

On the exterior, the house has a wonderfully hand-sculpted adobe zaguán with wood lintel, corbels, and gate. The latter is known as "Penasco- style" after similar designs found on doors in the village of Penasco, New Mexico. Some windows have Territorial Revival–style frames with pedimented lintels, and on the east and south facades are small nichos with wood grilles. The latter originally passed through to the interior and thus may have been used for cooling foods or beverages.

Among the few major changes Rush made was replacing the front door with a window and moving the entrance to the east side of the building under a portal, and she covered the earthen floors with a mixture of concrete and other material to give the appearance of packed adobe (or, as in the case of the library, red cement that was scored to give the effect of red floor tiles). The building originally shared a placita with the house next door, which Rush also owned and renovated. When she finally finished all the work, a Santa Fe newspaper writer exclaimed: "[Rush] has done a grand job of the places."[60]

In the 1920s Rush experimented with the traditional fresco technique of painting on wet plaster and used the walls of her Canyon Road home as her canvas.[61] Although faded somewhat from exposure to light, and dimmed by layers of soot and dirt, the lively and colorful frescoes still adorn her house today. She painted elaborate scenes on the corner fireplace and ceiling beam in her studio, and on small areas on walls throughout the house and gardens. She kept notebooks in which she chronicled her recipes for pigments and plaster; and in one she commented that "Architecture without polychromy is architecture incomplete."[62] Shortly after finishing the paintings in her home, Rush

Fireplace mural by Olive Rush in the studio of her Canyon Road home

Zaguán, Olive Rush House and Studio

gave a lecture at a local woman's club about how frescoes were perfectly suited to the Santa Fe style of architecture. In 1934 Rush completed a mural for the Public Works of Art Project in the Santa Fe Public Library on Washington Street (now the Fray Angélico Chávez History Library).

Objects once owned by Rush—including her easel, palette, *alacena* (built-in wall cabinet) containing the pigments she once used, and some rustic furniture—remain in the house. These items, as well as a photograph of the interior, indicate that Rush decorated her home with collections of Spanish Colonial furniture, Native American textiles, New Mexican artifacts, and Pueblo pottery (including work by San Ildefonso potter Maria Martinez). When *Sunset Magazine* featured Rush's studio in its April 1928 issue, the writer described the artist as having furnished her house "with striking effect, avoiding the bizarre and maintaining in every detail the individuality of the original dwelling, its historic importance and its native environment."[63]

After finishing the restoration of the two Canyon Road properties, Rush reestablished her active social life. As a Santa Fe gossip columnist explained, "Painter, Olive Rush is just having a grand time flinging teas these days. On Saturday she had up one lot, reported to be artists. On Sunday there was another of alleged archaeologists. We see all this entertaining as an expression of relief after the tedium [of] reconstructing her own home and the one next to it."[64]

Besides entertaining, Rush became busy with the Santa Fe Artists' Guild, which she helped cofound in 1933, and the Women Artists' Exhibiting Group. She also promoted and influenced the development of young Native American artists; in 1932 she supervised an important mural project at the Santa Fe Indian School. With her keen interest in preserving Santa Fe's historic architecture, she was an early member of the Old Santa Fe Association.

When Rush died in August 1966 at the age of ninety-three, she bequeathed her home to the Santa Fe Meeting of the Religious Society of Friends as a memorial to her parents, who were Quaker ministers.[65] The Friends continue to use the building today as a place of worship, and except for adding handicap access and a few other modern improvements, the group has preserved the architectural integrity of the site, in fond memory of Rush.

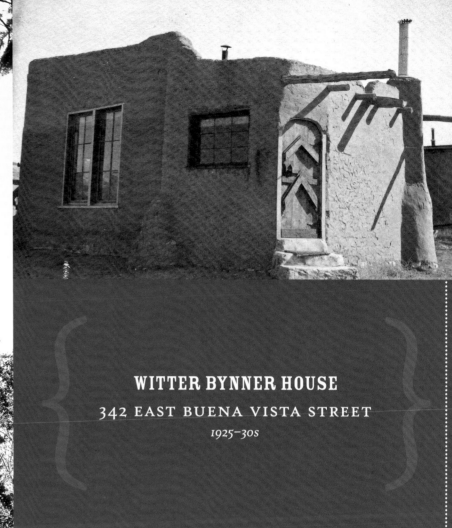

WITTER BYNNER HOUSE

342 EAST BUENA VISTA STREET

1925–30s

Santa Feans followed the essence of the Spanish Pueblo Revival style dictated by the city leaders when building their homes, but they also imbued them with distinctly unique qualities. As Santa Fe writer Ruth Laughlin Alexander said when describing poet Witter Bynner's house: "Your home is what I feel Santa Fe homes should be—the outer conformity to our native architecture and the inner expression of individual taste."[66]

Harold Witter Bynner (1881–1968) first visited Santa Fe in February 1922 to give his lecture "China Today" at Sunmount Sanatorium. He was forty-one years old and already a well-known poet, translator, and essayist. A bout of influenza led him to remain at Sunmount, where he convalesced and took part in poetry readings and literary discussions. Smitten with Santa Fe, Bynner decided to stay; in June he rented a small adobe home from painter Paul Burlin, one of the earliest members of Santa Fe's artists' colony.

The son of a wealthy New England couple, Bynner graduated from Harvard with honors in 1902 and then served as literary editor of

LEFT

Main facade, Witter Bynner House

ABOVE

Witter Bynner House, 1922

Courtesy of the Witter Bynner Foundation

ABOVE

Yin Yang fresco, Witter Bynner House

CENTER

Chinese dragon ceramic tile, Bynner House

RIGHT

Arched doorway and door with Chinese characters, Bynner House

OPPOSITE

Main facade, Witter Bynner House

....

the progressive New York magazine *McClure's*. He wrote for other important journals, traveled widely on the lecture circuit, and taught poetry at Berkeley. During his lifetime he produced more than thirty volumes of poetry and prose and knew many of the prominent writers, artists, composers, actors, and philosophers of his day.

After moving into his Santa Fe rental, Bynner immediately filled the house with paintings, large Chinese carvings, other decorative objects, and good friends. Among his first visitors was Frieda Lawrence, wife of famed author D. H. Lawrence. From the start Bynner wanted to buy the house, and in 1925, after almost losing it to Margretta Dietrich, Bynner was able to buy his favorite little "pink adobe."[67]

Around this time Bynner described how he felt about his new house and his new hometown: "I had found my own adobe, one of the oldest, with a broad beamed roof to shed homely dirt on me in windy weather and primitive rain in wet. I was above the troubled world. I was washed clean of the war. I was given communion each night when sunset would elevate the host on the Sangre de Cristo mountains. . . . I had found something not to be found elsewhere in These States, a town too much itself to be feverishly imitating its neighbors. Nothing strained, nothing silly, just an honest-to-God town, seasoned and simple, easily breathing its high air."[68]

The poet's home originally consisted of a small, crudely constructed three-room adobe that was situated on a bare plot of land on the outskirts of town. In the earliest photograph of the house it is hard to ignore the widely varying lengths of the protruding vigas—a result of the tree trunks being left just as they were when felled by an axe. Among the first changes he made were building a separate storeroom for his treasures, adding a bay window to his studio, hanging white curtains he had specially woven in Jocotepec, Mexico, and installing a Franklin stove in the main room for heating.[69]

In 1926 he added on three new adobe rooms, as well as a vault, a bathroom, and a study. Of the latter he wrote, "I am to have a study where papers may lie about as they like. It is to be upstairs, shut away from the rest of the house, but nearer the mountains."[70] For many years he called this new two-story structure the "O. Henry story," because it was financed by the sale of three O. Henry short stories that were given to him by the author.[71] The *New Mexican* reported on the remodel: "Witter Bynner is painting his College Street or rather Buena Vista Loma home and studio a peculiar color—some call it a brick red. Bynner has finished the interior in Chinese style, with Chinese carvings, silks, and satins. Why should not the exterior be brick-red? If some artist friend will now paint a few blue dragons on the walls, the house will be perfect."[72]

Over the following decades, Bynner bought adjacent plots of land and a house, and continued to remodel and add on rooms until the little pink adobe became an eccentric, rambling, eight-thousand-square-foot mansion of thirty rooms, surrounded by a meticulously groomed garden. The architecture of the single-story rooms with the two-story structure in the center reflected the favored Spanish Pueblo Revival style: flat roof, canales protruding from parapet walls, projecting viga ends, and adobe walls. Many rooms had traditional adobe and plaster corner fireplaces and ceilings with prominent exposed vigas. By 1929 a journalist claimed that Bynner's house was "one of the most beautiful places in Santa Fe" and "one of the most remarkable in America, a blending of Pueblo-Mission architecture with Chinese decoration."[73]

During his lifetime, Bynner displayed the art objects he collected on his travels: Chinese carvings, scrolls, and jade were hung on white walls; gold-painted woodwork was incorporated into rooms; colorful Navajo rugs were on the floor, and black and white Mexican serapes draped over couches; New England heirloom chests and silver graced some of the rooms; and Hispanic santos and American Indian pottery and baskets were displayed throughout. As the biographer James Kraft noted, "The house in details of architecture was at once Indian, Hispanic, and Chinese, and in time became a reflection of Bynner's character."[74]

The poet's interest in China stemmed from his two visits to the country between 1917 and 1921 and from his transla-

tion of the *Tao Teh Ching*. A few remnants of Bynner's Chinese decoration in the house can be seen today: the yin-yang symbol painted on the courtyard wall, a circular ceramic tile of a Chinese dragon, and Chinese characters on a door.

Bynner was a leading civic figure and a witty and charming host; his house was the scene of lively and sometimes scandalous social events. The *New Mexican* often reported on the gatherings. For example, in May 1928, the newspaper noted: "Witter Bynner entertained a number of literary and artist friends at a tea at his Chinese palace on College street yesterday afternoon."[75] The invitation lists for his parties were a veritable who's who of the Santa Fe and American literary scene of the era.[76] Among his guests were Robert Frost, Thornton Wilder, Willa Cather, Martha Graham, Georgia O'Keeffe, Ansel Adams, Edna St. Vincent Millay, and D. H. and Frieda Lawrence. The home, which he shared with his companion of thirty years, Robert Hunt, was indeed at the very center of Santa Fe's burgeoning art colony.

Bynner became an early member and trustee of the Old Santa Fe Association, the city's first historic preservation organization, and he wrote letters to the editor and essays on preserving Santa Fe's native architecture and cultural traditions.[77] His admiration for the rustic earthen architecture of New Mexico even influenced his poetry. In 1931 he wrote: "Here in this autumnal Spain / Adobes live with little rain, / And even crumbling seem to me / Sweeter than a spring can be / In any other place but this, / Where an eternal autumn is."[78]

At one time hoping to make his home a permanent "poet's residence" with a museum for his Chinese art collection, Bynner bequeathed his home to St. John's College.[79] In 1995 it was purchased by Ralph Bolton and Robert Frost, who lovingly restored the rambling adobe complex and opened it as the Inn of the Turquoise Bear.

Drawing Room   sleeping porch   flower garden continued
                                                 große Arbour

— Our Home (Continued
Santa Fe. N.M.
23ᵈ Sep. 1927

ACEQUIA MADRE HOUSE
614 ACEQUIA MADRE
1925–26

In 1927 famed writer, editor, and historic preservationist Charles Lummis called 614 Acequia Madre the "House of Three Wise Women."[80] The building is indeed the expression of three remarkable wise women, each of whom had a unique sense of style and avid interest in the preservation of art and architecture: Eva Scott Muse Fényes, her daughter, Leonora Scott Muse Curtin, and granddaughter, Leonora Frances Curtin Paloheimo. Over several decades, these highly educated and cultured women welcomed members of Santa Fe's artistic and literary communities, as well as other prominent visitors, to their home.

In the late 1880s, after suffering through a particularly bad blizzard in New York City, Eva Scott Muse Fényes saw a Santa Fe Railway advertisement of a burro and an adobe that lured her to Santa Fe.[81] Having suffered from a chronic cough since the blizzard,

ABOVE

Eva Scott Fényes, "Our House,
Santa Fe, N.M., 23 Sept. 1927."
Watercolor on paper

Courtesy of the Archives
at the Pasadena Museum of History

RIGHT

Territorial-style facade of
Acequia Madre House

Living room, Acequia Madre House

she traveled to the region primarily for its healthful benefits and like so many others ended up returning for extended periods of time and eventually making a home there. In 1922 she purchased a large alfalfa field for $1,700 on Acequia Madre—a road named after the irrigation ditch that runs alongside it (constructed in 1610). After subdividing the land, Eva, her daughter, Leonora, and granddaughter, Leonora Frances, built a main family home and four additional rental houses.

The first design for the house was created by famed California architect Wallace Neff and consisted of a two-story, Mediterranean-style structure with a barrel-tile roof, round arched openings, quatrefoil windows, and elaborate wrought-iron grills. Unable to reach an agreement with Neff and finding the style of house he proposed unsuitable for Santa Fe, the Fényes-Curtin women rejected the plans. At that time Carlos Vierra and others warned homebuilders, "Keep away from the tile roofs. Or we will be mixing up with California. The line between Santa Fe and California types should be held hard and fast."[82]

Eventually, after consulting with other architects, including William Penhallow Henderson, the women designed their Santa Fe compound themselves. Albuquerque architect A. Rossiter was hired to draw up plans based on their ideas. The final design reflects primarily the personal taste and aesthetics of Eva Fényes, who supervised every aspect of the building and furnishing of the house. When she was absent from Santa Fe, her daughter and granddaughter oversaw the project and sent frequent reports to Eva. In May 1925 Leonora S. M. Curtin wrote, "Our minds are so full of house plans that we can think of nothing else." And later that month: "The ground is so hard that a light team of horses could not plow it. . . . We succeeded in making a more or less correct line round the foundations. Today we shall have 2 teams and a stronger plow—as we plan to make all the adobes we can, where the house is to stand."[83] In a notebook Curtin recorded that the plowing and making of the adobes in situ cost a total of $343.[84]

The biographies of the women who built Acequia Madre are as interesting as the house. Few photographs of the three together exist, but one shows Eva and her daughter Leonora at San Ildefonso Pueblo meeting with famed potters Julian and Maria Martinez. The Fényes-Curtin women often visited the Indian pueblos of New Mexico. For instance, the *New Mexican* reported in September 1920: "Mrs. Thomas Curtin left with a party today for San Juan to attend the Indian dance given there."[85]

Eva Scott Muse Fényes (1849–1930), the daughter of wealthy New York publisher Leonard Scott, was a successful investor and an accomplished artist. Her first husband was U.S. Marine General W. S. Muse. She came to Santa Fe in the late 1880s, and after building a new adobe home on Hillside Avenue, she became an active member of the city's social life; among her acquaintances was archaeologist Adolph Bandelier. She later became an initial member of the Spanish Colonial Arts Society, which brought about a renaissance of the textiles, and wood and metal crafts of Hispano New Mexicans.

She met her second husband, Dr. Adalbert Fényes, while traveling and studying art in Egypt. Together they settled in Pasadena, California. At the urging of Charles Lummis, and because of her own interest in preservation, Eva spent more than thirty years documenting in watercolor the California missions and other historic adobe buildings.[86] Eva also sketched her own home, Acequia Madre House, shortly after it was completed in 1927. The watercolors serve as records of the original configuration of the house. For instance, in one sketch we can see where a sleeping porch was once located on the west side. Screened or glass-enclosed sleeping porches, where people could take advantage of Santa Fe's healthful air, were a popular feature in 1920s homes.[87]

Dining room, Acequia Madre House

Detail of fireplace, Acequia Madre House

Eva's daughter, Leonora, first came to Santa Fe in the late 1880s with her mother and developed a lifelong interest in the art and archaeology of Spanish and Native American New Mexico. After marrying lawyer Thomas E. Curtin of Santa Fe, she lived in Colorado Springs, where her husband developed railroads and resorts. Their daughter, Leonora Frances Curtin (Paloheimo), was born in 1903, and after Thomas Curtin's death in 1911, the two Leonoras moved to Pasadena to live with Eva. Together the three traveled around the world before designing their special retreat in Santa Fe, where they had spent summers and holidays for many decades.[88]

Leonora Frances Curtin (Paloheimo) played a major role in the preservation and revival of Spanish arts and crafts. She was a founding member of the Spanish Colonial Arts Society, opened the Native Market crafts store in Santa Fe, and with her husband, Y. A. Paloheimo, established El Rancho de las Golondrinas in La Ciénega, New Mexico—a living history museum of Spanish Colonial life. Leonora also became renowned for her research and books on the ethno-botany of New Mexico.

With its overall linearity and crisp formality, Acequia Madre is a classic example of the Territorial Revival manner. In September 1926, shortly after the house was completed, the *New Mexican* ran an editorial on the successful "crusade to stamp the Indian-Spanish character upon Santa Fe building," in which Acequia Madre was praised. "The large Fenyes-Curtin residence . . . shows an increasing trend toward the true Spanish colonial hacienda style as distinguished from the Pueblo," wrote the editor.[89]

The Fényes-Curtin women insisted on authenticity in the methods and materials used in constructing their house. Erected by Santa Fe builder Charles Campbell, the house consists of adobes mostly handmade at the site.[90] The adobe walls were plastered with mud (later stuccoed over), brick dentil coping was installed on the parapet, and the windows were adorned with pedimented lintels. The flat roof was initially topped by six inches of dirt for insulation. The Fényes-Curtin women included a few characteristics of the Pueblo Revival style, including a recessed porch with brown-stained columns and corbels at the front entrance, and protruding vigas over the sleeping porch (later remodeled).

Rossiter's specifications provide much information on the materials and techniques used to build the house. For example, the brickwork for the cornice is "Santa Fe, hard burned, common red brick"; the vigas in the spacious living room and dining room were "tooled with a broad axe or adz so as to appear hand hewn"; and the vigas in all other rooms are "common round vigas." Most of the interior woodwork is "kiln dried and carefully milled Oregon fir"; the floors in the dining and living rooms are "Bruce select oak"; and the interior paint was the "Sanbusco" brand.[91]

In addition, the specifications state that exterior adobe walls are sixteen inches in thickness, interior adobe walls are fourteen inches in thickness, and all the adobe bricks are set in mud mortar. And "Ceilings in rooms other than in living and dining rooms, exposed beams, corbels etc. shall be stained to give a weathered appearance, under the supervision of the Owner."

Over the years the Fényes-Curtin women ensured that any additions to the house and property were in keeping with the original style. In 1928 Leonora Frances Curtin (Paloheimo) wrote to her grandmother that the green pots they were considering buying for the garden "should be of primitive design so as not to look out of place and distract the eye."[92]

Like the original Territorial-style homes, the floor plan is flexible, with most rooms opening onto a central hallway. Initially the house consisted of three bedrooms, two bathrooms, a living and dining room, a kitchen, and one porch on the east side and one sleeping porch on the west side. A distinctive feature is the magnificent large arched entryway that leads from the living room into the dining room, which may reflect the influence of Wallace Neff, who typically used this detail in his homes.[93]

Interior walls have a smooth plaster finish and the woodwork is either painted or stained a dark brown. Some features, including the Arts and Crafts–style metal lighting fixtures in the living room, were ordered from companies in Pasadena. The Fényes-Curtin women were fairly economi-

cal in building the home; for instance, as noted on the blueprints for the house, they used stock fir-wood doors for the interior.[94] However, for the main entrance, the women hired a craftsman to make a replica of an antique door they had admired on "an ancient Colonial House on Palace Ave."[95] The massive green-painted door was constructed from fir with a panel design and eight overlights.

The fireplace in the living room has a distinct design, based on the collaboration of Eva Fényes and her artist friends Sheldon Parsons and George Cole. It consists of cement spiral columns ordered from Pasadena, California, and blue and white tiles that were purchased in 1924 in Valencia, Spain. The dominant hood is reminiscent of fireplaces in Spain and was typically used in Spanish Mission Revival homes designed by Neff and his contemporaries in 1920s California. An early photograph shows that a bearskin rug was once placed on the floor in front of the hearth.

Some rooms in the house had views of the mountain landscape—vistas that today are obscured by giant cottonwood trees planted on the grounds. Eva Fényes wrote in October 1926, shortly after moving in, "I am sitting by my 'picture window' looking at the mts. with their patches of golden aspen woods. Oh! The glorious sunshine. One gets up every morning, with a feeling of joy & thankfulness."[96]

Now owned by an operating foundation dedicated to the preservation of the house and grounds, Acequia Madre has retained all of its original architectural features, as well as the family's furnishings and art. The relatively simple design of the interior spaces serves as a backdrop for the antique furniture, paintings, and rare Spanish Colonial and American Indian art collected by the Fényes-Curtin women. Included are examples of Maria Martinez's pottery; very old objects purchased by Eva Fényes in Mexico and Spain; antiques from other European countries, including Germany and Italy; and reproduction Spanish furniture purchased in Pasadena.[97]

A particularly important feature of the interior is the handmade wood furniture, intricate tinwork, and textiles purchased in the 1930s at the Native Market, a cooperative for artisans making traditional Spanish New Mexican objects.[98] In addition to selling objects, the Native Market encouraged the revival of crafts by working closely with a training program in vocational schools throughout the state.

Many of the paintings in Acequia Madre were gifts from artists whom the family had supported in their early careers. Among them is Sheldon Parsons, whose painterly,

ABOVE

Acequia Madre House bedroom, with handcrafted wood beds and chests purchased from Native Market, Santa Fe

LEFT

Acequia Madre House, handcrafted tin chandelier, purchased from Native Market, Santa Fe

....

picturesque scenes of Santa Fe's landscape and architecture grace the walls. Works by Joseph Henry Sharp, Gustave Baumann, Gerald Cassidy, Oscar Borg, George Cole, and Julius Rolshoven are also in the home. The dining room contains a rare example of ceramic work by Frank Applegate. The house and collections of art are indeed an important legacy well worth preserving. As Bunny Pierce Huffman, director of the Acequia Madre House explains, "Not simply patrons, these women devised practical and energetic solutions to conserve and protect past cultures and give them a future."[99]

This five-thousand-square-foot adobe and its surrounding 2.6 acres were originally intended to be part of a center for anthropological studies—an ambitious project proposed and financed in 1928–29 by John D. Rockefeller Jr., philanthropist and heir to the Standard Oil fortune. It was to consist of thirty-eight buildings: laboratories, a museum, a Navajo building, research and administrative offices, a library, residential quarters, and service structures.[100] The building committee chosen to oversee the project specified the Spanish Pueblo Revival style for the proposed complex. A national architectural competition was held, and local architect John Gaw Meem was chosen as the winner. Only two structures were ever built—the administration/research building (now called the Laboratory of Anthropology on Museum Hill) and the director's residence. Due to the collapsed U.S. economy in the

LEFT

John Gaw Meem's Laboratory of Anthropology Director's Residence

ABOVE

John Gaw Meem's sketch of the Laboratory of Anthropology Director's Residence, ca. 1930

John Gaw Meem Drawings and Plans, University of New Mexico Center for Southwest Research

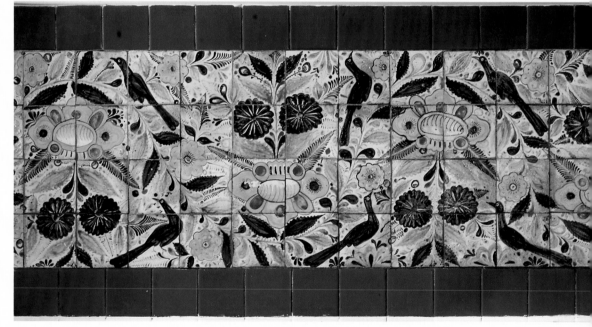

TOP LEFT

Detail of living room ceiling, alternating vigas and latillas, Laboratory of Anthropology Director's Residence

BOTTOM LEFT

Curving doorway, Laboratory of Anthropology Director's Residence

TOP RIGHT

Spacious living room (now museum gallery) with large corner fireplace, Laboratory of Anthropology Director's Residence

BOTTOM RIGHT

Mexican tile mural in former kitchen, Laboratory of Anthropology Director's Residence

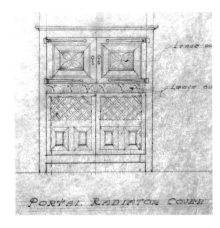

TOP LEFT
*Original tin light fixture, Laboratory
of Anthropology Director's Residence*

TOP CENTER
*Meem drawing for radiator cover, Laboratory
of Anthropology Director's Residence, ca. 1930*
John Gaw Meem Drawings and Plans, University
of New Mexico Center for Southwest Research

TOP RIGHT
*Meem radiator cover in the Laboratory
of Anthropology Director's Residence*

ABOVE
Alacena in former dining room

early 1930s, Rockefeller's grand plan was eventually
scrapped.

The first residents of the house were Jesse and Aileen
Nusbaum. Aileen (1889–1979) was a writer and artist, and
Jesse (1887–1975) served as the first director of the Laboratory of Anthropology from 1930 to 1935. Jesse was an archaeologist, photographer, architectural consultant, and
advocate of the new-old Santa Fe style. He supervised the
Palace of the Governors renovations and the building of the
art museum in the 1910s.

Since 2002 the building has housed the Museum of
Spanish Colonial Art. It is operated by the Spanish Colonial Arts Society, which was founded in the mid-1920s by
writer Mary Austin and artist Frank Applegate with the
mission to "preserve and revive" Spanish Colonial art. The
organization now owns more than three thousand religious
and utilitarian artifacts, dating from the sixteenth century
to the present, all of which pertain to the Spanish Colonial
history of New Mexico and the world. Bultos, retablos, textiles, straw appliqué, furniture, ironwork, and tinwork are
some of the many items on display.

The museum building is a fine example of John Gaw
Meem's Spanish Pueblo Revival–style residences in Santa
Fe.[101] As the city's premier architect in the early to mid-
twentieth century, he was perhaps the most influential figure in the architectural transformation of the city during
that time. The director's residence is also significant
because it represents Meem's special connection with the
Spanish Colonial Arts Society. Meem and his wife, Faith,
were active members of the society since its incorporation
in 1929, and John served on its first exhibitions committee.
Over the following sixty years, the Meems made major
donations to the collection, including 34 New Mexican
textiles and 147 bultos and retablos.

An engineer by training, Meem first came to Santa Fe in 1920 seeking a cure for tuberculosis. He stayed at the Sunmount Sanatorium, owned and directed by Dr. Frank Mera, and when his health improved he immersed himself in the study of historic New Mexican architecture. He never completed his architectural training and yet he flourished as one of the most important regional architects. In the end he designed numerous public buildings and around 150 houses in and around Santa Fe for wealthy, spirited clients.

Meem was also an active historic preservationist: in 1947, as chairman of the City Planning Commission, he assisted in protecting the character of downtown Santa Fe by helping develop the city's first master plan. And as the chairman of the New Mexico Society for the Restoration and Preservation of New Mexico Mission Churches, he oversaw the restoration of dozens of historic mission churches, including those at Acoma, Laguna, and Zia pueblos.

Built for about $35,000, the director's residence was completed by the general contractors Edward Lembke and Company. The layout of the residence is a classic Meem design: the asymmetric yet balanced building is entered through a picturesque portal, the family bedrooms and service functions are in separate wings, and a sunroom (portal with removable windows) along the south facade leads to a patio with garden views of Sunmount Mountain.

Because the house was originally intended for the director of the Laboratory of Anthropology, who would have used it to entertain visitors and host receptions, Meem designed a series of rooms that allows for the easy flow of large numbers of people, as well as a formal living room that could comfortably accommodate a large group. Meem gave the living room regional character by designing an elaborate ceiling of regularly spaced hand-hewn vigas and diagonally placed latillas, and placing a large adobe fireplace in the corner.[102]

The light-filled house also provides easy access to the outdoors, for Meem typically opened out his floor plans to create sheltered courtyards and terraces. In the residence/museum building he created a long, deep covered porch or sunroom with multiple doors and windows leading to a flagstone patio that offers spectacular views of the piñon- and juniper-studded hills.

The house is constructed of hollow terra-cotta blocks laid to simulate the irregular contours of adobe walls. Locally referred to as "pentile," because it once was made at

TOP

Meem preliminary sketch of fireplace and sitting area, Laboratory of Anthropology Director's Residence, ca. 1930

John Gaw Meem Drawings and Plans, University of New Mexico Center for Southwest Research

BOTTOM

Cozy corner with fireplace and banco, Laboratory of Anthropology Director's Residence

John Gaw Meem, ca. 1930s

John Gaw Meem Collection, University of New Mexico Center for Southwest Research

. . . .

the state penitentiary in Santa Fe, the blocks were striated, so the mortar adhered better to the surface. The building was then completed with a coat of adobe-colored stucco in the smooth finish that Meem preferred. A number of the windows have Territorial-style trim.

The building illustrates the architect's signature features. Meem liked shapes that imitated the soft, rounding curves of adobes—visible in the curvy, uneven silhouette of doorways, windowsills, and fireplaces throughout the residence/museum. His drawings for the building show exactly where he wanted the plaster to be uneven and of different thicknesses, again in imitation of adobe. In Meem's bid specifications for this residence he warned the contractors that "The chief characteristics of this building are irregular contours of its wall surfaces and silhouettes. . . . In general, the masonry is to reflect primitive adobe and therefore is to be laid more by eye than by plumb, square and level. Deviation from the straight line are shown on drawings."[103]

Like many architects and builders in 1930s Santa Fe, Meem purchased tiles and other decorative architectural fea-

tures from Tony Taylor's shop, Old Mexico.[104] The blue, green, and yellow Mexican tile mural in the original kitchen of the house (now the gift shop) portraying birds and flowers likely came from this source.[105] Meem also arranged for the lighting fixtures in this building, which consisted of nineteenth-century New Mexican tin sconces that were electrified, as well as sconces of "typical Mexican design" made by a craftsman named Sweringen.[106] Most of the original fixtures are now in storage, except for two tin fixtures with red and green painted decoration that are installed in the museum's entrance hall.

Meem's drawings for the interior include the design and placement of every handmade decorative detail, including the corbels for the front portal, doors, cupboards, fireplace grilles, a hood for the stove, doors, and shelving. In addition, he created at least six different designs for covers to hide the unsightly hot water radiators in the house. Some of the shields are quite elaborate, with solid and open panels filled with spindles.

When designing residences like this one, Meem replicated the built-in furniture, such as bancos, wall niches, and shelves of colonial New Mexico homes. For example, in the dining room (now an exhibit room) of this building is an alacena from a home in northern New Mexico.[107] Built-ins such as this were also a popular feature in the space-saving, early-1900s Craftsman bungalows.

At one end of the sunroom in this building is a cozy sitting area consisting of a fireplace and adjoining built-in adobe banco. Meem made several preliminary sketches of the area, suggesting it was an important feature. He generally liked to include as many of these social areas as possible in his homes. After meeting with one client he noted, "Provide as many terraces, portales, and nooks as possible so as to make the whole interesting in appearance and inviting to lounge in."[108]

DOROTHY S. MCKIBBIN HOUSE
1099 OLD SANTA FE TRAIL
1936

In the early 1930s, during weekends off from her job at the Spanish and Indian Trading Company in Santa Fe, Dorothy S. McKibbin toured rural northern New Mexico and photographed and sketched the distinctive features of crumbling old houses.[109] When it was clear a building was being torn down, she searched through piles of debris to salvage corbels, vigas, window frames, gates, doors, and any other interesting fragments. Back in Santa Fe, she purchased additional antique furniture and tinwork made in New Mexico from various shops near the plaza.

McKibbin collected and safely stored all these photographs, sketches, and decorative pieces in preparation for her Santa Fe dream home. In 1936 her ambitions came true. In April of that year, McKibbin, a widow and mother of a five-year-old, purchased one and a half acres of land in the sandy, piñon-studded hills near Sunmount Sanatorium (where she had once stayed as a patient). She commissioned Katherine Stinson Otero (1891–1977) to draw up the plans for a home based on the typical Hispanic farm and ranch

LEFT

*Living room, Dorothy
McKibbin House*

ABOVE

*Portal and facade,
Dorothy McKibbin House*

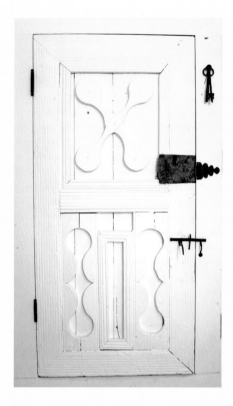

Door details, Dorothy McKibbin House

houses of late-nineteenth and early-twentieth-century New Mexico.[110] A famous pioneer aviator and the first woman to skywrite, fly airmail, and fly solo at night, Stinson Otero traveled to Santa Fe in 1920 to receive treatment for tuberculosis at Sunmount Sanatorium. She settled permanently in the city, married prominent New Mexico politician Miguel A. Otero Jr. in 1928, and turned to remodeling and designing homes after meeting and becoming friends with the architect John Gaw Meem.[111] She never received professional training as an architect and considered herself an "artist-designer," and yet during her lifetime her work received wide recognition and gained numerous awards in statewide design competitions.[112] For instance, in 1930 the home she designed for herself and her husband on East Manhattan Avenue won "best example of a new residence costing between $8,000 and $10,000" by a distinguished panel of judges, including Meem, Carlos Vierra, and others.[113]

According to the current owners of the house, who knew Dorothy well, McKibbin liked to tell a story about how she walked around the property with the builders and drew marks in the earth to delineate the floor plan. This may be true, but Stinson Otero did eventually make detailed architectural drawings for the house, as she did for the other

buildings she designed.[114] She made notations for the number of vigas needed in the ceilings, the measurements for recessed radiators with wood grill fronts, the exact shape and location of fireplaces, and other crucial information.

The house Stinson Otero designed replicated the traditions that McKibbin eagerly sought: thick adobe walls; a U-shape plan; a flat, built-up earthen roof; a partially enclosed patio; and front and rear portals. The front portal, supported by hand-carved corbels, is particularly impressive at sixty-five feet long and ten feet wide (see page 225). Originally the entire exterior was mud plastered in the traditional manner, but later, possibly during the 1940s when labor was scarce in Santa Fe, most of the surfaces were stuccoed. However, at present, the walls under the front and rear portals, where they are protected from the elements, still have smooth, straw-tempered mud-plaster finishes—red hued on the front and yellow hued in the rear. The earth used in the plaster came from a deposit at the base of La Bajada Hill outside Santa Fe.[115]

A remarkable series of photographs was taken of the house during construction, providing valuable information concerning the authentic methods used.[116] The shots portray a crew of workmen peeling aspen latillas for the living room

Dorothy McKibbin's photograph of zigzag molding on window and door of a house in Pojaque, New Mexico, 1930s
The McKibbin collection of Mary and Curtiss Brennan

Zigzag window detail, Dorothy McKibbin House

Dorothy McKibbin's photograph of a window under a portal in a Galisteo, New Mexico, house, 1930s
The McKibbin collection of Mary and Curtiss Brennan

Window detail, Dorothy McKibbin House

Corner fireplace, Dorothy McKibbin House

ceiling; adobes being made with mud and straw; adobes being laid in courses for the walls; the screening and throwing up of dirt on the roof; and the positioning of vigas and latillas in the living room ceiling. As all the images illustrate, the dirt used for the roof and the adobes came directly from the land surrounding the house.

A tiny notebook in which McKibbin scribbled remarks about the house gives us further information on the construction process.[117] We learn, for instance, that the house cost a little over $9,000 to build; the number of adobe bricks used was 16,996; and the cost of making those adobes was a mere $442. She listed the names of the carpenters, made drawings of furniture she wanted constructed, noted names of adobe plasterers (Simon Apodaca, $3 per day and Fred Abeyeta, $2 per day), listed expenses for the project ($60 for "spindles & rails," $40 for "red portal," $125 for stone, $85 for "hauling adobes"), and mentioned sources for santos and tinwork. She even included recipes for "fixative for adobe," furniture and floor polishes, and a solution "to kill bedbugs." Another recipe was for calcimine whitewash, a traditional finish McKibbin used on the walls throughout the interior.

Included in the notebook are a few drawings of architectural details and notations of where all the doors were to be placed; some of the doors are identified by style or place of origin (such as Mora or Apodaca, New Mexico). This remarkable collection of handcrafted doors with folk designs is among the many decorative elements that McKibbin rescued from deteriorated rural homes and had Stinson Otero incorporate into the house. They range in date from the seventeenth to nineteenth century. Also, the square-adzed lintels and uniquely carved zapatas of the portal along the south facade date to the early nineteenth century and are from a house in Belen, a village on the lower Rio Grande.[118]

In addition, some wooden features are replicas inspired by details in older houses. Sometime before building her house, McKibbin took photographs of an old adobe house in Pojaque, a rural village north of Santa Fe, that had a window and door with "zigzag" lintels.[119] She had a carpenter replicate this unusual detail for a window in her Old Santa Fe Trail house. She also took a photograph of a window frame in a historic house in Galisteo, another small rural village south of Santa Fe, which was later replicated twice in the McKibbin home.

On the interior are several pieces of tinwork that McKibbin collected for the house, as well as exquisitely hand-molded corner fireplaces (based on photographs McKibbin took of hearths in rural New Mexico homes) and a spacious living room with a traditional New Mexico ceiling of latillas and vigas.

In 1943 McKibbin began working for the Manhattan Project in Los Alamos, New Mexico. Located on a mesa top, it was where the first atomic bombs were created. With an office at 109 East Palace Avenue in Santa Fe, Dorothy became known as the official "gatekeeper" to the project—no one could go through the gate at Los Alamos without a pass from her. She met top scientists from around the world, including J. Robert Oppenheimer, the physicist who directed the building of the atomic bombs and who became one of her closest friends. "We sensed the excitement and suspense of the Project, for the intensity of the people coming through the office was contagious," McKibbin later wrote.[120]

Her gracious home on Old Santa Fe Trail became an oasis and "safe house" for Oppenheimer and other scientists, where they could stay overnight, hold meetings, and dine together in absolute secrecy.

McKibbin stayed on at 109 East Palace until her retirement in 1963. Twenty-three years later her house was listed on the New Mexico State Registry of Historic Places.

TOP
Workmen peeling aspen latillas for the ceiling, 1936

CENTER
Workman making adobes with mud and straw, 1936

BOTTOM
Workmen laying adobes in courses for the walls, 1936

TOP
Workmen screening and throwing up dirt for the roof, 1936

BOTTOM
Workman positioning the vigas and latillas in the ceiling, 1936

All images: The McKibbin collection of Mary and Curtiss Brennan

ACKNOWLEDGMENTS

I COULD NOT HAVE completed this enormous book project without the assistance of many kindhearted and knowledgeable individuals. First and foremost, Steve Larese—friend, colleague, and photographer extraordinaire—deserves the most recognition and biggest thanks of all. His cheerfulness, advice, patience, and photography skills made him the perfect project partner. Remarkably he never said "no" and kindly put up with my last-minute craziness. Thank you, Steve!

Secondly, I am grateful to my superb editor, Alex Tart, whose sage advice, guidance, patience, and friendship made the nerve-racking process of writing this book much less difficult and much more rewarding. And my gratitude to designer Sara Stemen, who has once again produced a stunning layout.

I am also indebted to Elaine Bergman, executive director, Historic Santa Fe Foundation (HSFF), who answered my millions of questions and opened up the HSFF archives to me; Daniel Kosharek, photo archivist, Palace of the Governors, who cheerfully put up with my last-minute photo requests and guided me through the museum's extensive collection; John W. Murphey, architectural historian and state and national register coordinator for the New Mexico Historic Preservation Division, Santa Fe, who was so helpful with many aspects of my research; and Bunny Pierce Huffman, director of Acequia Madre House, for sharing all she knew about the historic house under her care and for being so understanding and supportive.

Additionally, I am extremely grateful to the colleagues who wrote such insightful essays for the book: Jim Hare, executive director, Cornerstones Community Partnerships; and Audra Bellmore, curator, the John Gaw Meem Archives of Southwestern Architecture and assistant professor, Center for Southwest Research.

Thank you to the following kind souls who were instrumental in providing answers to my research requests, or arranging for tours of historic properties, or loaning images for the book: Ana Archuleta, art assistant to Gerald Peters; Alexa K. Hokanson, director of marketing and communications at La Posada; Patricia Lucero, Clerk, Historic Preservation Division, Santa Fe; Cordelia Thomas Snow, archaeologist, Santa Fe; William Field, director, and Robin Farwell Gavin, chief curator, Museum of Spanish Colonial Art, Santa Fe; Father Tien-Tri Nguyen of Santuario de Guadalupe Church; Stephen Post, deputy director, Office of Archaeological Studies, Museum of New Mexico; Tomas Jaehn, Fray Angélico Chavéz History Library; Nick Rugen of the Historic Santa Fe Foundation; Tom Appelquist, architect; Bettina Raphael of the Olive Rush Home and Studio–Santa Fe Religious Society of Friends Meeting House; Laura Holt, librarian, McElvain Library, School for Advanced Research, Santa Fe; Laura Verlaque, collections manager, Research Library and Archives, Pasadena Museum of History; and the staffs at the Santa Fe Public Library, the New Mexico State Library and State Records Center & Archives, and the Center for Southwest Research at the University of New Mexico.

To all the house owners who so generously invited me into their homes and into their lives, and shared as much information on their historic properties as they could, I am eternally grateful. This book would not have been as comprehensive or as successful without your assistance.

And a special thank you to Carolyn MacArthur, Ana Matiella, Dan Stubbs, Alex Pennington (and Bob, too), for their unwavering friendship and support. Oh, and of course, there is the ever-patient, always-loving husband of mine, Martin Booker, without whom this book never would have seen the light of day.

SELECTED BIBLIOGRAPHY

BOOKS

Armstrong, Patricia Cadigan. *Bronson Cutting, 1910–1927*. Albuquerque: University of New Mexico, 1959.

Dary, David. *The Santa Fe Trail: Its History, Legends, and Lore*. New York: Alfred A. Knopf, 2000.

Drumm, Stella M. *Down the Santa Fe Trail and into Mexico: The Diary of Susan Shelby Magoffin, 1846–47*. Lincoln and London: University of Nebraska Press, 1982.

Duchscherer, Paul. *The Bungalow: America's Arts and Crafts Home*. New York: Penguin Studio, 1995.

Foote, Cheryl J. *Women of the New Mexico Frontier, 1846–1912*. Albuquerque: University of New Mexico Press, 2005.

Jaehn, Tomas. *Germans in the Southwest, 1850–1920*. Albuquerque: University of New Mexico Press, 2005.

Keleher, William A. *New Mexicans I Knew: Memoirs, 1892–1969*. Albuquerque: University of New Mexico Press, 1983.

Lancaster, Clay. *The American Bungalow, 1880–1930*. New York: Dover Publications, Inc., 1985.

Markovich, Nicholas C., Wolfgang F. E. Preiser, and Fred G. Sturm, eds. *Pueblo Style and Regional Architecture*. New York: Van Nostrand Reinhold, 1990.

Seth, Sandra, and Laurel Seth. *Adobe! Homes and Interiors of Taos, Santa Fe and the Southwest*. Stamford, Connecticut: Architectural Book Publishing Company, 1988.

Sommer, Robin Langley, and David Rago, eds. *The Arts and Crafts Movement*. Edison, New Jersey: Chartwell Books, Inc., 1995.

Warren, Nancy Hunter. *New Mexico Style: A Sourcebook of Traditional Architectural Details*. Santa Fe: Museum of New Mexico Press, 1995.

JOURNAL ARTICLES

Anonymous, "Barrio de Analco," *Bulletin of the Historic Santa Fe Foundation* 8, no. 1 (June 1981): 2.

Anonymous. "The Santa Fe Celebration," *Harper's Weekly*, July 14, 1883 (page 445).

Bohme, Frederick G. "The Italians in New Mexico," *New Mexico Historical Review* XXXIV, no. 2 (April 1959): 98–111.

Boyd, E. "Domestic Architecture in New Mexico," *El Palacio* 79, no. 3: 12–29.

Bunting, Bainbridge. "El Zaguan," *Bulletin of the Historic Santa Fe Foundation* 3, no. 1 (March/April 1977): 1–4.

Bunting, Bainbridge, and John P. Conron. "The Architecture of Northern New Mexico," *New Mexico Architecture* 8, nos. 9 & 10 (October 1966).

Conron, John P. and R. Patrick Christopher, "The Architecture of Santa Fe: A Survey of Styles," *New Mexico Architecture* 20, no. 5 (September–October 1978): 12–35.

Hewett, Edgar L. "Santa Fe in 1926," *Papers of the School of American Archaeology*, no. 39 (1917): 8–12.

López, Alejandro. "The Enjarradora Folk Art Tradition of Northern New Mexico," *Adobe Journal*, no. 8 (Winter 1992): 30–33.

Purdy, James H. "The Carlos Vierra House," *Bulletin of the Historic Santa Fe Foundation* 5, no. 1 (January 1979): 1–12.

_____. "The Fort Marcy Officer's Residence—A Case for Renovation," *New Mexico Architecture* 17, no. 4 (July–August 1975): 12–23.

Spears, Beverley. "Santa Fe's Westside/Guadalupe Historic District: Hispanic Vernacular Versus Pueblo Revival," *New Mexico Architecture* 31, no. 5 & 6 (September/October–November/December 1990): 9–13.

Sze, Corinne P. "A Martyr to Progress: The Tin Roof Comes to New Mexico," *Bulletin of the Historic Santa Fe Foundation* 29, no. 1 (Autumn 2002): 1–24.

_____. "The Harry Howard Dorman House," *Bulletin of the Historic Santa Fe Foundation* 28, no. 1 (November 2001): 1–21.

_____. "The Santa Fe Railway's Santa Fe Passenger Depot," *Bulletin of the Historic Santa Fe Foundation* 20, no. 1 (February 1992): 1–11.

Valdez, Arnie and Maria. "Hispanic Contributions to the Adobe Architecture of New Mexico," *Adobe Journal*, no. 8 (1992): 36–41.

NOTES

Abbreviations in Notes

CSWR: Center for Southwest Research, University Libraries, University of New Mexico, Albuquerque, New Mexico

HPD: Historic Preservation Division, Department of Cultural Affairs, Santa Fe

HSFF: Historic Santa Fe Foundation

SF-DNM: Santa Fe *Daily New Mexican* newspaper

SF-NM: Santa Fe *New Mexican* newspaper

INTRODUCTION

1. Susan E. Wallace, "Among the Pueblos," *The Atlantic Monthly* 46, no. 274 (August 1880): 215.
2. José Antonio Esquibel, "Founders of the Villa de Santa Fe," *La Herencia* 55 (Fall 2007): 44.
3. "The Borrego House," HABS No. NM-14, typescript report, 1940, 2, HSFF files. The Victorian-era features of this fireplace surround are no longer visible; a recent owner stuccoed over the features.
4. "Conversations in Santa Fe with Lewis Mumford, no. 2," *New Mexico Architect* 5, nos. 1 and 2 (January–February 1963): 5.
5. Ernest Ingersoll, "La Villa Real de Santa Fe," *Harper's New Monthly Magazine* 60, no. 359 (April 1880): 678.
6. "Santa Fe Artists Exhibit Paintings," SF-NM, 26 August 1916.
7. Santa Fe *Daily New Mexican*, 8 October 1889.
8. Charles F. Lummis, "The Land of Poco Tiempo," *Scribner's Magazine* 10, no. 6 (December 1891): 760, 762, 764.

CHAPTER ONE

1. John L. Kessel, *Spain in the Southwest* (Norman: University of Oklahoma Press, 2002), 98.
2. To "puddle" adobe the Indians laid down stiff, damp courses of mud about eight to ten inches deep, one on top of another, allowing each course to dry before placing the next course on. It was a painstaking, slow process.
3. James A. Abert in William A. Keleher, *Abert's New Mexico Report, 1846–47* (Albuquerque: Horn & Wallace Publishers, 1962), 61–62.
4. Stephen S. Post, "Buildings Lost and Found: Eighteenth-Century Foundations of a New Museum," *El Palacio* 111, no. 4 (Winter 2006): 40–41, 90.
5. It was 80,000 bricks, according to Max L. Moorhead in "Rebuilding the Presidio of Santa Fe, 1789–1791," *New Mexico Historical Review* XLIX, no. 2 (April 1974): 129. But according to a letter written by Pedro de Nava in 1791, it was 100,000 bricks. See SANM I:1238 or "Santa Fe Historic Plaza Study II," typescript, Cross-Cultural Research Systems for the City of Santa Fe, 1992, 40.
6. Joseph P. Sanchez, "The Peralta-Ordóñez Affair and the Founding of Santa Fe," in David Grant Noble, ed., *Santa Fe: History of an Ancient City* (Santa Fe: School for Advanced Research Press, 1989), 28.
7. Chris Wilson, *The Myth of Santa Fe: Creating a Modern Regional Tradition* (Albuquerque: University of New Mexico Press, 1997), 33.
8. Ibid., 34.
9. Eleanor B. Adams and Fray Angelico Chavez, eds., *The Missions of New Mexico, 1776: A Description By Fray Francisco Atanasio Dominguez* (Albuquerque: University of New Mexico Press, 1956), 40.
10. Ibid., 11.
11. "Santa Fe Historic Plaza Study II," 38.
12. Adams and Chavez, 39–40.
13. "Santa Fe Historic Plaza Study II," 34; original source SANM I: 169.
14. Wilson, 36.
15. "Santa Fe Historic Plaza Study II," 34; original source SANM I: 482.
16. Public Survey Office Document, 2 June 1738, Spanish Archives of New Mexico I: 521, Translations, roll 4. New Mexico State Library and Archives, Santa Fe.
17. Wilson, 37.
18. Ibid., 98.
19. Ibid.
20. Post, 90.
21. Museum of Spanish Colonial Art, Santa Fe, NM, exhibition brochure, "La Casa Delgado/The Delgado Home."
22. Wilson, 39.
23. Boyd C. Pratt, "A Brief History of the Practice of Architecture in New Mexico," *New Mexico Architecture* 30, no. 6 (November-December 1989): 8.
24. Quoted in John L. Kessell, "Not That Remote: Diego de Vargas and His Household in Santa Fe," *El Palacio* 109, no. 1 (Spring 2004): 29.
25. Moorhead, 128, 132.
26. "Santa Fe Historic Plaza Study," typescript, Cross-Cultural Research Systems for the City of Santa Fe, 1992, 42.
27. Emily Abbink, *New Mexico's Palace of the Governors: History of an American Treasure* (Santa Fe: Museum of New Mexico Press, 2007), 60.
28. Wilson, 41–42.
29. Abbink, 9.
30. Charles D. Biebel, "Civic Buildings," in New Mexico Historic Preservation Division, Office of Cultural Affairs, *Recording Vanishing Legacy: The Historic American Buildings Survey In New Mexico, 1933–Today* (Santa Fe: Museum of New Mexico Press, 2001), 96.
31. Abbink, 25.
32. Interview with Cordelia Thomas Snow, 7 March 2008. See also Cordelia Thomas Snow, "When the Palace of the Governors

Had a Second Story," *La Crónica de Nuevo México*, no. 35 (April 1993): 2–3.

33. Post, 40–41, 90.

34. Abbink, 40.

35. I am grateful to Cordelia Snow for telling me about this source. Report of the Cabildo to Felix Martinez, 13 July 1716, Spanish Archives of New Mexico II, no. 253, New Mexico State Records Center and Archives, Roll 5, Frames 564–67.

36. Spanish Archives of New Mexico II, no. 307, New Mexico State Records Center and Archives, Roll 5, Frames 1004–15.

37. Ibid. and Snow, 2.

38. Adams and Chavez, 40.

39. Abbink, 25.

40. "Santa Fe Historic Plaza Study II," 42. Original in SANM I: 1272.

41. Ibid., 43. This is based on Antonio Barreiro's 1832 account of the plaza.

42. Marian Russell, *Land of Enchantment* (Albuquerque: University of New Mexico Press, 1981), 46.

43. Snow, 2.

44. "Santa Fé," *Harper's Weekly* (13 September 1879): 733.

45. *American Anthropologist*, 1905.

46. Quoted in James H. Purdy, "The Oldest House, Application for Registration, New Mexico State Register of Cultural Properties, Santa Fe," 24 August 1976, HPD files.

47. "The 'Oldest House,'" typescript, no date, HSFF files. Thanks to Cordelia Thomas Snow for leading me to sources about tree ring dating.

48. Original deed dated 22 February 1859, in Santa Fe County Court House; copy in HSFF files.

49. "The 'Oldest House,'" typescript, no date, HSFF files.

50. See Bennett, number 10743; see Wittick, number 15845; and Brown, number 111462; Chase, number 14044 and 56982; Jackson, number 49170, all at the Palace of the Governors Photo Archives.

51. William G. Ritch, *Illustrated New Mexico, Historical and Industrial* (Santa Fe: The Bureau of Immigration, 1885), 153.

52. Quoted in Lansing B. Bloom, ed., "Bourke on the Southwest," *New Mexico Historical Review* (July 1935): 319.

53. Wayne L. Mauzy, ed., "Fort Marcy and Santa Fe in 1889: The Journal of Caroline Douglass," *El Palacio* 67, no. 5 (October 1960): 169.

54. SF-DNM, 29 February 1892.

55. SF-DNM, 22 July 1898.

56. Tom Sharpe, "Landmark redux: One of Santa Fe's oldest structures gets a makeover," SF-NM, 16 May 2003.

57. "See Oldest House and Rare Old Curios," SF-NM, 2 April 1928.

58. See "The Gregorio Crespin House," typescript, HSFF files, and Bryant Bannister to Edwin Ferdon, 17 January 1962, HSFF files.

59. "The Gregorio Crespin House," typescript, HSFF files.

60. Biographical data is from James H. Purdy, "National Register of Historic Places Inventory—Nomination Form for the Gregorio Crespin House," 30 January 1973, Historic Preservation Division.

61. The Historic Santa Fe Foundation, *Old Santa Fe Today* (Santa Fe/Albuquerque: Historic Santa Fe Foundation/University of New Mexico Press, 1991), 42.

62. The history of the structure is also drawn from James H. Purdy, "National Register of Historic Places Inventory—Nomination Form for The Gregorio Crespin House," 30 January 1973, Historic Preservation Division.

63. Katherine Van Stone Mayer, "132 East De Vargas Street," typescript, 3 July 1961, HSFF files.

64. The beams are illustrated in Brother B. Lewis, *Oldest Church in U.S.: The San Miguel Chapel* (Santa Fe, 1968).

65. Rexford Newcomb, *Spanish-Colonial Architecture in the United States* (New York: J. J. Augustin, 1937; reprint, New York: Dover Publications, Inc., 1990), plate 41.

66. Estevan Rael-Galvez, in a lecture entitled "Of Mud and Memory: Narrative of Place," presented in 2008, St. Francis Auditorium, Santa Fe.

67. Jason S. Shapiro, *Before Santa Fe: Archaeology of the City Different* (Santa Fe: Museum of New Mexico Press, 2008), 20, 31.

68. For further information on Santa Fe's earliest inhabitants and their building types see Stephen S. Post, "Ancient Santa Fe: Ten Thousand Years of High Desert Living," in David Grant Noble, ed., *Santa Fe: History of an Ancient City* (Santa Fe: School for Advanced Research Press, 2008): 1–13.

69. Jerilou Hammett, Kinglsey Hammett, and Peter Scholz, *The Essence of Santa Fe: From a Way of Life to a Style* (Santa Fe: Ancient City Press, 2006), 14.

70. Quoted in Stephen Trimble, *The People: Indians of the American Southwest* (Santa Fe: School for Advanced Research Press, 1993): 44.

71. Post, 10.

CHAPTER TWO

1. Biographical information on Manuel Armijo was drawn from Janet Lecompte and Joseph P. Sánchez, "When Santa Fe Was a Mexican Town, 1821–1846," in David Grant Noble, ed., *Santa Fe: History of an Ancient City* (Santa Fe: School for Advanced Research Press, 2008), 63–64.

2. Emily Abbink, *New Mexico's Palace of the Governors: History of an American Treasure* (Santa Fe: Museum of New Mexico Press, 2007), 69.

3. Lecompte and Sánchez, 60.

4. Ibid., 61.

5. Santa Fe Historic Plaza Study II," typescript, Cross-Cultural Research Systems for the City of Santa Fe, 1992, 44.

6. Ralph P. Bieber, ed., *Adventures in the Santa Fé Trade* (Lincoln: University of Nebraska Press, 1995), 92.

7. Information relating to the Palace's appearance in this time period is from Abbink, 68.

8. Lecompte and Sánchez, 58–59.

9. Josiah Gregg, *Commerce of the Prairies* (J. and Henry G. Langley, 1844; reprint: Norman, Oklahoma: University of Oklahoma Press, 1990), 144.

10. All information concerning this code is drawn from John O. Baxter, "Civic Reform in Santa Fe, 1845," *Bulletin of the Historic Santa Fe Foundation* 10, no. 3 (October 1982): 1–4. The original document: Mexican Archives of New Mexico, Communications of Local Officials, 1845, State Records Center and Archives, Santa Fe, NM.

11. Sally Ventres, "Historic Guadalupe Neighborhood Association," *Bulletin of the Historic Santa Fe Foundation* 24, no. 1 (March 1997): 10.

12. Ralph Emerson Twitchell, *The History of the Military Occupation of the Territory of New Mexico, from 1846 to 1851* (Denver: The Smith-Brooks Co., Publishers, 1909), 209.

13. Corinne P. Sze, ed., *Within Adobe Walls: A Santa Fe Journal* (Santa Fe: The Historic Santa Fe Foundation, 2001), 15.

14. Lynn Cline, "House's past enriches the present," SF-NM, 1 December 1996.

15. All early data on the Vigil property is drawn from "Donaciano Vigil House," National Register of Historic Places Inventory—Nomination Form, 1969, HSFF files.

16. For a good description of the various restoration efforts see Myra Ellen Jenkins, "The Donaciano Vigil House," *Bulletin of the Historic Santa Fe Foundation* 12, no. 3 (December 1984): 1–9.

17. Lynn Cline, "House's past enriches the present," SF-NM, 1 December 1996.

18. There is some debate as to which property the woodwork came from. In her own book,

White says St. Michaels, but subsequent studies suggest it was the Loretto. Some of the Lumpkin doors were "left lying around outside" and not installed until Charlotte White and Boris Gilbertson restored the house in the 1960s. Sze, 30.

19. The 1960s restoration is well documented in Sze, *Within Adobe Walls*.
20. Sze, 70.
21. SF-DNM, 10 March 1882.
22. "Sena Plaza" brochure, HPD files.
23. Bieber, 92–93.
24. SF-DNM, 30 June 1869.
25. *The New Mexican Review*, 19 July 1883.
26. Charles D. Biebel, "Civic Buildings," in New Mexico Historic Preservation Division, Office of Cultural Affairs, *Recording a Vanishing Legacy: The Historic American Buildings Survey in New Mexico, 1933–Today* (Santa Fe: Museum of New Mexico Press, 2001), 95.
27. SF-DNM, 27 July 1868.
28. SF-DNM, 10 April 1869.
29. SF-NM, 10 September 1900; 2 October 1909.
30. Chris Wilson, *The Myth of Santa Fe: Creating a Modern Regional Tradition* (Albuquerque: University of New Mexico Press, 1997), 183.
31. SF-DNM, 5 June 1889. Wilson, 244.
32. Wilson, 245.
33. The Sena house also underwent renovation work in 1982, 1984, and 1990-91. See "125–137 East Palace Avenue," New Mexico Historic Building Inventory—Santa Fe Resurvey 1995, HSFF files.
34. SF-NM, 3 April 1926.
35. Edna Robertson and Sarah Nestor, *Artists of the Canyons & Caminos, Santa Fe: Early Twentieth Century* (Santa Fe: Ancient City Press, 2006), 105.
36. Ibid., 106.
37. SF-NM, 15 September 1926.
38. Daria Labinsky and Stan Hieronymus, *Frank Applegate of Santa Fe: Artist and Preservationist* (Albuquerque: LPD Press, 2002), 64, 93.
39. Wilson, 245.
40. The span at Giusewa, a mission now in ruins adjacent to Jemez Pueblo, was thirty-three feet. See G. Kubler, *Religious Architecture of New Mexico* (The Rio Grande Press, reprint 1962), 43.
41. Bainbridge Bunting, *Early Architecture in New Mexico* (Albuquerque: University of New Mexico Press, 1976), 55.

CHAPTER THREE

1. William A. Keleher, *Abert's New Mexico Report: 1846–47* (Albuquerque: Horn & Wallace, Publishers, 1962), 45.
2. Chris Wilson, *The Myth of Santa Fe: Creating A Modern Regional Tradition* (Albuquerque: University of New Mexico, 1997), 53.
3. Keleher, 5.
4. Ibid., 46.
5. Ibid.
6. Ibid., 42.
7. Paul Horgan, *Lamy of Santa Fe: A Biography* (New York: The Noonday Press, 1988), 123.
8. Keleher, 57.
9. Emily Abbink, *New Mexico's Palace of the Governors: History of an American Treasure* (Santa Fe: Museum of New Mexico Press, 2007), 78.
10. Ibid., 71-72.
11. Keleher, 57.
12. Horgan, 119.
13. David Remley, ed., *Adios Nuevo Mexico: The Santa Fe Journal of John Watts in 1859* (Las Cruces, New Mexico: Yucca Tree Press, 1999), 9.
14. SF-DNM, 7 October 1872.
15. Wilson, 53.
16. LeRoy R. Hafen, ed., *Ruxton of the Rockies* (Norman, Oklahoma: University of Oklahoma Press, 1950), 180.
17. Anna Maria de Camp Morris Diary (hereafter Morris Diary), 12 July 1850, Morris Collection, University of Virginia Library, Charlottesville, Virginia, microfilm reel M547.
18. W. W. H. Davis, *El Gringo: New Mexico and Her People* (New York: Harper, 1857; reprint, Lincoln: University of Nebraska Press, 1982), 234.
19. Davis, *El Gringo*, 40-41.
20. The house was eventually torn down in the early 1900s to make way for the New Mexico Museum of Art. Marian Russell, *Land of Enchantment: Memoirs of Marian Russell Along the Santa Fe Trail* (Albuquerque: University of New Mexico Press, 1981), 52.
21. Jane Lenz Elder and David J. Weber, *Trading in Santa Fe: John M. Kingsbury's Correspondence with James Josiah Webb, 1853-1861* (Dallas: Southern Methodist University Press/DeGolyer Library, 1996), 24, 28 n.50, 37. See also, SF-DNM, 24 July 1868, about his work for Judge Houghton.
22. Santa Fe *Weekly Gazette*, 22 May 1858.
23. Built in the 1860s-1870s, this house is named after two famous families associated with it: archaeologist Adolph Bandelier, who rented the house with his wife Josephine from 1885 to 1891, and Henry Kaune, founder of Kaune's grocery store in 1896, who rented

the house in 1891 and then later purchased it. During the renovation of the house in 2003, much of the original fabric of the building was lost. For more on the house see Corinne P. Sze, "The Kaune-Bandelier House," *The Bulletin of the Historic Santa Fe Foundation* 21, no. 2 (November 1993): 1–14.
24. Boyd C. Pratt, "A Brief History of the Practice," *New Mexico Architecture* 30, no. 6 (November-December 1989): 8.
25. Wilson, 54.
26. Santa Fe *Gazette*, 11 May 1861.
27. Ellen Williams, *Three Years and a Half in the Army, or History of the Second Colorados* (New York: Fowler and Wells Company, 1885), 32, 14-17.
28. SF-DNM, 18 August 1868.
29. SF-DNM, 15 April 1869.
30. As described by Don Demetrio Perez to Benjamin Read, "Santa Fe Historic Plaza Study," typescript, 1992, 45.
31. SF-DNM, 7 April 1869.
32. See their advertisements, Santa Fe *Weekly New Mexican*, 11 October 1870; 25 November 1872.
33. SF-DNM, 11 October 1872.
34. Wilson, 99.
35. Morris Diary, 7 July 1850.
36. John M. Kingsbury to James Josiah Webb, 28 March 1856, in Elder and Weber, 37.
37. Kingsbury to Webb, 29 December 1855, in Elder and Weber, 30.
38. Kingsbury to Webb, 13 March 1859, in Elder and Weber, 150.
39. Morris Diary, 8 July 1850.
40. Morris Diary, 22 November 1850.
41. SF-DNM, 16 July 1868; 30 July 1868.
42. SF-DNM, 7 October 1872.
43. Sister Blandina Segale, *At the End of the Santa Fe Trail* (Columbus, Ohio: The Columbian Press, 1932; reprint: Albuquerque: University of New Mexico Press, 1999), 97.
44. Anonymous, "Mud Roofed Houses," SF-DNM, 5 August 1868.
45. SF-DNM, 24 August 1872.
46. SF-DNM, 23 August 1872.
47. SF-DNM, 29 August 1872.
48. "Prize-winning houses in Santa Fe Architectural Competition," *El Pasatiempo*, 31 August 1930.
49. Margretta Stewart Dietrich, *New Mexico Recollections, Part II* (Santa Fe: Vergara Print. Co., 1961), 16.
50. Kate Chapman interview with Historic Buildings Survey team, 1940. Among the other changes she made were new pine floors, new fireplaces and wall partitions in some rooms, etc. See "The Borrego House,"

HABS No. NM-14, typescript report, 1940, p. 1, HSFF files.

51. Kate Chapman and Dorothy N. Stewart, *Adobe Notes, Or, How To Keep The Weather Out With Just Plain Mud* (Taos: The Laughing Horse Press, 1930), 5, 7.

52. Charlie R. Steen, Historic Preservation Advisor, National Park Service, who analyzed beam ends from one room in the Borrego House wrote: "This room is thought to have been built in the eighteenth century and then was remodeled sometime in the last half of the nineteenth century. The roof had a bad case of dry rot and had to be replaced and Miss Sylvia Loomis of The Old Santa Fe Association asked if it would be possible to get some dates from the timbers. . . . The beams were removed by the workmen and cannot be identified as to their original positions." Charlie R. Steen to Bryant Bannister, 16 September 1969, Old Santa Fe Association Papers, Fray Angélico Chavéz History Library, AC 174, Box 3, fold. 1.

53. All early data and all deeds concerning the house are compiled in: Ina Sizer Cassidy, "A History of The Borrego House," typescript, HSFF files.

54. The date the sala and portal were added is from "The Borrego House," HABS No. NM-14, typescript report, 1940, p. 2, HSFF files.

55. Dietrich, 16.

56. The east window has lost its shutters and both sets of windows are no longer double hung.

57. Beatrice Chauvenet, *John Gaw Meem: Pioneer in Historic Preservation* (Santa Fe: Historic Santa Fe Foundation/Museum of New Mexico Press, 1985), 97.

58. Old Santa Fe Association, "Fact Sheet, The Borrego House," typescript, HSFF files.

59. Remley, 148.

60. I am grateful to John Murphey for this information on the faux-brick technique.

61. Corinne P. Sze, "Lord Hovey's Brick," typescript, 2002, p. 23, HSFF files.

62. Another faux-brick façade was constructed on the Gregorio Crespin property on East De Vargas Street.

63. I am grateful to Elaine Bergman, executive director, HSFF, for providing this information in email correspondence with the author, 5 June 2008.

64. Santa Fe *Weekly Gazette*, 20 February 1858; 6 March 1858; 22 May 1858.

65. Remley, 50. See inventory of Oliver Hovey's possessions upon his death in 1862, Sze, 25.

66. Remley, 17.

67. Ibid.

68. Kingsbury to Webb, 27 October 1857, in Elder and Weber, 67.

69. Kingsbury to Webb, 6 November 1859, in Elder and Weber, 187.

70. According to the 1860 Census and Oliver Hovey's will and testament. See Sze, 24.

71. Sze, 71.

72. See Hope Curtis' photographs of the restoration process in the *Bulletin of the Historic Santa Fe Foundation* 4, no. 1 (May/June 1978).

73. All early information on the house is from Sze, 23–24.

74. The Mexican tiles in the hearths were likely added in the early twentieth-century renovation.

75. Santa Fe *Weekly New Mexican*, 5 January 1875.

76. SF-DNM, 7 April 1869; Santa Fe *Weekly New Mexican*, 1 November 1870.

77. SF-DNM, 21 November 1872; 22 June 1875.

78. Juan Bautista Moya first purchased this land in 1816, as part of a larger parcel along the Santa Fe River.

79. Santa Fe *Weekly New Mexican*, 5 January 1875.

80. Corinne P. Sze, "The James L. Johnson House (El Zaguan)," *Bulletin of the Historic Santa Fe Foundation* 25, no. 1 (March 1998): 2.

81. According to Elaine Bergman, executive director of the HSFF, quoted in Paul Weideman's "The bones of El Zaguán date to 1816," Santa Fe *New Mexican Real Estate Guide* (January 2008): 31.

82. "Johnson Place on Canyon Road, Famed For Beautiful Garden, To Become Elite Summer Hotel," SF-NM, 1 May 1928.

83. Unless otherwise noted, all references to the recent El Zaguán restoration are from Weideman, 31.

84. I am grateful to Elaine Bergman, executive director, HSFF, for this information.

85. Dietrich, 14.

86. "Johnson Place on Canyon Road, Famed For Beautiful Garden, To Become Elite Summer Hotel," SF-NM, 1 May 1928.

87. Dietrich, 15.

88. SF-NM, 23 September 1933; 4 June 1936.

89. Undated newspaper clipping, "El Zaguan, Historic Old Baca Place, New and Attractive Hotel," [ca. 1930], HSFF files.

90. Mimi B. Voegelin, "The Juan Jose Prada House: A Private Residence At 519 Canyon Road, Santa Fe, New Mexico," *Archaeology Notes No. 13* (Santa Fe: Museum of New Mexico Office of Archaeological Studies, 1990).

91. According to Robert Nestor, who restored the property in the mid-1980s, the windows are authentically Territorial and are among the oldest details of the house. Voegelin, 21.

92. Voegelin, 6.

93. Ibid., 18.

94. Dietrich, 12.

CHAPTER FOUR

1. SF-DNM, 1 October 1880.

2. SF-DNM, 9 September 1872.

3. SF-DNM, 30 March 1878; 5 September 1891.

4. Anonymous, "Tin for Roofing," SF-DNM, 1 December 1877.

5. SF-DNM, 21 July 1875.

6. Anonymous, "Tin for Roofing," SF-NM, 1 December 1877. As the newspaper reported, in 1877, "Messrs. Irvine & McKenzie" installed new tin roofs on "Messrs. Johnson & Co.'s" store, "W. H. Manderfield's dwelling house, J. G. Schuman's new two-story business house, Felipe Delgado's new two story business house, and the one Irvine & McKenzie are doing business in," and "that portion of the 'Palace' building comprising the Territorial Library and Legislative Assembly rooms." For Franz, see SF-DNM, 2 September 1882.

7. SF-DNM 1872; 11 October 1872.

8. SF-DNM, 21 June 1873.

9. See *Albuquerque Journal North*, 26 September 1984.

10. J. W. Schomisch, "Old house gets new historic role," Santa Fe *New Mexican*, 11 June 1986.

11. William Ritch, territorial secretary, was responsible for the renovation. SF-DNM, 9 March 1878.

12. Ernest Ingersoll, "La Villa Real de Santa Fe," *Harper's New Monthly Magazine* 60, no. 359 (April 1880).

13. Quoted in Matthew Edward Gallegos, "The Arts and Crafts Movement in New Mexico, 1900–1945," master's thesis, School of Architecture, University of Virginia, May 1987, 11.

14. Captain John G. Bourke Diary, 16 April 1881, quoted in Lansing B. Bloom, ed., "Bourke on the Southwest," *New Mexico Historical Review* (July 1935): 311.

15. Santa Fe *New Mexican*, 3 March 1881.

16. Hubert Howe Bancroft, *History of Arizona and New Mexico, 1530–1888* (Albuquerque: Horn and Wallace, 1962), 790.

17. James C. Massey and Shirley Maxwell, "The Mania for Mansards," *Old House Journal*, article archive, www.oldhousejournal.com.

18. "Santa Fe Historic Plaza Study II," typescript, 1992, 49.

19. SF-DNM, 26 October 1886.

20. SF-DNM, 30 April 1886.

21. SF-DNM, 8 November 1887.

22. SF-DNM, 5 September 1891.

23. SF-DNM, 15 January 1882; 3 June 1886; 18 April 1888; 21 March 1888; 8 March 1890.

24. Captain John G. Bourke Diary, 16 April 1881, quoted in Bloom, 311.

25. Ibid., 303.

26. SF-DNM, 14 November 1889.

27. SF-DNM, 23 July 1868.

28. Anonymous, "Old Hotel to Become New," SF-NM, 18 August 1911. Room rates were advertised in SF-DNM, 17 October 1882.

29. See for example SF-DNM, 24 August 1886.

30. SF-DNM, 26 April 1889.

31. See for example the ad for Las Vegas Hot Springs, SF-DNM, 2 September 1882.

32. SF-DNM, 6 October 1882.

33. SF-DNM, 29 August 1889.

34. Eva Scott Muse Fényes Inventory of Home, Hillside Avenue, Santa Fe, NM, 16 May 1891, Pasadena Museum of History, F-C-P Papers, Box 13, Folder 8.

35. SF-DNM, 27 May 1886.

36. Anonymous, "Notes of Progress," SF-DNM, 26 October 1886.

37. SF-DNM, 19 April 1889; 20 April 1889.

38. SF-DNM, March 1881.

39. *Biennial Report of the Board of Commissioners and Superintendent of the New Mexico Penitentiary* (Santa Fe: New Mexican Printing Company, 1894), 19.

40. SF-DNM, 11 May 1886.

41. SF-DNM, 26 May 1886.

42. SF-DNM, 13 April 1888.

43. SF-DNM, 27 May 1886.

44. SF-DNM, 12 May 1886.

45. Catron was the leader of the notorious Santa Fe Ring, a group of powerful ranchers, businessmen, and politicians that controlled the economic and political life of New Mexico during the Territorial period. Kinglsey Hammett, *Santa Fe: A Walk Through Time* (Layton, Utah: Gibbs Smith, Publisher, 2004), 31.

46. SF-DNM, 17 October 1891.

47. Ernest Peixotto, "The City of the Holy Faith," *Scribner's Magazine* LX, no. 3 (September 1916): 324.

48. SF-DNM, 9 October 1891; 16 October 1891; 23 October 1891.

49. SF-DNM, 3 April 1889; 9 April 1889.

50. SF-DNM, 7 September 1891.

51. Beginning about 1868, the east extension of Palace Avenue was gradually built on a *ciénega* (marshland). Using oxcarts, stones were brought to the marsh and sunk into dry mud, creating a foundation on which the houses and streets were later built. I am grateful to John Schaffer, who leases the Spiegelberg House for his gallery business, for this information.

52. Santa Fe *Weekly New Mexican*, 23 September 1873.

53. SF-DNM, 22 July 1868.

54. Biographical information on Willi Spiegelberg is mostly drawn from Tomas Jaehn, *Jewish Pioneers of New Mexico* (Santa Fe: Museum of New Mexico Press, 2003), 6.

55. SF-DNM, 20 August 1872.

56. Anonymous, "The Spiegelberg Nuptials," Santa Fe *Daily New Mexican*, 2 January 1875.

57. Flora Spiegelberg, "Reminiscences of a Jewish Bride of the Santa Fe Trail, Part I," *Jewish Spectator* (August 1937): 22.

58. Santa Fe *Daily New Mexican*, 23 September 1880.

59. It may have been built by the same artisans who built the Francisco Hinojos House at 335 East Palace Avenue, as the two buildings have similar architectural details. James H. Purdy, "The Willi Spiegelberg House," *Bulletin of the Historic Santa Fe Foundation* 4, no. 1 (May/June 1978): 3.

60. I am grateful to John Schaefer for renovation details. For further information see Michael Coleman, "Renovated Home," Albuquerque *Journal North*, 25 June 1998.

61. Flora Spiegelberg, "Reminiscences of a Jewish Bride of the Santa Fe Trail, Part II," *Jewish Spectator* (September 1937): 25.

62. Biographical information on Flora is drawn from Jaehn, 6, 63.

63. For further details on ownership see Purdy, 5–6.

64. SF-DNM, 6 October 1882.

65. He moved his store to the new building in late October of 1882. SF-DNM, 26 October 1882.

66. SF-DNM, 26 October 1882.

67. SF-DNM, 22 September 1886.

68. The fireplaces were brought to Santa Fe in 1899 from Solomon Luna's house in Los Lunas, New Mexico. See photograph files of the HPD and James H. Purdy, "The A. M. Bergere House National Register of Historic Places Inventory—Nomination Form," 1975, HPD.

69. His ad in the SF-DNM, 4 June 1889, lists his "Factory at Residence, Prospect Hill." His ad in the 13 September 1889 issue lists his store in the Griffin block and says "repairing a specialty." Both ads say he was an engraver, as well.

70. It was sold at Spitz's jewelers, Mondragon & Bros., and George W. Hickox & Co. See for example the advertisements on the front page of the SF-DNM, 7 June 1889.

71. Their income was also augmented by the jams and jellies made by Christina and her daughters from the fruit trees growing on the property. Marian Meyer, "She Triumphed in a Man's World," *The Santa Fe Reporter*, 22 May 1985.

72. I am grateful to Burke Denman, current owner of the house, for showing me the photographs in his collection.

73. The new portion of the porch reportedly came from the De Vargas Hotel on Water Street. See James H. Purdy, "The Hayt-Wientge Mansion," *Bulletin of the Historic Santa Fe Foundation* 2, no. 1 (Spring–Summer 1976): 13.

74. For restoration details see Dr. Michael Weber, "The History of the Hayt-Wientge House," typescript, no date, HSFF files, and the following newspaper clippings: "House on the Hill," Albuquerque *Journal North*, 28 August 1982, and Rosanna Hall, "Couple to renovate 1870s home," [ca. 1976], HSFF files.

75. The house was also rewired, replumbed, and equipped with a gas furnace. Sometime toward the end of the renovation, in the early 1980s, a single-story apartment wing was added to the north, with a stucco facade.

76. The address was originally 217 Rosario Boulevard.

77. SF-DNM, 7 October 1872. See also Jaehn, 18.

78. SF-DNM, 3 June 1886.

79. Anonymous, "Our Jobbing Trade," SF-DNM, 10 April 1889. See also Elizabeth Nordhaus Minces, "The Family: Early Days in New Mexico," typescript, August 1890, 3.

80. Minces, 9–10.

81. Ibid., 3.

82. SF-DNM, 7 October 1872.

83. M. F. Cummings, *Cummings' Architectural Details, Containing 387 Designs and 967 Illustrations…* (New York: Published by Orange Judd & Co., 1873; reprint, Watkins Glen, New York: The American Life Foundation & Study Institute, 1978).

84. SF-DNM, 9 March 1882.

85. SF-DNM, 9 February 1882.

86. SF-DNM, 21 August 1886.

87. Previous to the Nasons, the house was owned by Lawrence and Edna Rich Elliott, who married in 1920 and lived there for the following ten years. Information concerning ownership after the Staabs was provided by Alexa K. Hokanson, director of marketing, La Posada de Santa Fe Resort & Spa. See also Minces, 9.

88. SF-DNM, 30 August 1886.

89. The other surviving example is the 1885 Montezuma Hotel, north of Las Vegas, New Mexico.

90. SF-DNM, 19 June 1886.

91. SF-DNM, 7 August 1886.

92. SF-DNM, 25 June 1886.

93. SF-DNM, 12 May 1886.

94. SF-DNM, 27 May 1886; 26 October 1886.

95. SF-DNM, 4 June 1882.

96. The drawings of the windows are surprisingly different than what appear in the house today and may or may not be accurate. The students responsible were B. R. Morgan, T. Cochrell, T. A. Shelden. See Polhemus House, ID no. 60, Bainbridge Bunting Collection of Measured Drawings, CSWR.

97. Henry Hudson Holly, *Modern Dwellings in Town and Country* (New York: Harper & Brothers, Publishers, 1878), 117. One source suggests the staircase was built by Chinese railroad workers who lived in a camp across the street, but I was only able to find mention of one Chinese man living in Santa Fe in 1882 and he was working at a laundry. See Lynn Hunter Cline, "B&B Is a House Full of History," SF-NM, 8 October 1995.

98. Ownership data is from James H. Purdy, "The George Cuyler Preston House," *Bulletin of the Historic Santa Fe Foundation* 1, no. 2 (1975): 2.

99. SF-DNM, 23 March 1888; 26 April 1888.

100. Author's interview with Connie Hesch, great-granddaughter of Phillip Hesch, Santa Fe, 6 August 2008.

101. Myra Ellen Jenkins, "Hesch House, Application For Registration, New Mexico State Register of Cultural Properties, Santa Fe," 27 September 1972, HPD files.

102. Biographical information on Hesch is from: Obituary, Santa Fe *New Mexican*, 26 October 1914. Obituary, Riverbank, California *Review*, November 1914, in the collection of Connie Hesch, Santa Fe; and Mary J. Straw Cook, *Loretto: The Sisters and Their Santa Fe Chapel* (Santa Fe: Museum of New Mexico Press, 2002), 53–54.

103. SF-DNM, 8 November 1887. A photograph of the saw mill is in the collection of Connie Hesch, Santa Fe.

104. SF-DNM, 2 April 1888 (supplement to the paper).

105. SF-DNM, 26 April 1888.

106. SF-DNM, 13 November 1889.

107. Author interview with Connie Hesch, great-granddaughter of Phillip Hesch, Santa Fe, 6 August 2008; Cook, 54.

108. Myra Ellen Jenkins, "Hesch House, Application For Registration, New Mexico State Register of Cultural Properties, Santa Fe," 27 September 1972, HPD files.

109. "Improvement Notes," SF-DNM, 23 July 1889.

110. The cellar and foundation for the house may have been completed the previous year. See SF-DNM, 13 April 1888.

111. For instance, in April of 1889, even though their bid was the lowest ($8,408), Digneo & Brothers lost the bid to build Mr. Kahn's brick business block on the plaza to Berardinelli & Palladino (who bid $8,500.). See SF-DNM, 20 April 1889; 22 April 1889. And in September of that year Digneo & Brothers lost again to that same firm for B. Seligman's new residence. See SF-DNM, 14 September 1889.

112. General laborers at that time earned only about $1 per day. SF-DNM, 2 April 1888 (supplement to the paper).

113. "Improvement Notes," SF-DNM, 23 July 1889.

114. See real estate transfer notes and "Round About Town" column in SF-DNM, 26 April 1889 and 2 May 1889.

115. One is located one half block east at the corner of Paseo de Peralta and Weber Street and another is located at 512 Weber. John O. Baxter, "The Digneo-Valdes House," *Bulletin of the Historic Santa Fe Foundation* 4, no. 2 (September/October 1978): 3.

116. Sand bricks were made of sand, water, and clay and burned in a kiln.

117. National Register of Historic Places Nomination Form.

118. Paul Horgan, *Lamy of Santa Fe: His Life and Times* (New York: The Noonday Press, 1975), 117.

119. Bishop Juan B. Lamy, letter to members of Central Council for the Propagation of the Faith, 25 August 1866, printed in Louis H. Warner, *Archbishop Lamy: An Epoch Maker* (Santa Fe: Santa Fe New Mexican Publishing Corporation, 1936), 173.

120. SF-DNM, 6 June 1882.

121. For further information on his house see Myra Ellen Jenkins, "Archbishop Lamy's Chapel," *Bulletin of the Historic Santa Fe Foundation* 15, no. 1 (November 1987): 1–8.

122. SF-DNM, 16 June 1875. Kalsomine—usually called calcimine—generally consisted of zinc oxide, water, glue, and a coloring agent, and was used on interior plastered surfaces. Such paints were typically made with whatever materials were available locally; in Santa Fe this type of paint usually included lime.

CHAPTER FIVE

1. Rexford Newcomb, *The Spanish House for America* (Phil: J. B. Lippincott Company, 1927), 46.

2. Atchison, Topeka and Santa Fe Railway Co., *Old-New Santa Fe and Roundabout* (ATSF: 1912), 12, 16.

3. SF-NM, 21 August 1909; 6 October 1909.

4. Carl D. Sheppard, *Creator of the Santa Fe Style: Isaac Hamilton Rapp, Architect* (Albuquerque: University of New Mexico Press, 1988), 46.

5. SF-NM, 8 June 1909.

6. SF-NM, 1 August 1911; 18 September 1911.

7. Chris Wilson, *The Myth of Santa Fe: Creating a Modern Regional Tradition* (Albuquerque: University of New Mexico Press, 1997), 115.

8. Sylvanus Griswold Morley, "Keeping a City Old," *Santa Fe Trail* 1, no. 2 (August 1913), 93-95.

9. Sylvanus Griswold Morley, "Santa Fe Architecture," *Old Santa Fe* 2, no. 3 (January 1915): 284.

10. SF-NM, 18 August, 1913.

11. Anonymous, "Architecture Must Stick to Traditions, says Carlos Vierra," SF-NM, 30 July 1929.

12. Atchison, Topeka and Santa Fe Railway Co., 12.

13. His last name was Farah, which he dropped shortly after arriving in the U.S. See Jill White, "A Home with a Past," SF-NM, 31 May 1988.

14. The biographical data on Nathan Salmon is conflicting, especially concerning the dates he arrived in the United States and Santa Fe. I have drawn my information from two sources: White, "A Home with a Past," which features an interview with Nathan's grandson, Nathan Greer; and Anonymous, "Walled Solidarity: the Salmon-Greer House," *Bulletin of the Historic Santa Fe Foundation* 13, no. 1 (July 1985): 2–3.

15. Elias John Greer was born in Beirut, Lebanon, in 1889, as Elias John Arab; he changed his name to Greer following his marriage to Salome. See White, "A Home with a Past."

16. White, "A Home with a Past."

17. SF-NM, 2 September 1908; 31 March 1910; 17 August 1916.

18. Obituary for Mrs. Nathan Salmon, SF-NM, 31 August 1931.

19. Steve Jordan, "Metal Shingles," *Old House Journal*, website article archive, www.oldhousejournal.com.

20. Anonymous, "Walled Solidarity," 5.

21. Ibid., 6.

22. Ibid., 3.
23. Ibid.
24. I am grateful to Alexis K. Girard, great-granddaughter of Nathan and Petra Salmon, for this and other biographical information on the family.
25. Kathy Haq, "Title Firm Renovating Greer Home for Offices," *Albuquerque North*, 24 September 1988.
26. "Will Put Up Big Building, Salmon States," SF-NM, 23 April 1928.
27. SF-NM, 16 September 1911.
28. Atchison, Topeka and Santa Fe Railway Co., 16.
29. Corrine P. Sze, "The Bronson M. Cutting House," *Bulletin of the Historic Santa Fe Foundation* 16, no. 1 (September 1988): 7–8.
30. Bainbridge Bunting, *John Gaw Meem: Southwestern Architect* (Albuquerque: A School of American Research Book/University of New Mexico Press, 1983), 80.
31. Bronson M. Cutting, letter to Dear Papa, 1 August 1910, copy in Lowitt Papers MSS 589BC, Box 1, Folder 11, CSWR. Original in the Manuscript Collection, Library of Congress.
32. Curtiss was displeased, for example, when he discovered that searching for old timber and making adobe bricks and other specialty materials would take a long time. Louis Curtiss, letter to Bronson Cutting, 28 July 1910. The original correspondence is in the Bronson Cutting Papers, Manuscript Division, Library of Congress. See also Sze, 3, and footnotes page 11.
33. SF-NM, 15 October 1910; Richard Lowitt, *Bronson Cutting: Progressive Politician* (Albuquerque: University of New Mexico Press, 1992), 24.
34. Unknown, letter to Louis Curtiss, 14 October 1912, AC 237, Box 1, fold. 8, Fray Angélico Chávez History Library, Santa Fe, NM.
35. Anonymous, "Thomas MacLaren, Architect," Cragmor Historic Preservation website, www.uccs.edu/~cragmor/people/maclaren/maclbio.html.
36. Cutting, letter to Dear Papa, 11 October 1910, copy in Lowitt Papers, MSS 589BC, Box 1, Fold 1, CSWR. Original in Manuscript Collection, Library of Congress.
37. "Olivia M. Cutting's Notes & From Her Diary," Lowitt Papers MSS 589, Box 1, Folder 12, CSWR.
38. Lowitt, 24.
39. MacLaren, who was generally restrained in his use of decorative embellishments on facades, used a similar combination of rounded arches and curvilinear gables in the Chambers Ranch in Colorado.

40. Sze, 5.
41. Other changes made to the house: in 1932 the library was expanded to the south according to plans drawn by John Gaw Meem. In 1951 the Archdiocese of Santa Fe bought the property to use as an orphanage and made some changes. And the open land once surrounding the house has dwindled in size and been largely developed since Cutting owned the property. His former carriage house has been remodeled as a residence.
42. Sze, 5.
43. Anonymous, "Gets Big Tank," SF-NM, 7 April 1911.
44. Lowitt, 29, 332 fn. 14.
45. Anonymous, "Building Activities in Santa Fe," SF-NM, 5 June 1936.
46. George Fitzpatrick, ed., *New Mexico Magazine Home Plan Book* (Santa Fe: New Mexico Magazine, 1940; reprint 1947).
47. Newcomb, 34.
48. Many thanks to Jay Payne, owner of Casa de Estrellas, for information relating to the building and recent renovation of the complex.
49. SF-NM, 12 August 1916.
50. The current owner of the house says this type of building tile brings the outdoor temperature indoors (cold in the winter, hot in the summer) and makes any remodeling very difficult.
51. "Encouraging," SF-NM, 15 September 1926.

CHAPTER SIX

1. Sylvanus Griswold Morley, "The Most Selfish Thing for Santa Fe," ca. 1912, typescript, Guide to the Santa Fe City Planning Board Records, 1912–1914, AC 237, Box 1, Folder 6, Fray Angélico Chávez History Library and Photo Archives.
2. Ruth Laughlin, "Santa Fe in the Twenties," *New Mexico Quarterly* XIX, no. 1 (Spring 1949): 62.
3. Carlos Vierra, "Our Native Architecture in Its Relation to Santa Fe," *Papers of the School of American Archaeology*, no. 39 (1917): 7.
4. Bainbridge Bunting, *John Gaw Meem: Southwestern Architect* (Albuquerque: A School of American Research Book/University of New Mexico Press, 1983), 6.
5. SF-NM, 29 June 1903.
6. Lewis Publishing Company, *An Illustrated History of New Mexico* (Chicago: The Lewis Publishing Company, 1895), 212.
7. Anonymous, "Santa Fe Sunlight Twice as Strong as That of Florida," SF-NM, 2 May 1928.
8. SF-NM, 3 April 1915.

9. Anonymous, "Accommodations Should Be Provided," SF-NM, 5 September 1900.
10. SF-NM, 10 September 1908.
11. SF-NM, 10 June 1909.
12. Anonymous, "Remarkable Finds by Hewett Party," SF-NM, 2 September 1908.
13. SF-NM, 11 May 1909.
14. SF-NM, 5 May 1910.
15. Sylvanus Griswold Morely, "Santa Fe Architecture," *Old Santa Fe* 2, no. 3 (January 1915): 300.
16. Now called Marian Hall, the building was renovated and has only traces of the original interior and exterior.
17. Agnesa Lufkin Reeve, *From Hacienda to Bungalow: Northern New Mexico Houses, 1850–1912* (Albuquerque: University of New Mexico Press, 1988), 167.
18. Arrol Gellner, *Red Tile Style: America's Spanish Revival Architecture* (New York: Viking Studio, 2002), 15.
19. According to Karen Walker, current owner of the building, Stan Davis of Davis Construction dated this bungalow circa 1911–12 and believed this and other bungalows on the street were built for the Santa Fe Railway.
20. SF-NM, 18 August 1913.
21. See "Dudrow House," Application for Registration, New Mexico State Register of Cultural Properties," HPD files.
22. See for example SF-NM, 6 August 1910.
23. "Commerce Chamber Head Tells Why You Should Do Your Buying in Santa Fe," SF-NM, 8 June 1934.
24. SF-NM, 16 June 1913; 22 July 1926.
25. SF-NM, 2 January 1913.
26. SF-NM, 8 June 1909.
27. Robert Henri, "An Artist's Impressions of Santa Fe," *Art & Archaeology* VII, nos. 1–2 (January–February 1918).
28. SF-NM, 11 April 1920.
29. Anonymous, "Clearer Definition Needed of the Santa Fe Style," SF-NM, 12 July 1926.
30. August Reingardt's houses were often noted in the Santa Fe *New Mexican*. For example, see 12 May 1909, which describes a modern five-room brick cottage built by him on Marcy Street.
31. Tom Milligan, "Housing Demolition Fight May Be Too Late," *Albuquerque Journal North*, 20 November 1991.
32. Pancho Epstein, "Preserving Santa Fe's historic character," SF-NM, 8 May 1994.
33. This information was written on the back of a photograph of the house in the Palace of the Governors Photo Archives.
34. *Santa Fe Telephone Directory, Spring 1926* (Santa Fe: The Mountain States Telephone & Telegraph Company, 1926), 5.

35. Paul Duchscherer, *Inside the Bungalow: America's Arts & Crafts Interior* (New York: Penguin Studio, 1997): 19.

36. Biographical information on Dorman is from "The Harry Howard Dorman House," typescript, HSFF files.

37. Bronson M. Cutting, letter to Dear Mamma, 13 July 1910. Copy in Lowitt Papers, MSS 589 BC, Box 1, Folder 11, CSWR. Original in Manuscript Division, Library of Congress.

38. Albuquerque *Morning Journal*, 4 March 1912.

39. Ibid.

40. I am grateful to Ed Crocker for this information.

41. The construction details were drawn from Jerome Iowa, "Harry H. Dorman House," typescript, n.d., New Mexico HPD.

42. The current owners, Ralph and Francis Sanders, have restored the battens and the walls separating the living and dining rooms, and other interior details that were removed when the Unitarian Universalist Fellowship Church owned the property in the 1970s.

43. Anonymous, "Big Real Estate Boom on in Santa Fe," SF-NM, 14 June 1913.

44. The property history was supplied by the current owner, Brigette C. Buynak.

45. Anonymous, "Beautiful Modern Homes Being Built in Santa Fe," SF-NM, 30 July 1919.

46. Family data is drawn from Corinne P. Sze, "Elizabeth and Henry Berchtold House," typescript, 6 December 2001, 1, 3.

47. When interior designer Susan Trowbridge opened an antique store in the Berchtold House in 2000, she retained the original features of the exterior and interior. Sze, 5.

48. Sze, 4.

49. *Santa Fe Telephone Directory*, 11. *New Mexico Business Directory* (1921–22).

CHAPTER SEVEN

1. SF-NM, 17 July 1909.

2. Arrol Gellner, *Red Tile Style: America's Spanish Revival Architecture* (New York: Viking Studio, 2002), 58.

3. Anonymous, "Only One May Be Oldest," *Bulletin of the Historic Santa Fe Foundation* 10, no. 2 (May 1982): 5–6

4. Bainbridge Bunting, *John Gaw Meem: Southwestern Architect* (Albuquerque: A School of American Research Book/University of New Mexico Press, 1983), 8–9.

5. Carlos Vierra, "Our Native Architecture in Its Relation to Santa Fe," *Papers of the School of American Archaeology*, no. 39 (1917): 5.

6. Ibid., 5–6.

7. Anonymous, "Spanish Portale for Palace of Governors," SF-NM, 15 August 1913.

8. Twitchell, Ralph E., *The City Different: Descriptive Guide to Santa Fe and Vicinity* (Santa Fe: Chamber of Commerce, 1913), n.p.

9. Anonymous, "The Santa Fe Pamphlet," SF-NM, 1 August 1911.

10. SF-NM, 14 August 1913.

11. Anonymous, "Old-New Santa Fe Plans Are Adopted," SF-NM, 20 August 1913.

12. "Vierra Encourages Santa Fe Style," SF-NM, 27 April 1918.

13. See advertisement for Santa Fe Builders Supply Company in *New Mexico Magazine* (May 1936): 8, George Fitzpatrick, ed., *New Mexico Magazine Home Plan Book* (Santa Fe: New Mexico Magazine, 1940; 1957 reprint).

14. Vierra, 2.

15. They were sold at P. Hesch, Jr. & Son in Santa Fe. SF-NM, 16 August 1913.

16. See the advertisement in *New Mexico Magazine* (May 1936): 7.

17. SF-NM, 15 September 1926.

18. Chris Wilson, *Facing Southwest: The Life and Houses of John Gaw Meem* (New York: W. W. Norton & Company, 2001), 19.

19. City of Santa Fe, New Mexico, "Camino Del Monte Sol Architectural Historic Survey," 1984, typescript, 22–23.

20. Rexford Newcomb, *The Spanish House for America* (Phil: J. B. Lippincott Company, 1927), 34.

21. M.B., "The Century-Old Studio of an Artist," *Sunset Magazine* (April 1928): 51, HSFF files.

22. Nancy Cook Steeper, *Dorothy Scarritt McKibbin: Gatekeeper to Los Alamos* (Los Alamos, New Mexico: Los Alamos Historical Society, 2003), 32.

23. Anonymous, "World Travelers Choose Old Santa Fe for Fine Homes," SF-NM, 2 October 1933.

24. Ibid.

25. Anonymous, "Building Activities in Santa Fe," SF-NM, 5 June 1936.

26. John Gaw Meem, letter to Cyrus McCormick, 12 October 1931, John Gaw Meem Job Files, Box 5, folder 2, job #130, Cyrus McCormick, Jr. residence at Nambe, CSWR.

27. Molly H. Mullin, *Culture in the Marketplace: Gender, Art, and Value in the American Southwest* (Durham: Duke University Press, 2001), 47, 72.

28. City of Santa Fe, New Mexico, "Camino del Monte Sol Architectural Survey," 1984, typescript, 29.

29. Marit K. Munson, ed., *Kenneth Chapman's Santa Fe: Artists and Archaeologists, 1907–1931* (Santa Fe: School for Advanced Research Press, 2007): 61.

30. Margretta Stewart Dietrich, *New Mexico Recollections, Part II* (Santa Fe: Vergara Print. Co., 1961), 17.

31. Elizabeth White, letter to Elizabeth Shepley Sergeant, 1923, John Collier Papers, microfilm reel 5.

32. SF-NM, *El Pasatiempo* insert, 31 August 1930.

33. Witter Bynner, "A City of Change," *Laughing Horse*, Fiesta Number (September 1924).

34. Vierra, 2, 4.

35. Anonymous, "How Santa Fe Is Working to Keep Old Building Types," SF-NM, 31 August 1930.

36. The design bears little similarity to his Old Pecos Trail home. See Agnes Lufkin, "The 'New-Old Santa Fe Style' of 1915," *Bulletin of the Historic Santa Fe Foundation* 10, no. 3 (October 1982): 6.

37. For a description of the arrangement Springer made with the Vierras see James H. Purdy, "The Carlos Vierra House, National Register of Historic Places Inventory—Nomination Form," 1979, HPD.

38. "Carlos Vierra Dies," SF-NM, 20 December 1937.

39. Vierra's former studio now includes a sleeping loft, and in 1982 an indoor tennis court was added to the house. For a list of the changes see Purdy, "The Carlos Vierra House" 1979, HPD.

40. Anonymous, "Beautiful Modern Homes Being Built in Santa Fe," SF-NM, 30 July 1919.

41. Rexford Newcomb, *The Spanish House for America* (Phil: J. B. Lippincott Company, 1927), 22; *Spanish-Colonial Architecture in the United States* (New York: J. J. Augustin, 1937; reprint, New York: Dover Publications, Inc., 1990), 7, 14, plate 108.

42. "Carlos Vierra Dies," SF-NM, 20 December 1937.

43. Meem borrowed the six photo albums which eventually became part of his permanent office library. See Wilson, *Facing Southwest*, 21.

44. Subsequent owners: 1979, Larry D. Hays and C. Eugene Law; 1982, Gladys and Julius Heldman.

45. SF-NM, 21 December 1937.

46. Corinne P. Sze, "The Frank Leonard Smith House," *The Bulletin of the Historic Santa Fe Foundation* 20, no. 3 (November 1992): 1.

47. Anonymous, "Clearer Definition Needed of the Santa Fe Style," SF-NM, 12 July 1926.

48. Anonymous, "Leonard Smith Passes Away; Spent Fortune," SF-NM, 26 April 1924.

49. City of Santa Fe, New Mexico, "Camino del Monte Sol Architectural Survey," 1984, typescript, 35.

50. Rexford Newcomb, "Santa Fe, The Historic and Modern," *The Western Architect* (January 1924): 6, and plate 13.

51. Anonymous, "Leonard Smith Passes Away; Spent Fortune," SF-NM, 26 April 1924.

52. Anonymous, "Artistic Adobe," *Indianapolis News*, 25 August 1921. HSFF files.

53. Stanley L. Cuba, *Olive Rush: A Hoosier Artist in New Mexico* (Muncie, Indiana: Minnetrista Cultural Foundation, 1992), 43.

54. Ibid., 45.

55. Sylvia Loomis, "Application for Registration, New Mexico State Register of Cultural Properties," 17 June 1977, HPD, Santa Fe.

56. Anonymous, "Artistic Adobe," *Indianapolis News*, 25 August 1921. HSFF files.

57. Olive Rush Studio, ID no. 52, Bainbridge Bunting Collection of Measured Drawings, CSWR.

58. Bainbridge Bunting, *Taos Adobes: Spanish Colonial and Territorial Architecture of Taos Valley* (Taos: Fort Burgwin Research Center and the Museum of New Mexico Press, 1964; reprint, Albuquerque: University of New Mexico Press, 1990), 2.

59. The students who did these drawings were R. L. Peters and A. T. Clawson. Olive Rush Studio, ID no. 52, Bainbridge Bunting Collection of Measured Drawings, CSWR.

60. Undated, untitled newspaper clipping [ca. early 1930s], HSFF files.

61. Anonymous, "Long, Slow Silent Past Is Like the Sky Overhead…So Says Miss Olive Rush," SF-NM, 28 April 1928.

62. Olive Rush, "Technical Art Notes," ca. 1920s, Olive Rush Papers, 1879–1967, Archives of American Art, Smithsonian Institution, Box 2, Folder 36.

63. M.B, "The Century-Old Studio of an Artist," *Sunset Magazine* (April 1928): 51. HSFF files.

64. Undated, untitled newspaper clipping [ca. early 1930s], HSFF files.

65. Rush was instrumental in forming the Santa Fe Meeting and offered her studio and garden for Friends Meetings during her later life. See Sylvia Loomis, "Pertinent Facts Concerning the Ownership of the Olive Rush Studio as Bequeathed to the Santa Fe Monthly Meeting of Friends," typescript, 1 August 1975, HSFF files.

66. Ruth Laughlin Alexander, "On Hal's Birthday," SF-NM, 12 August 1956.

67. See Witter Bynner, letter to Annie Louise Bynner Wellington, 31 October 1924, Houghton Library, Harvard University, bms Am 1891.1 (167) #149; and Corinne P. Sze, "The Witter Bynner House," *Bulletin of the Historic Santa Fe Foundation* 20, no. 2 (September 1992): 8–9.

68. Witter Bynner, "A City of Change," *Laughing Horse*, Fiesta Number (September 1924).

69. Witter Bynner, letter to Annie Louise Bynner Wellington, 7 June 1925, Houghton Library, Harvard University, bms Am 1891.1 (167) #153; and 28 October 1925, bms Am 1891.1 (167) #161.

70. Witter Bynner, letter to Annie Louise Bynner Wellington, 29 June 1926, Houghton Library, Harvard University, bms Am 1891.1 (758) #233.

71. James Kraft, *Who Is Witter Bynner?: A Biography* (Albuquerque: University of New Mexico Press, 1995), 16–17.

72. B. B. D., "Among the Literati," SFNM, 14 June 1926.

73. Undated, untitled newspaper clipping [ca. 1920], HSFF files.

74. Kraft, 58.

75. SF-NM, 5 May 1928.

76. See for example, "Witter Bynner Entertains 150 Guests This Afternoon at Tea," SF-NM, 1 August 1936.

77. For example, see "A City of Change," *Laughing Horse*, Fiesta Number (September 1924).

78. Published in *The New Mexico Quarterly* I, no. 1 (February 1931).

79. Unidentified, undated newspaper clipping [ca. 1929], HSFF files; Kay Bird, "For sale: spacious home; history included," SF-NM, 29 July 1988, HSFF files.

80. Charles Lummis, letter to Leonora Frances Curtin, 13 January 1927, Acequia Madre House Archives, Santa Fe.

81. Corinne P. Sze, "The Fenyes-Curtin House," typescript, 1994, HSFF files.

82. Anonymous, "Clearer Definition Needed of the Santa Fe Style," SF-NM, 12 July 1926.

83. Leonora S. M. Curtin, letter to Eva Scott Fényes, 15 May 1925; Leonora S. M. Curtin to Eva Scott Fényes, 11 May 1925, Acequia Madre House Archives, Santa Fe.

84. "Santa Fe Expenses 1925," Pasadena Museum of History, F-C-P Papers, Box 13, Folder 13.

85. SF-NM, 8 September 1920.

86. She pasted approximately 2,500 watercolors into fifteen bound volumes that are now in the collection of the Pasadena Museum of History, Pasadena, California.

87. In 1930 the sleeping porch was made into a library and office by architect Irving Parsons, and a new porch was added, which was also later enclosed.

88. Eva Fényes enjoyed the house for only a few years before her death in 1930; the elder Leonora Curtin lived there extensively from 1930 to 1972; after the younger Leonora married Y. A. Paloheimo in 1946, she and her family mostly stayed at El Rancho de las Golondrinas until after her mother's death, and then Acequia Madre House became her primary Santa Fe residence.

89. SF-NM, 15 September 1926.

90. The SF-NM reported on 31 July 1925 that "countless adobes" were being made on the land.

91. A. Rossiter, "Specifications for a residence to be constructed on Acequia Madre Road in Santa Fe, New Mexico, for Mrs. Eva S. Fényes," [1925], Acequia Madre House Archives, Santa Fe.

92. Leonora Frances Curtin, letter to Eva Scott Fényes, 26 April 1928, Acequia Madre House Archives, Santa Fe.

93. See for example the Neff interior in Rexford Newcomb's *The Spanish House for America* (Philadelphia: J. B. Lippincott Company, 1927), 118.

94. According to Rossiter's "Specifications," [1925], doors on the blue prints "marked 'Top glass' shall be 'Universal' No. 751 doors with florentine glass" and "the door in bedroom marked 'Fr' shall be 'Universal' design No. 982," Acequia Madre House Archives.

95. Eva Fényes, letter to Boyses [Adalbert Fényes], 6 October 1926, Pasadena Museum of History, F-C-P Papers, Box 12, Folder 14.

96. Eva Fényes, letter to Boyses [Adalbert Fényes], 25 October 1926, Pasadena Museum of History, F-C-P Papers, Box 12, Folder 14.

97. Some of Eva Fényes' pottery collection was given to the Indian Arts Research Center, School for Advanced Research, Santa Fe.

98. The shop was on Palace Avenue from 1934 to 1937 and on College Street from 1937 to mid 1940. For further information see Sarah Nestor, *The Native Market of the Spanish New Mexican Craftsmen, Santa Fe, 1933–1940* (Santa Fe: The Colonial New Mexico Historical Foundation, 1978).

99. Bunny Pierce Huffman, director of Acequia Madre House, interview by the author, 17 June 2008.

100. For more information on the complex, see Bunting, *John Gaw Meem*, 80.

101. The primary changes made to the design after it was converted into a museum are: the two-car garage was turned into public restrooms, the maids' rooms were reconfigured into offices, the kitchen now houses the gift shop, bathrooms and bedrooms were opened up to create larger exhibition spaces, a new collections stor-

age and conservation and study center was added on. Also, many of the original doors and light fixtures were placed in storage.

102. Architectural historian Bainbridge Bunting suggested that the primary source of inspiration for this residence was Byne and Stapley's *Spanish Interiors and Furniture* (1928). He said the numerals found on one of Meem's sketches for the house matches the plate and figure numbers in the book. This author compared the two and did not find a direct correlation. See Bunting, *John Gaw Meem*, 137.

103. Bid specifications for job 138–2, A Director's Residence for the Museum and Laboratory of Anthropology, page 10, John Gaw Meem Papers, MSS 790, Box 6, CSWR, UNM, Albuquerque, NM.

104. William Field, director of the Museum of Spanish Colonial Art, interview by the author, 7 March 2008.

105. Ibid.

106. "Light Fixtures for Director's Residence Memo," 16 June 1931, John Gaw Meem Papers, Box 6, Folder 4, CSWR.

107. Usually Meem designed these features himself, but Bill Field, director of the Spanish Colonial Art Museum, believes this one was salvaged from a building in Las Trampas or Truchas, small villages north of Santa Fe.

108. Quoted in Wilson, *Facing Southwest*, 94.

109. Nancy Cook Steeper, *Dorothy Scarritt McKibbin: Gatekeeper to Los Alamos* (Los Alamos, New Mexico: Los Alamos Historical Society, 2003), 39.

110. The land and house cost $10,000, according to Steeper, 40–41. McKibbin's father may have helped with the purchase. See also SF-NM, 5 August 1936, which lists McKibbin's building permit.

111. Obituary, SF-NM, 10 September 1977.

112. Agnesa Lufkin, "The Gay-Wagner House: Hand-made Space," *New Mexico Architecture* 20, no. 4 (July–August 1978): 10.

113. SF-NM, 31 August 1930.

114. See Katherine Stinson Otero Architectural Drawings, CSWR.

115. Betsy Swanson, "National Register of Historic Places Inventory-Nomination Form," HPD, Santa Fe.

116. Photographs in the collection of Mary and Curtiss Brennan.

117. Dorothy McKibbin House Notebook, 1936, copy owned by Mary and Curtiss Brennan.

118. Betsy Swanson, "National Register of Historic Places Inventory-Nomination Form," HPD, Santa Fe.

119. I am grateful to Mary and Curtiss Brennan for sharing information and these photographs.

120. Steeper, 77.

INDEX